THE RISE OF MERCHANT BANKING

FINANCE, MONEY AND BANKING

THE RISE OF MERCHANT BANKING

STANLEY CHAPMAN

Routledge
Taylor & Francis Group

LONDON AND NEW YORK

First published in 1984

Reprinted in 2006 by
Routledge
2 Park Square, Milton Park, Abingdon, Oxon, OX14 4RN
or
270 Madison Avenue, New York, NY 10016

First issued in paperback 2010

Routledge is an imprint of Taylor & Francis Group

© 1984 Stanley Chapman

The publishers have made every effort to contact authors and copyright
holders of the works reprinted in the *Economic History* series. This has not
been possible in every case, however, and we would welcome
correspondence from those individuals or organisations we have been
unable to trace.

These reprints are taken from original copies of each book. In many cases
the condition of these originals is not perfect. The publisher has gone to
great lengths to ensure the quality of these reprints, but wishes to point out
that certain characteristics of the original copies will, of necessity, be
apparent in reprints thereof.

British Library Cataloguing in Publication Data
A CIP catalogue record for this book
is available from the British Library

The Rise of Merchant Banking
ISBN 978-0-415-37863-5 (hbk) (Volume)
ISBN 978-0-415-48948-5 (pbk) (Volume)
ISBN 978-0-415-37850-5 (subset)
ISBN 978-0-415-28619-0 (set)

Routledge Library Editions: Economic History

The Rise of Merchant Banking

The Rise of Merchant Banking

Stanley Chapman

Pasold Reader in Business History
University of Nottingham

London
GEORGE ALLEN & UNWIN
Boston   Sydney

George Allen & Unwin (Publishers) Ltd,
40 Museum Street, London WC1A 1LU, UK

George Allen & Unwin (Publishers) Ltd,
Park Lane, Hemel Hempstead, Herts HP2 4TE, UK

Allen & Unwin Inc.,
9 Winchester Terrace, Winchester, Mass 01890, USA

George Allen & Unwin Australia Pty Ltd,
8 Napier Street, North Sydney, NSW 2060, Australia

First published in 1984

British Library Cataloguing in Publication Data

Chapman, S.D.
    The rise of merchant banking.
1. Banks and banking—England—London—
History
I. Title
332.66′09421′2   HG3000.L82
ISBN 0-04-332094-5

Library of Congress Cataloging in Publication Data

Chapman, Stanley D., 1935–
    The rise of merchant banking.
Includes bibliographical references and index.
1. Merchant banks—History.   I. Title.
HG1970.C46   1984   332.66′095   84–6204
ISBN 0-04-332094-5

Set in 10 on 11 point Plantin by V & M Graphics Ltd, Aylesbury

Contents

List of Tables

Preface

A large number of histories of particular merchant banks have been published in recent years but, surprisingly, there has never been a history of this important sector of our national economy, and of its financial influence in the international economy. The reasons are not far to seek. Most of the histories have been privately published by banks that, for the sake of their prestige or that of their founding families, have commissioned journalists, novelists and retired executives for the task. The authors of a recent successful textbook on *Modern Merchant Banking,* both of whom spent their careers with leading houses, described the work of these 'professional authors' as so many 'historical novels', and the heroic tradition in which some have been written certainly lends substance to this contention. A business history stands or falls by its context, and few of these have any inkling of the economic history of the period. The better sort of business history, such as Ralph Hidy on the Barings, Bertrand Gille's unfinished work on the French Rothschilds, or Dr E. J. Perkins's book on Brown Bros & Co, has been written on the continent or in the USA and consequently is not directly concerned with the situation as seen from the City of London.

This scholarly neglect of a vital international power cannot fairly be ascribed to the lethargy or lack of interest of historians. The fact is that, for obvious reasons, the banks have to safeguard the confidentiality of their records (many of which are the records of their customers) and it is only very recently that they have begun to grant access to the historic part of this material. So far as merchant banks are concerned, academic researchers, and ultimately the reading public at large, must be grateful to Baring Bros and N. M. Rothschild & Sons for taking the lead in appointing full-time professional archivists to list and administer access to the confidential business records. Most other merchant banks have readily co-operated in the Business Archives Council (BAC)'s survey of banking records, ably conducted by Dr M. John Orbell of Baring Bros. The BAC survey has drawn attention to very large stores of records elsewhere, not least to those of what is now the largest merchant bank in the City, Kleinwort, Benson & Co. In writing this book my greatest debt is to Dr Orbell, whom I am happy to record as a former research student and research assistant, who first went to the City to examine part of the incredibly rich archive of the Bank of England for me.

The basic plan of this book is quite simple. The first four chapters are devoted to a broad survey of the origins, types and evolution of the family business that came to call themselves merchant banks. The remaining six chapters consider a variety of themes central to the merchant banking scene. I have not felt able, within the compass of one modest volume, to embark on the wider subject of the national and international political influence of the merchant banks. The subject is evidently a very large one in which some research is underway by those whose main interest is political history, and here I write as a business historian. I have a quantity of material on nineteenth-century international finance and imperialism but plan to publish it elsewhere. Some critics will wonder why I have cut off my story so early as 1914. The answer is simply that the banks are unwilling to grant general access to more recent records, and consequently archivists have not given priority to their listing. As soon as records become more accessible I hope to carry forward the story commenced in this book. In the mean time, I have tried to indicate the future significance of some developments at various points through my text. Research on the subsequent period is already going ahead where access to records can be obtained; in particular, a commissioned history of Kleinwort, Benson Ltd, taken down to 1961 and written in partnership with Dr Stefanie Diaper of the University of Bath, is already with Oxford University Press.

In an international business like merchant banking it is inevitable that a large quantity of records will be found in repositories round the world. I am grateful to record financial support to visit various centres, particularly to Kleinwort, Benson Ltd for a tour of various US libraries, to the University of Nottingham to visit Budapest to establish contact with scholars in Eastern Europe, to De Beers Ltd for a tour of South African universities, to the Israeli Historical Society for a week in Jerusalem, and to the SSRC and DAAD (West Germany) for generous grants in aid of research expenditure and travel. However, most of my research time has been spent running round the City after archives, and at Guildhall Library where Dr Hollaender, Chris Cooper and their team have built up an unrivalled collection of banking records. In a period of austerity in the universities, I am equally grateful to acknowledge tenure of a Nuffield Fellowship in 1982–3 to allow adequate time to write up my accumulated research. These few comments by no means exhaust my list of obligations to others, but much personal help has come from City people who, I believe, would prefer to remain anonymous; it would probably be best not to attempt to list them all here. I trust that they, and others, will not think that the omission of a string of such names is any indication of lack of gratitude on my part.

Financial history is not a particularly prominent subject in universities, but the handful of devotees have given me stalwart support. In particular I am pleased to acknowledge the advice of Professor Christopher Platt (St Antony's College, Oxford), Professor Leslie Pressell (University of Kent), Dr Philip Cottrell (University of Leicester), Dr Yousef Cassis (Geneva), Professor Frank King (Hong Kong University), Professor Jacob van Klaveren (Frankfurt University) and Dr John Killick

(University of Leeds). In the course of many travels, and in the 'free market' of national and international academic conferences, I have swapped masses of details with colleagues, archivists, research students and many others; I would be hard pressed to list them all, but I remember many of their conversations with pleasure. Thank you all for your varied contributions, however considerable or modest they may be.

S. D. CHAPMAN
August 1983

1 The Evolution of Merchant Roles in Eighteenth-Century Finance

It is well known that during the seventeenth and most of the eighteenth century international finance was centred on Amsterdam. The Dutch were then the carriers of international commerce and in conducting this business their commission merchants acquired increasing expertise in the finance of trade. By degrees British merchants learned to bypass Amsterdam, while the rise of the heavily protected British home industry gradually dispensed with several sorts of foreign imports, particularly of linens and paper. As competition between Dutch and British merchants intensified, it inevitably happened that those on the losing side found it easier to shift their accumulated capital into financial dealings. Consequently Amsterdam merchants became the first masters of the various financial techniques and developments which, in the course of the nineteenth century, became identified with the emergent profession of merchant banker. It will be helpful, at the opening of this book, to identify developments at the period they became familiar to most British merchants.[1]

Eighteenth-Century Dutch Influences

Professor Charles Wilson, whose writings on Dutch trade and finance opened the subject up to British historians, explains that much of the trade to and from Amsterdam was conducted by commission merchants, that is agents who sought out customers but did not own the commodities in which they traded. This enabled them to trade on less capital and, by degrees, introduced them to shipping agency and acceptance credit, a most important development in the history of international trade. Acceptance credits worked in this way: during the eighteenth century it became an established practice for smaller merchants finding their way into international trade (such as many British merchants were doing at the time) to ask the established houses to endorse their trade bills so as to make them acceptable without question to foreign exporters, or to bankers at home and abroad. The long-established practice (which still continues) is for the importer to draw a three months or six months bill of exchange on its accepting house, the bill maturing when payment becomes due from the customer. The accepting house concerned receives the bill and may hold it to maturity or (as increasingly happened in the course of growing specialisation) discount it with one of the financial intermediaries that made a trade of this function. When the bill matures the importer's remittance is paid direct to the accepting house for the account of his customer. This self-liquidating instrument for financing trade can readily be renewed on a 'revolving' basis, but meanwhile offers the accepting house the opportunity of maintaining his liquidity and operating on a moderate capital. It is impossible to say exactly when this practice became widespread, but several London merchants were acting as agents for Dutch financiers in the 1660s, quite likely on the basis of this kind of credit.[2]

The actual buying and selling of bills of exchange, usually referred to in the literature as the function of foreign exchange, was also centred on Amsterdam for most of the eighteenth century. It was largely conducted by the city's colony of Sephardic Jews, who connected it with the precious metals trade between London and Amsterdam. The Jews had secured the trade because they had developed such expertise and such reliable chains of international correspondents that they were able to prosper on thin profit margins. And of course the exchange business followed on easily from the traditional economic pursuits of the Jews, for deficiencies on one side or the other had to be settled in coin and bullion. At a period when a large array of gold and silver coins were used to make settlements, money-changing itself had for centuries been a distinct specialism. In later chapters of this book we shall see that this ancient Jewish specialism survived well into the nineteenth century.[3]

The wealth of Amsterdam also gave rise to another financial specialism, that of lending to foreign governments. Already in the seventeenth century the Dutch were lending substantial sums to Brandenberg, Denmark, Sweden, Hamburg, Bremen, Emden, East Friesland and the Empire. At the end of the century when the Dutch Stadtholder, William of Orange, became William III of England, Scotland and Ireland, he borrowed heavily in Amsterdam to fight his continental wars. During the course of the eighteenth century successive British administrations drew on the same source, and William concluded that Dutch money was indispensable to the British government. Sweden, Russia and the German states also contracted a sequence of loans in Amsterdam, and after 1780 bold attempts were made to develop the financial tie with New York. The details need not detain us here, but two features of the system should be noted for their future importance. Transfer of money for investment, or of interest earned or won on successful speculations, was made through agents by means of the established commercial instrument, that is the bill of exchange, so that the loan business was quite conveniently run in harness with that of the merchant. We shall see that this duality continued well into the nineteenth century in London as well as Amsterdam. Secondly, particular firms specialised in the state issues of particular countries, for which they distributed prospectuses and recruited other financial supporters to share a sequence of loans. The best-documented instance of the maintenance of such a connection is Hope & Co.'s ten loans to the Swedish crown (1767–87) and eighteen loans to Russia (1788–93) but there are numerous other cases on record. Thirdly, the loan contractors assumed the responsibility for retailing the bonds not only on the Amsterdam bourse and in the Netherlands, but also throughout Europe. The loan business was from the outset essentially an international one.[4]

The connections between Amsterdam and London were maintained at various levels. Each was the most important European trading partner of the other, while the Dutch merchants' lending was largely focused on the British government and the largest part of the foreign-held part of the national debt owed to Dutch creditors. But in the context of this book, the more interesting connection was the personal and family ties that developed to span the two capitals. The commitment of numerous Amsterdam merchants to trade and investment in London was so considerable that, from the early eighteenth century, they began to send younger sons or other members of their families to act as agents and factors for them, and by the middle of the century a considerable Dutch colony was collecting around Austin Friars in the City of London. In the second quarter of the eighteenth century there was an exodus of Dutch Jews to London, usually beginning, like the Gentile houses, with a younger son, with the branch house growing to strong independence as the volume of business continued to grow. A few of the most successful immigrants, like the Van Necks, acquired landed estate and entered the ranks of the English aristocracy. There were others again that, coming of more modest backgrounds, owed their ascendancy in England to the patronage of richer houses in Amsterdam. The best-known case of this kind of development is that of Barings, a family of Dutch origin that prospered in the textile trade, first in Exeter then London, with the support of Hopes of Amsterdam.[5]

It is convenient to label the kind of family business that operated simultaneously in two or more centres of trade as an 'international house'. This kind of business structure was familiar from at least the late Middle Ages, but the expansion of international trade in the eighteenth and nineteenth centuries gave it great impetus. While the Dutch operated it with striking success, ethnic trading groups that had been dispersed by religious persecution were more tenacious in holding to it as it had become a way of life for them. From French historians we are familiar with the activities of the 'international Huguenots' whose family dynasties linked Geneva, Berne, Frankfurt, Amsterdam and Paris with London, and who 'practically monopolised the financial relations between England and France' in the eighteenth century. Already at the mid-century the Huguenots who had settled in London were intermarrying with Dutch Protestants.

During the French Wars (1793–1815), the Dutch, French and Sephardic Jewish *émigrés* were overtaken by a new wave of international trading families. Ashkenazi Jews from Hamburg, Frankfurt, Berlin and Leipzig were attracted to London by the dramatic growth of the British textile trade as well as by a greater degree of religious toleration. Other German merchants, sometimes with Huguenot backgrounds, joined the growing community when Napoleon occupied Frankfurt and Hamburg (1806–12). These were followed after the war by an influx of 'Greek' merchants, the religious minority in the Ottoman Empire. Their trading stations had reached as far west as Amsterdam in the late eighteenth century, but it was the renewal of persecution that led a sequence of families to settle in London, Manchester and other northern textile centres. These waves of immigration brought not only mercantile experience and capital, but also specific expertise in trading to export markets hitherto lightly touched by British-based enterprise. The fusion of this experience with the financial techniques that the British adopted from the Dutch will form one of the main themes of this book.[6]

The financial needs of the British government during the French Wars proved to be a hothouse for the rapid development of a home-grown species of loan contractors. Dealing in government stocks became a major activity; according to the Bank of England ledgers, the number of people dealing in bonds rose from 430 in 1792 to 726 in 1812, but most of the business was effectively handled by as few as 10 loan contractors. The major contractors included Boyd, Benfield & Co., originally Paris bankers, J. J. Angerstein, who came of a Hanoverian merchant family, Peter de Thelusson, a typical Huguenot merchant and financier, David Ricardo, of Dutch Jewish descent, and the Goldsmid brothers, who were Ashenazi Jews. This list is intended to illustrate ethnic variety rather than cover the entire spectrum.[7] At the end of the war the most successful contractors were Sir Francis Baring, Exeter-born son of the Dutch immigrant already mentioned, and N. M. Rothschild, a younger son of a Frankfurt Jewish dealer in coins who moved into the trade in printed cottons. Their firms became leaders and pace-setters in the postwar economy, so their story will be dealt with in greater detail in the next chapter. For the moment it is sufficient to notice that they stood in the long tradition of merchants who united their trade with sporadic ventures into 'pure' finance.[8]

It may seem surprising on the face of it that, considering the impressive growth of the British economy and British overseas trade in the eighteenth century, the country should remain a debtor nation to the Netherlands for so long. Actually economists are quite familiar with the concept of young and expanding economies being in deficit on balance of trade, but in this particular instance there is a more significant point. Through the eighteenth century British merchants were devoting increasing resources to providing long credits for the development of the rapidly growing American colonies and their successor, the United States. At the end of the eighteenth century the British merchant trading there seldom saw his capital back within three years, and sometimes it was four or five. Dutch acceptance credits in London were typically three or six months, and despite a drive to win American markets after 1776, Amsterdam merchants were unwilling to accede to the liberal system by which the British retained their grip on the North American market. In specific commodity terms, printed textiles are said to have been the most important article of international trade in the eighteenth century; much of the production was concerned with the Dutch financing the export of German linens to London where they were printed, while London merchants financed the export of popular lines across the Atlantic. This is only one example, but it serves to illustrate the notion that Amsterdam was used to support the growth of the British overseas trade. However, this general proposition tells us nothing of the functions of British merchants and manufacturers in relation to the finance of overseas trade, a matter which must now be given closer attention.[9]

The Finance of Trade in the Early Industrial Revolution

The financial dependence of British manufacturers on importers and other merchants can be glimpsed in the correspondence of a few leading firms of the period. Matthew Boulton, the famous Birmingham toymaker (and later partner with James Watt in marketing the separate condenser steam engine) was in partnership with a merchant called Fothergill until his death in 1782. Fothergill travelled all over the continent looking for markets, and borrowed money from various German merchants in the 1760s and 1770s. Similarly Josiah Wedgwood, the famous potter, was in partnership with a merchant called Thomas Bentley, who found the earliest foreign orders for their goods from Hamburg merchants and their inland connections. One such firm, Grammer & Wright of Munster, wrote in 1769, 'what goods you send us the value will be accepted by an eminent house in Amsterdam at the usual credit of twelve months'. A parallel theme can be discerned in the trade of a number of the provincial textile regions. Some of the exports from Liverpool were part of a triangular system of trade and credit involving sales of American produce to the continent. Payment for these goods was usually made by such continental houses as Hope & Co. and Sylvanus Bourne & Co. of Amsterdam. The Devon serge industry, like calico printing, was evidently nurtured by the enterprise and wealth of Amsterdam, Hamburg and Frankfurt merchant houses, prominent among which were Huguenot families such as Passavant and Du Fay. Norwich and Leeds appear to have benefited from similar connections.[10]

However, most manufacturers who exported already drew on London rather than continental houses. Wedgwood explained to an Italian customer 'that being a manufacturer only in an inland county, neither travelling myself nor employing any agent to do it for me, my foreign correspondents name me a good house, generally in London, to accept my draft for the amount of goods.' In much the same way, Boulton & Watt sought London and Liverpool merchant guarantors for the overseas sales of their patent steam engines, but allowed foreign orders to be guaranteed by merchants in that country. 'You will observe', James Watt jun. wrote in 1795, 'that the sums [engine prices] we have specified are to be paid upon the delivery of the materials at Hull, and that we undertake no foreign orders without having a guarantee in their country, being engineers not merchants.' Similarly, McConnel & Kennedy, the early leaders of the fine spinning industry in Manchester, refused to meet foreign orders without the guarantee of a London merchant. The same theme can be found in the correspondence of West Riding woollen manufacturers of the period.

Towards the end of the eighteenth century, there are signs that many more manufacturers were taking the initiative in establishing their own connections abroad, particularly in the more familiar North American market, and were now less dependent on external finance. One of the most informative sources on this is the journals of Joshua Gilpin, an American paper manufacturer who toured the manufacturing districts of Britain in the middle 1790s. In the Potteries he recorded

> The number of houses now engaged in the manufacture are nearly 150, each house is generally confined to some particular kind [of ware] according to the line in which their business extends, as those who supply the home demand, those for Germany, France, West Indies, and America, require such different wares to each market that no-one could engage to make them all; they therefore apply themselves separately to make for the different markets to which they extend their trade. ... Many of the manufacturers export to orders on their own credit from the Continent but to America they generally require an English house to be drawn to the extent of the credit.

The usual twelve months' credit was allowed. In Nottingham, the principal seat of the hosiery industry, Gilpin noted

A large trade is carried on from Nottingham direct to America by the manufacturers. They ship their goods chiefly by London but also by Liverpool and Hull; they prefer the last, the goods are delivered at either place at the charge of the manufacturer. Mark Huish is the most established merchant in Nottingham ... he supplies most of the good houses in Philadelphia with hosiery on twelve months' credit.

In Leicester, Gilpin called on John Pares, the partner of James Heygate, London hosier and banker, and found that his house also 'give 12 mo. credit paid to their agent in America or 9 mos. remitted here.'

In the fastest-growing textile regions of Lancashire and the West Riding of Yorkshire, numerous fustian manufacturers in the cotton districts and clothiers in the woollen districts were encroaching on merchant functions to find their own markets abroad. This was part of an energetic extension of functions that was characteristic of the 'new frontier' manufacturing regions, for the organisers of the domestic system were simultaneously integrating backwards into mechanised spinning. In 1784 Bailey' *Northern Directory* listed thirty-five cotton and yarn merchants, among whom only one indicated that he had manufacturing interests. The Manchester section of the *Universal British Directory* (1794) listed sixty firms who combined manufacturing and mercantile functions, and a recent analysis of the origins of the forty-three biggest cotton mill owners in the industry shows that numbers of 'country manufacturers' (that is organisers of the domestic system and calico printers in the villages around Manchester) also became merchants. A parallel process of simultaneous forward and backward integration was evident in Leeds and its region, though the growth in the woollen industry was not so spectacular as that of cotton. A few of the biggest merchant-manufacturers evidently sold in several world markets; Lingards, for instance, sold their fustians and other cottons direct to agents in Russia, Italy, the United States and Prussia, while Peels, the calico printers, had an extensive sale in North America and continental Europe, employing both resident agents and travellers working on commission. Other firms, in a more modest way of business, evidently specialised or rather pursued a limited connection abroad. Thus William & Samuel Rawlinson, also trading in partnership with an Italian called Alberti, exported 'much to the Continent, especially Italy and Germany, some to W. Indies, not much to America', while Samuel Greg found the main outlet for his fustians in an agent in Philadelphia (USA), and Robinsons & Heywood appear in the 1794 directory as merchants and 'Manufacturers of African Goods'. Other merchant-manufacturers from Manchester and Leeds attempted to find their own customers at the continental fairs. William Radcliffe of Mellor (Stockport), who began his working life as a handloom weaver and was employing a thousand country weavers before the end of the century, sold first to visitors from Berlin and Copenhagen, then at the Frankfurt and Leipzig Fairs. Meanwhile his neighbour Samuel Oldknow, the pioneer of the muslin manufacture, took leave of his dependence on his London wholesaler to sell at the great fairs. The clear implication of this rapid regional survey is that in the most energetic period of growth in the late eighteenth century, numerous manufacturers were becoming merchants and financing their own export drive.

In the 1780s and 1790s the northern industrial regions also set the pace in the provinces by sending partners to reside in foreign commercial cities. Occasionally agents abroad were invited to become a member of the family partnership, but it appears to have been more usual to follow the London practice of sending a junior partner to prove himself abroad, as when Longsdons & Morewood (one of Arkwright's Derbyshire connections) sent John Morewood to St Petersburg in 1784, or Wardle & Tillards, Manchester cotton manufacturers and Liverpool merchants, sent William Tillard to take charge of their trade in Jamaica, or the Fergusons of Halifax, Ogdens of Leeds and Thompsons of Rawdon left their respective family clothing businesses in Yorkshire for New York. The premier Liverpool merchant houses sent junior partners to North America for two or three years at a time, while leading New York, Philadelphia and Baltimore merchants sent their sons to Britain for training. Young migrants in both directions sometimes settled, and in a few notable cases became the leading houses in their adopted towns. The counterpart of this well-known migration of enterprise to and from the New World was the settlement of increasing numbers of European – mostly German – merchants in the rising industrial towns. Before the end of the eighteenth century at least fifteen foreign merchants and manufacturers had settled in Manchester, and two of them were among the biggest millowners in the cotton industry. Their numbers were not sufficiently large to make a major impact on the rapidly-rising provincial trade before 1815, but growing numbers were nurtured by more substantial compatriots in London, and a few reached the stature of major finance houses during the ensuing half-century.[11]

The emergence of this new breed of merchant-manufacturers in the provincial industrial regions was facilitated by the increase in size, wealth and expertise of the merchants of Liverpool. Already in the 1790s there was specialisation by export destination and by commodities in a similar way to that defined by Mortimer for London; Gilpin listed ten American merchant houses, eleven West Indian merchants, a dozen corn merchants and a number of American shippers. Liverpool shippers provided a service for manufacturers with customers abroad, while the merchants assumed the role of their London antecedents by purchasing on their own account from inland manufacturers or from the various trade warehouses that stocked goods for export. Thus Sparling & Bolden, who exported woollen goods, printed cottons, carpets, hosiery, linens and a variety of other manufactured goods to Virginia, drew their supplies from a circle of firms in Manchester, Halifax, Colne, Rochdale, Leeds, Wakefield, Kendal, Keswick and Mansfield. They followed the trade practice of paying in bills on London at two or three months' date. London merchant houses, acting in effect as bankers, accepted bills for consignments to America and other markets from all parts of the world, and paid the drafts of foreign merchants to the order of British manufacturers. Bills on London houses also financed the purchase of cotton and other Liverpool imports, so the port was financially dependent on its southern rival.[12]

So it was that, although London did not set the pace of industrial development at this period, it emerged as the financial fulcrum of the country. It had been steadily gaining ground on Amsterdam for much of the century, but in the last two decades several developments accelerated this process. The diversion of capital across the Atlantic during the American War of Independence curtailed the supply to London, and the French Wars almost severed it altogether, forcing London into independence. Meanwhile the 'take-off' of British industrialisation further reduced British dependence on Dutch supplies and opened up other export markets. The position at the turn of the century was clearly defined by Henry Thornton, a London banker:

> Bills are drawn on London from every quarter of the Kingdom, and remittances are sent to the Metropolis to provide for them, while London draws no bills, or next to none, upon the country. London is, in this respect, to the whole island, in some degree what the centre of a city is to the suburbs. ... London also is become, especially of late, the trading metropolis of Europe, and, indeed of the whole world; the foreign drafts, on account of merchants living in our out-ports and other trading towns, and carrying on business there, being made, with scarcely any exceptions, payable in London.[13]

In a word, London had entirely superseded Amsterdam in the financing of British domestic and foreign trade. The spectacular development of that trade was to multiply further the role of the City in international finance.

New Specialisation: the Rise of Commission Agents and Accepting Houses, c.1800–36

A combination of circumstances in the closing years of the French Wars led to the bankruptcy, enervation or retirement of many of the old merchants of London, Liverpool and Bristol, and the simultaneous withdrawal of a large number of northern manufacturers who had ventured into overseas marketing. In their place there emerged new kinds of specialists, commission agents resident in foreign commercial centres (but usually having a partner or agent in Britain), and accepting houses, that is wealthy merchants who were graduating to pure finance and providing the credits for manufacturers to send their goods to agents abroad. The commission agents were characteristically young men of modest capital who went to seek their fortunes abroad. At the end of the French Wars most of those selling British goods appear to have been British born, but during the next twenty years, and particularly after 1825, the European and North American markets were increasingly served by the junior partners of United States, German, Greek and other foreign merchant houses who came to British industrial towns to buy their own goods. British commission agents moved out into the less-developed and more geographically remote markets, particularly Latin America and the Orient, no doubt hoping for less competition and more profit. The exporting manufacturer so far declined that by the 1850s it could be said that 'at least seven-eighths or three-fourths' of the entire export business of Lancashire and Yorkshire was conducted by 'foreign houses' (that is commission agents), and a parallel change seems to have taken place in other manufacturing regions. This far-reaching change in the structure of trade and its finance is clearly central to the main theme of this book and so needs to be examined in a little more detail.

The initial cause of this change was the ruin of numerous old merchant houses as a result of the American Revolutionary War and the Napoleonic War. The American War drove numerous houses into bankruptcy, especially after the Netherlands entered the war against Britain in 1780. The figures are startling enough – seventeen London merchants bankrupt in 1781, twenty-five in 1782, and thirty-eight in 1783 – but they are not the whole story. The bigger houses survived, but some never regained their former prosperity. In 1784 Lord Sheffield claimed that the liberal credits granted by London houses to the USA had bankrupted three-quarters of them. The losses of the Napoleonic War are not so precisely documented, but it is clear that the continental blockade caused merchants to turn to Latin America, and there were severe losses in Buenos Aires in 1806 and Rio in 1808-9. The American War of 1812-14 caused extensive losses in Glasgow and Liverpool, and the postwar flooding of the European market led to further losses in 1815-16 and 1819. Lévy-Leboyer maintains that 90 per cent of London's continental houses were eliminated after the war, while in Manchester four out of five manufacturers (many no doubt with marketing interests) disappeared during the twenty years or so of war. Some of the names that left the pages of the directories in these years no doubt included those who, like the

Peels and Arkwrights, retired to landed estates.[14]

Increasing postwar competition was the consequence not only of a new generation of fortune-hunters, but also of the introduction of new types of trading organisations. London had harboured a colony of foreign merchants from the Middle Ages, but the settlement of foreign commission agents in the provincial centres of industry was a consequence of the French Wars. Young Rothschild and his countrymen brought a tradition of cash buying when the market was low, small profit margins, volume trade and rapid turnover of stock that set a cracking pace in Manchester and by degrees brought most of the continental trade into their warehouses. Backed by Frankfurt and Hamburg capital, their resources were often superior to local merchants served by Manchester's underdeveloped banking system. Other young German merchants that settled in London at this time and subsequently emerged as merchant bankers were J. H. Schröder in 1802, E. H. Brandt in 1805, Frederick Huth in 1809 and Frühling & Goschen in 1814. S. L. Behrens, Leo Schuster and other migrants developed from a Manchester base, along with several firms of Huguenot origin.[15]

Another development of the war years was the wholesale warehouse serving the exporter. They had already made their appearance by the period of the compendious *Universal British Directory* (1793–8), and specialised in particular lines such as cotton twist, hosiery and lace, carpets and earthenware. In the fastest-growing sector of trade, textiles, the cheap-selling warehouse business was increasingly dominated by a handful of firms, about a dozen in London by the middle 1830s. The doyen of this movement was James Morrison of Todd, Morrison & Co., who made a fortune in bulk purchase of cheap cotton and worsted goods, which he appears to have sold through his connections in North and South America. Morrison's bills were readily cashed by banks, and as Morrison, Cryder & Co. he briefly became one of the leading accepting houses.[16]

British and foreign commission agents were also encouraged by the emergence of a group of wealthy Anglo-American acceptance houses specialising in the finance of particular branches of trade. The leading firms were Barings, Brown, Shipley & Co., and (until 1836) the 'three W's' (Wiggin, Wilson and Wildes), all specialising in transatlantic finance, and a few firms of European origin, notably Rothschilds, Huths and Lizardis. A number of the best-known accepting houses were founded on fortunes made in the textile trade, Barings in Exeter and the East India Co., Browns in the Philadelphia linen trade, Rothschild and Wiggin in Manchester, Morrison and Wilson in Liverpool, the Huguenot houses Souchay and Du Fay in selling textile prints abroad. Most based themselves in London but had offices or partners in Liverpool; however, until the 1860s several maintained their headquarters in the northern centres of trade. The acceptance houses were prepared to advance up to two-thirds of the invoice to recognised clients for limited periods, 3–4 months for sales in North America, and up to 12 months for oriental markets.[17]

A handful of wealthy manufacturers continued to invest capital in overseas trading adventures, but most were restrained by modest and uncertain profit margins. Thus, to take one example, by the middle 1830s the Glasgow cotton trade was almost all for export, yarns ('cotton twist') being sent principally to Germany, with some to Russia and the Orient. But though the industry had 'fallen into the hands of large capitalists' who carried on their operations in multi-storey steam-driven mills, few indeed contemplated shipping on any terms, as this branch of business was left 'almost exclusively in the hands of middlemen and yarn agents who cannot do without advances' from financiers. Henry Houldsworth, who had been in the industry since 1799 and employed 1,400–1,500 hands, explained that profits had been so low since 1826 that it was not possible to accumulate capital. Similarly, in Lancashire less than thirty firms regularly shipped goods to the Orient on their own account, that is, about 2 per cent of the firms in the cotton industry. The remainder either shipped occasionally (when they had a surplus to dispose of), or sold to export warehouses or entrusted their goods to commission agents.[18]

The relationship between the acceptance houses and the commission agents moving into the newly opening centres of commerce is vividly illustrated in Vincent Nolte's *Reminiscences of a Merchant's Life*. Nolte, who was born in Hamburg and trained as a merchant in Nantes, was sent by Hope & Co. (the Amsterdam banking house) to New Orleans in 1805. Arriving only three years after the USA had purchased Louisiana from Napoleon, he found that

> The mercantile class was made up of four or five French establishments ... three Scotch county houses, one German concern, and eight or ten commission houses lately opened by young American merchants from New York, Philadelphia and Baltimore ... there was not a single house there possessed of any capital worth mentioning.

By contrast, Nolte was soon well-placed financially, for Barings lent him £6,000 capital and credit of £10,000 to return to New Orleans to open a new commission house in 1812. As the leading exporter to Le Havre as well as Liverpool, Nolte was able to secure 'more or less extensive connections with all the great bankers of Paris', including Hottinguer & Co. and Jacques Lafitte. His principal rivals in New Orleans were 'four Scotch houses' who worked together to a common plan 'arising more out of an instinctive feeling of their common interest than from any regular arrangement entered into between them'. They were men of little capital, but secured large credits abroad 'through the influence of the central capitalists in Glasgow'. The methods of financing commission agents described by Nolte seem to have become fairly general in the first half of the nineteenth century.[19]

All the acceptance houses in London employed 'corresponding clerks' in their offices, many of them of foreign birth. They were an élite of educated men, having served a mercantile apprenticeship abroad, and earned £250 to £400 or even £500 a year. (As a comparison, cotton mill managers earned about £130 pa at the period.) Towards mid-century most first-class merchant houses employed ten to fifteen and sometimes twenty clerks; Rothschilds employed forty to fifty while Barings had forty clerks in London and twenty in Liverpool. 'The Rothschilds, the Barings, the Heaths, the Huths, and other great houses display a spirit of liberality towards their clerks; and from connexions made in these firms, several of them have been enabled to get into business for themselves', a City commentator observed at this time. The best-known north of England merchants can be observed exercising a similar patronage. Almost all of the small firms have disappeared without evidence of the scale of their operations, but the numerous printed circulars announcing their foundations all carry a list of references directing potential customers to one or more of the above firms, together with Souchays, Schröders and other eminent patrons. The experienced clerk setting up as a commission agent needed the support of an acceptance house because (as one of them explained to Morrison, Cryder & Co. in 1836) 'the shippers and manufacturers in England generally require an advance' so that the agent had to raise credit through 'some London or Liverpool House'. The acceptance banker maintained an intimate knowledge of his scattered constituents by 'calling in' new partners from the more successful merchants and agents in provincial centres and abroad.[20]

Postwar developments in the cotton trade were followed, at varying intervals of time, by similar changes in other branches of overseas commerce. In Birmingham the commission agent had eclipsed the old-style general merchant by 1927, according to the Bank of England's agent there. His description of the new system shows the precise relationship of agent, customer and financier:

There are persons in Birmingham who are designated as merchants but who act rather as agents having in fact few or no mercantile transactions of their own. Many of these agents are highly respectable in their character and conduct, although generally speaking not possessed of much property. They are paid by a commission on the transactions which they effect and for the most part, when they receive orders from abroad, particularly from America, they are furnished with bills on London and Liverpool [merchant] houses, with which they pay for goods purchased for their correspondents. These bills are frequently drawn by the bank of the U.S. and generally on the most eminent houses in this country, such as Baring Brothers & Co., Thomas Wilson & Co., Finlay, Hodgson & Co., Thomas Dickinson & Co. and others, and in Liverpool on Cropper, Benson & Co., Sands, Hodgson & Co., W. & G. Maxwell, Maury, Latham & Co., W. & J. Brown & Co., and others. The paper which these mercantile agents negotiate is held in high estimation by the banks here [in Birmingham], and is perhaps on the whole considered the best in the market.

In other words, Birmingham commission agents depended on London and Liverpool accepting houses for their export finance. The agents operated on a modest scale because the industry they served was a conglomerate of small workshops; according to information collected for the Bank of England the average annual returns of the Birmingham manufacturers did not exceed £3,000 each at this time.[21]

To summarise, it may be said that there were three overlapping phases in the changing functions and relations of merchants, manufacturers and financiers:

(1)   For most of the eighteenth century, London merchant enterprise strengthened its leadership over provincial and continental rivals, reinforced by the immigration of branches of wealthy houses from the continent and from the English provinces. As the volume of trade and competition increased, so did the rate of turnover, but the roles of merchants, factors, brokers, middlemen and other metropolitan specialists continued along established lines. The value of Liverpool's trade overtook that of London early in the nineteenth century, but the northern centre of trade remained dependent on the London money market. The growing commercial power of London benefited provincial firms, for as London succeeded Amsterdam as the premier centre of international finance, manufacturers were able to seek all their financial guarantees in the British capital.

(2)   The period from about 1780 to 1825 saw the leading London and provincial industrialists gradually taking initiatives in marketing, often beginning with connections in the United States and the West Indies and increasingly backed by the financial resources of well-established mercantile houses in London or one of the continental centres. In the textile and iron industries, the manufacturers' assumption of mercantile roles can be seen as part of a wider process of the extension of entrepreneurs' functions on the 'new frontiers' of British industrial expansion. However, a large turnover of firms, heavy losses in exporting and the emergence of specialisation within

the heavily industrialised regions, reduced this development to small proportions. As profit margins declined, an increasing proportion of manufactured goods was sent for export, and as export markets became more dispersed, the numerous small family firms that conducted most of British industry were seldom able to assume the financial burden of marketing abroad. The handful of firms that continued to do so were obviously exceptional, and even the wealthiest of them ran into financial difficulties at one time or another. Only merchants with a secure base in the home market could risk building integrated manufacturing and mercantile enterprises.

(3) The period from about 1825 saw the rapid rise of the accepting houses, eminent merchants that took the financial risk of exporting. The London houses were augmented by another wave of wealthy continental and American merchants during the Napoleonic War, and by more migrants from the provinces. The crises of 1825–6 and 1836–7 checked, but did not arrest this development. The acceptance houses encouraged the establishment and financed the growing corps of commission agents and small general merchants that dispersed across the five continents in the first half of the nineteenth century. There were more British firms abroad than those of any other country, and financial support from London offers the main reason.

2 Market Leaders: Rothschilds and Barings

In the last chapter the emergence of Barings and Rothschilds as the two dominant houses in the City of London was referred to. Clearly the development of these outstanding firms exercised an influence, for better or worse, throughout the British money market, so that their record and characteristics require close attention. In this chapter the salient features of these concerns is surveyed from the Napoleonic War to the First World War with particular reference to those features which either were emulated by younger or smaller houses or provided openings for new competitors. Similarities and contrasts between the two are also emphasised.

The existing literature acknowledges the predominance of the two

Table 2.1 *Comparison of loans contracted by N. M. Rothschild & Sons and Bring Bros, 1815–1904*

	Baring Bros				N. M. Rothschild & Sons			
	Foreign & colonial Commercial government, state & city				*Foreign & colonial Commercial government, state & city*			
	No. of issues	*Amount £m.*	*No.*	*Amount*	*No. of issues*	*Amount £m.*	*No.*	*Amount*
1815–37	5	43.2	0	0	24	105.5	2	10
1839–59	8	20.8	1	2.0	16	106.8	8	29.4
1860–90	62	560.7	41	69.4	43	896.5	22	55.2
1891–1904	20	69.4	26	59.1	27	200.7	9	19.0

Sources: Jules Ayer, *A Century of Finance, 1804–1904: the London House of Rothschild* (1905); Private list of Baring Bros & Co.'s issues; Fenn's *Compendium of the English & Foreign Funds*, 12th edn (1876)

Notes: (1) The total nominal value of each issue has been counted, even where there are known to have been syndicated partners; where the records differed the Baring's figures were accepted as they agreed with *Fenn on the Funds.*

(2) When a government issue was announced as being for railways, it has been classified as government rather than commercial.

Currency equivalents: $ = 4s 6d (C. Fenn, p. 477) Nepolitan Ducat = 39d (P. Kelly, *Universal Cambist* (1831), II, p. 19). 121 fl. = £10 (C. Fenn, p. 116).

firms and appears to infer their approximate equality, though without reference to any comparative data. The figures for issues (Table 2.1) have been available for some years and leave no doubt that, with one small exception, Rothschilds kept well ahead of their rival throughout the period. Data on acceptances, which have only recently become available, emphasise even more strongly the early lead taken by Barings and retained by that house through the century. Barings obviously chased Rothschilds hard in the 1870s and 1880s, and almost overtook them, but the Baring crisis of 1890 dramatically reduced the business of this house, and they slipped several places down the 'league table'. Adequate comparison also calls for a tabulation of commissions and profits on merchanting, but unfortunately there is nothing at present available to meet this need. It is only possible to say that N. M. Rothschild and his successors were much less interested in commodity trade, while Barings retained a strong interest, at any rate during the period from 1828 to 1882, when Joshua Bates and Russell Sturgis were in turn senior partners there. Overall, these broad comparisons reflect the differing capital of the two houses noticed in Table 2.2.

Table 2.2 *Comparison of acceptances of N. M. Rothschild & Sons and Baring Bros at key dates, 1825-1913 (£m.)*

	Rothschilds	Barings
1825	0.30	0.52
1850	0.54	1.90
1890	1.39	c.15.00
1900	1.47	4.53
1913	3.19	6.63

Sources: N. M. Rothschild & Sons: annual ledgers, VI/10/0-113 (1815-1914). The series is incomplete before 1824 and the 'Bills Payable' (Acceptances) account does not commence until this year.

Baring Bros 1825, 1850, annual ledgers. 1890 in L. S. Pressnell, 'Gold reserves, banking reserves and the Baring crisis', in C. R. Whittlesey and J. S. G. Wilson (eds), *Essays in Money and Banking* (Oxford, 1968), p. 200

Subsequent data from T. Skinner's *The London Banks* (1891 et seq.).

Note: 'Acceptances' here means liabilities on acceptances at year end, *not* total acceptances given during the year.

Rothschilds

N. M. Rothschild was an entrepreneur of quite outstanding business ability, while his sons and grandsons could not match his genius, so that the founder's main policies were continued without major revision down to the First World War. All of the texts have placed much emphasis on the unity and integration of the five Frankfurt brothers, but while a large volume of transactions continued to flow between them, and an almost daily correspondence maintained between them and their successors down to 1914, this interpretation fails to give adequate recognition to the independence of the founder of the London enterprise. He stood in the central tradition of the Jewish brokers and exchange merchants, with their large volume of dealings through the principal European centres, their reputation for probity and regularity in all their dealings, their Yiddish correspondence with fellow Jews and their highly competitive profit margins.[1] His brothers were loyal lieutenants during the period of his dramatic spurt into the front rank (1814–18) but apart from James had no outstanding ability so that he could have been served almost as well by other Jewish firms connected with his father's house. The important distinction between the continental view of the Rothschilds (which until recently has informed most of the literature) and the British one was made at NM's death by the *Gentleman's Magazine*. 'The five houses were conducted nearly in common, except that in London, which was under the exclusive direction of its nominal chief.'[2] From the first, London was a law unto itself, and the most authoritative modern historian of the Paris house, Bertrand Gille, endorses the point. NM's outstanding success was achieved by specialisation; he never interested himself in anything much beyond bills, bonds and bullion. He repudiated his early career interest in merchanting, he missed out on English railways and he avoided all industrial business. Unlike his younger brother James, he never became a *grand homme d'affaires*.

NM's single-minded dedication to financial business in the narrow sense is relatively a novel point so will bear a little elaboration. As early as 1815 he wrote to a Frankfurt cousin, Jacob Stern, insisting that his 'chief business is in the banking line only', and that he was not prepared to devote any time to commodity transactions which he had passed on to his brothers-in-law Reiss, Sichel and Worms in Manchester.[3] In 1819, when a British government commission asked him about sending manufactures to France, he replied, 'I do no business but in banking business, loans, and so forth.'[4] His ledgers show that after the French Wars he retained only a basic network of agents and correspondents, 'first-class' houses located in key financial centres across Europe – Behrens, Oppenheimer and Hecksher in Hamburg, Eichthal in Augsburg, the Seehandlung and Benecke Bros in Berlin, Bethmann in Frankfurt, Osy and Ezechiels in Rotterdam, Braunsberg in Amsterdam, Steiglitz in St Petersburg, and so on. Most but not all were Jewish; almost all were bankers of distinction in their own right. The intention was obviously to maintain a business that combined simplicity and safety (that is an elite of safe correspondents) with large turnover.

NM deviated from this policy only in two or three relatively minor ways, the first of them quite well known. In 1824 he took the lead in the formation of the Alliance Insurance Company, a joint-stock company with the enormous capital of £5m. which succeeded in offering some rivalry to Lloyds.[5] The private insurance underwriters replied by electing a succession of senior partners of Rothschilds' rivals (Barings and Frühling & Goschen) as the Chairman of Lloyds Committee for half the century (1851–1901).[6] NM meanwhile became increasingly involved in providing various kinds of credits from import – export merchants, particularly for a number of German firms with bases in Manchester from which they imported raw cotton and exported yarns and piece goods to the continent. This business appears to have developed from NM's close connection with Levy Behrens & Sons of Hamburg, Manchester and Leeds. When Rothschild's relatives failed to make a go of the Manchester trade, he looked to Behrens' son who had recently settled there to maintain his interest. Another strong connection was made with Du Fay, a Huguenot house based in Frankfurt that had opened a branch in Manchester about 1802. Behrens, Du Fay and the other German houses in turn granted credits to some of Manchester's leading manufacturers of the day; the details of this system are examined in Chapter 7. The London house had a large part of the world trade in quicksilver, thanks to a major stake in the Almaden mines in Spain, and associated smelting houses. When new sources of supply appeared in Mexico they lost money in Spain, but transferred their interest to the New World by sending out an agent to Mexico City, so sustaining their leadership.[7]

In the 1840s, when the new generation was settled firmly in the saddle, interest in Manchester temporarily waned in favour of such promising transatlantic opportunities. Commercial credits were heavily reined in at the crisis of 1848, though this did not prevent the family losing a great deal of money. When Arnstein & Eskelles of Vienna failed with £600,000 liabilities that year, the Rothschilds' losses were so heavy that Belmont, their New York agent, believed they would go bankrupt.[8] It is easy to suppose that it was this traumatic experience that made Baron Lionel and his two brothers less willing to take risks than their father had been, but the firm's records in London and Paris show their caution in evidence from the beginning of their period that they were in control.

It is well known that the Rothschilds were centrally involved in railway development on the continent from an early date, but Gille has emphasised that this interest scarcely touched the London branch of the family.[9] While Baron James in Paris was enthusiastic for the new investment possibilities, the correspondence of his nephews in London shows that they were at best lukewarm, principally on the grounds that involvement was more trouble and risk than it was worth. Soloman

Rothschild's investment in the Witkowitz ironworks in the 1840s was not shared with his London nephews.[10] The continental Rothschilds' connections with railway building introduced the London house to the export of rails at an early date, but if the letter books of the Dowlais Iron Works are anything to go by, the field was soon more strongly occupied by Barings, Huths, Devaux, Peabody and other accepting houses.[11] To be fair to the second generation in London, their uncle James in Paris was not unequivocal in his support of railway development, as a letter from NM's third son (Nathaniel II) in 1847 clearly shows:

> I regret to observe that the Baron [James] has been making a row about the [joint] accounts; he is a queer fish but is terribly bothered about the railways and roads so you must not be angry with him ... our worthy uncle is very nervous when he thinks of the enormous sums we hold belonging to the railway companies and which can be called whenever they like – that is, in the event of liquidation.[12]

Moreover, through this younger brother, the London partners had direct experience of the trials of railway financing at the period. Another letter of 1847 is very revealing:

> You have no idea how plagued we are by the different railroad concerns; first the Northern falls (300 francs), then Marseille–Avignon, and now St Germain. I cannot advise you too strongly to steer clear of all sorts of concerns and affairs in which you risk money and where you have the entire management. I am sick of all railways and coal companies and everything else.

The advice was evidently taken very seriously, not least as Nathaniel was making similar complaints in the early 1860s.[13]

Another instance in which it is possible to probe the apparent conservatism of the second generation partners occurs in 1839, when they declined to join a syndicate of English and French bankers formed to make good the outflow of gold from the Bank of England.[14] This seems all the more surprising in view of NM's and James Rothschild's large sales of gold to the Bank in the late 1820s. An explanation is offered by a letter from Anselm Soloman in Frankfurt

> Do not take any rash step in a large operation. Your mother tells me that Herries told your good father in her presence to mind and not trust the Bank without any guarantee ... as the Bank being involved in difficulties may stop suddenly. ... Mind, my good cousins, that you are not your good father, that you do not have his influence and that he was capable of acting in other ways than prudence might dictate to you.[15]

It may seem preposterous to suppose that the Bank of England would have been allowed to stop payment, but at the time Joshua Bates of Barings had no doubt that the risk was not only real but also imminent. 'It cannot be denied that, but for the exertions of my House, the Bank of England would have stopped payment', he recorded in his private journal.[16]

Another area in which the second generation appeared to be sluggish was in their responding to opportunities in the USA. August Belmont, who was appointed their agent in 1837 after J. L. & J. Josephs went into liquidation, was constantly urging the London house to take up some new and profitable venture, but his proposals were often spurned or neglected. There was a rather better response after Baron Alphonse toured the USA in 1852 and enthusiastically pointed out the large market for US railroad bonds in Germany, but Belmont's letters to London continued to show more frustration than sense of progress or achievement. In despair he addressed Baron 'Natty' Rothschild (the young third generation) in 1870:

I have for the last few years offered to your house a variety of transactions and negotiations, all of which were safe and without risk, some of them paying handsome commissions and others which would have made brilliant profits. You have invariably rejected all my propositions, so that our correspondence becomes unprofitable and stagnant while other firms have taken hold of the business which you declined and not only have made a great deal of money by it but have obtained a position of importance which they could not have acquired otherwise ... if you do not wish to enter into any large negotiations of loans for states, cities, or railroads, no matter what my conviction of their safety may be, you had better let me know so.[17]

In this case, there seems to be a signal failure to respond to NM's leadership, for he had worked hard to secure his 1834 appointment as the US government's banker in Europe, driving off Barings and Willink of Amsterdam, and the loss of this agency in 1843 was more to do with a change in administration in Washington than in leadership at New Court. Belmont's leading role in the Democratic Party did not help matters; it was not easy to secure government patronage as Barings always seemed to be on the inner track. A typical letter, written in 1849, sadly reports that 'With all this [work] I have but little hope of success because, as I told you before, the administration is entirely in the hands of Barings' friends.'[18]

However, there were few political restraints in the 1850s and 1860s, when the US appetite for capital appeared insatiable. Belmont was not quite so infallible as his 1870 letter suggests – at one period, for instance, he was all for backing Vanderbilt's railway projects – but there can be little doubt that not only Barings, but also a sequence of other Anglo-American houses took business that Rothschilds might easily have had. Part of the explanation is that the London partners personally disliked Belmont, but never agreed to anyone to replace him as their agent.[19] (In this connection it is interesting to notice that they did not always get on with their other important agent at the period, Weisweller of Madrid). Significantly Rothschilds did best in the USA in one of their traditional lines, that of dealing in bullion. When gold was discovered in California in 1849, a family connection (Davidson) was sent out, and through him the London house quickly became the major London importer. By 1851 Belmont was forwarding twice as much as Barings and Browns together. The gold rush attracted new US bankers like Lazards and Seligmans to California, but for another generation they were not in the same league as the Rothschilds. Ten years after the first discoveries, Belmont was still making 'heavy shipments' at a profit of $\frac{3}{8}-\frac{1}{2}$ per cent after insurance. In the late 1840s other agents were sent to New Orleans and Havana and a modest trade built up in tobacco, cotton, sugar, coffee and grain.[20]

It might be supposed that this restraint in the USA was the obverse of a strong continuing commitment in Europe, and this is at least partly true. Rothschilds' ledgers show that most of their accounts continued to be in Europe, while their acceptances showed impressive (if somewhat erratic) growth in the second and third generations. But even in safe European business, New Court remained highly cautious. Shortly before his death in 1868, Baron James wrote to his London nephews

> I thoroughly dislike it that we are too restrictive in matters of business and that we did not negotiate the Swedish loan [taken by Raphaels], I would have liked to conclude it; this kind of loan is generally taken up in the issuing country and consequently but a mere advance business.[21]

When Baron Alphonse succeeded his father as head of the Paris house, he continued to show more enterprise than his London cousins. Acceptances fell away during Baron Lionel's last years, but this was probably due to his failing health as they picked up again when the new generation assumed control.

Apart from the bullion trade and loans to Brazil, N. M. Rothschild & Sons showed little interest in opportunities outside Europe until after the death of Baron Lionel in 1879. The third generation took some new initiatives at the beginning of their long reign at New Court, though largely in the trade in which their family had already shown most interest over the years, that in precious metals and diamonds. Their most conspicuous success was achieved in South Africa. From 1882 a stream of technical and financial experts was diverted from California to

Kimberley and the Rand, and the family began to take a small speculative interest in mining shares, which in the early 1880s were at a low level. But Rothschilds' celebrated sponsorship of the De Beers diamond monopoly (1888) was not such a bold venture as it may seem, for the merger initiative in fact began with the Paris Erlangers, and Rothschilds' syndicate was paid £250,000 for advancing £750,000 for the key purchase. Moreover, Cecil Rhodes and his De Beers board were regularly in conflict with their bankers, so the real value of the South African connection was soon recognised as shipping, refining and marketing gold for Wernher, Beit & Co., which by 1900 had overtaken the Standard Bank as the leading Rand dealers. The De Beers' issue of 1889 was arranged by Rothschilds' most able clerk of the period, Hamburg-born Carl Meyer, who became a director of the company in 1888 and deputy chairman from 1901 until his death in 1921. However, far from capitalising on his expertise, the Rothschild brothers declined to offer him a partnership in the bank, or even procuration, instead allowing their most dynamic rival, Sir Ernest Cassel, to capture Meyer for his Egyptian and other projects.[22]

The Rothschild group bought a 20 per cent interest in the lucrative Rand Mines Ltd, but the initial connection was between Wernher Beit & Co. and the continental Rothschilds, rather than their English cousins. Similarly the Rothschilds' well-known interest in the Russian (Baku) oil industry and the building of the Trans-Caucasian Railway (1883) was the outcome of Baron Alphonse's enterprise and it seems that London had little to do with it. It is, moreover, significant that the British-based oil companies, Marcus Samuel & Co. (Shell) and Frederick Lane, were supported by the Paris Rothschilds and not by their London cousins. Similarly, Rothschild support of the famous Rio Tinto mining company was based in Paris, not London.[23]

The fairest assessment of the policy of the second and third generation of London Rothschilds is that, fraternising with European royalty, entertained and flattered by the peerage, and considered financially inviolate by the commercial aristocracy of the age, they had little need to search for new business in the USA or trouble themselves with risky ventures in the old world.[24] As Baron Alphonse wrote to his London cousins in 1872, 'Notwithstanding the many new banking houses, the governments always turn to us.'[25] Such was their prestige, they could maintain the upward momentum of their business without taking any client that suggested the possibility of significant risk. It was an ideal business environment in which to operate, and the London Rothschilds did not care to look for trouble outside it. A pen-portrait of Baron Lionel just before his death in 1879 records how 'He held his usual [daily] business levée in New Court. ... he sat in the arm chair from which he controlled the exchanges of Europe', and received a string of supplicants for credit. This patronising relationship between banker and client, characteristic of the accepting houses at the period, was maintained well into the twentieth century.[26]

In the second and third generations the business was progressively simplified to minimise administration and eliminate risks. The number of ledger accounts was reduced from 115 in 1835 (the last full year before NM's sudden death) to 41 at the turn of the century, with the earlier concentration on the German states and Low Countries turning to Russia, southern Europe (Austro-Hungary, Italy, Spain and the Balkans), Latin America and the USA. Following a visit to Russia in 1873–4, Baron Edmond wrote to his London cousins that the 'Minister of Finance particularly is very pleased with himself and his connection with our Houses, enabling him to conclude his loans by a mere exchange of telegrams.' By 1900 a handful of favoured clients accounted for much of the turnover, three St Petersburg financial agencies (£14.4m.), three Latin American banks (£7.2m.) and M. Guggenheim & Sons of New York (£7.1m.). (Meyer Guggenheim was a Swiss Jew who found his way into New York's financial élite through his good luck and shrewdness in the US silver and copper mining.)[27] In 1885 Baron Alphonse Rothschild had complained to his London cousins about the Frankfurt house having made themselves the 'satellite' of Hansemann and his Discontogesellschaft, a house 'not of our standing', but by 1900 N. M. Rothschild & Co.'s largest business in Germany (£2.2m.) was being conducted through this joint-stock bank. The old private banks (Warburgs, Bleichroders, Behrens and Mendelsohns) maintained their accounts but were steadily diminishing in overall importance.[28]

A dozen years after NM's death, a well-known City journalist fairly observed that while the banker's sons inherited his business, 'they do not inherit his position in the stock market. They are competitors for government loans, but though with the name remains a certain amount of its former power, they do not appear willing to entertain the extensive and complicated business in which their father delighted.' When Lord 'Natty' Rothschild died in 1915, the ever-sober *Times* recorded that 'He was not a man of genius in the sphere of finance like his father, and in a still higher degree his grandfather.' Even so, his younger brothers 'were somewhat eclipsed by the masterful character of Lord Rothschild', who pontificated over his following of stockbrokers in much the same way that his father had done. A. R. Wagg, who became a partner in Helbert Wagg, Rothschilds' principal stockbrokers, in 1903, recorded that 'everybody was in considerable awe of Baron Lionel', while 'the manners of Lord Rothschild were not calculated to put a person at all sensitive at his ease.' Private records reinforce the picture of growing autocracy within the firm and aloofness to almost all other firms outside. In 1905 Carl Meyer wrote, 'One after the other of the principal employees retires finding it impossible to get on with Alfred [de Rothschild] who is becoming more unbearable than ever to the staff and treats men of 30 years service like office boys.' The brothers lunched regularly together at New Court, often calling in the experts who served them, but the names of other merchant bankers seldom figured in the invitation lists.[29]

Incredibly, no outside partners were brought into the business until the 1960s, so there were scarcely any critics of this autocracy and not surprisingly a failure to innovate. In addition to De Beers, Rothschilds in volved themselves in company promotion in the late 1880s with the Burma Ruby Mines and the Manchester Ship Canal, but found the business more troublesome than they expected and retired from the scene.[30] The later Ship Canal issues were shared with Barings, who now took the initiative in this area, though not always (as will be seen below) without losses. Rothschilds also issued stock for the armaments industry (Maxim Nordenfeld, 1888) and maintained an avuncular eye on Vickers' activities, but the latter's letter books reveal no sustained or specific correspondence on policy matters or special ventures.[31] From 1890 Rothschilds were less active as an issuing house as the Brazilian revolution of 1889 was 'a cause of serious anxiety to Lord Rothschild'. He 'often said that the trouble was largely due to the excessive growth of the practice of underwriting, which made it fatally easy to bring out almost any loan.' It was no doubt for this reason and the general caution induced by the Baring crisis that he declined for some years to take the initiative in Chinese and Japanese loans to be raised in London in the fifteen years or so before the First World War. This of course was the opportunity of the Hong Kong & Shanghai Banking Corporation, and for specialist stockbrokers like Panmure Gordon, from whom 'Natty' Rothschild belatedly acquired a holding in Japanese stock. More generally, we may accept *The Times's* verdict in 1915 that 'It is probably true that London as a money centre, though enormously powerful, was not so powerful as it would have been if Rothschilds had thought fit to initiate and control some of the big new business of the last 25 years' (1890–1915).[32]

Barings

The main contrast between Barings and Rothschilds is in the area of commodity dealing and mercantile outlook. While Rothschilds concentrated on those commodities traditionally of interest to Court Jews (bullion, mercury, diamonds and so on), Barings remained *general merchants* until well into the nineteenth century. There was a relatively slack period from Sir Francis Baring's death in 1810 to Joshua Bates's appointment as partner in 1828, but otherwise the most striking feature of Barings's activity was a continuing diversity. The partners were interested not only in the great staples of world trade of the period – tea, sugar, coffee, indigo and cotton – but also in virtually every commodity on which advances were made, shipping arranged and insured, or large volumes bought and sold on their own account, or on joint account, or on commission. At one time or another the partners can be observed trading in copper, flour, grain, hemp, hides, iron, rice, rum, saltpetre, spices, tallow, tin, tobacco and wool, and this list is by no means exhaustive. In fact the only commodities in which they were less than prominent were those requiring highly specific expertise, such as gold and mercury, and even here they did not allow Rothschilds's leadership to go unchallenged.[33]

The principal change that took place when Bates took control of the commercial side was that some of the traditional lines that harked back to the Barings' early years in Exeter were dropped. The Barings came to London originally as woolstaplers and cloth merchants, and one branch of their business that was still supposed to be most valuable consisted in making advances on and selling wool of great Russian and East European landowners and merchants. Bates found these had gradually fallen into the habit of drawing credits more and more in anticipation of future shipments and by his time drawing on bales which would have to grow on the backs of sheep unborn, and he persuaded his partners to abandon these speculative long-term credits. His caution brought much criticism but he was vindicated in the Leipzig crisis of 1834, when the houses that had continued it and devoured Barings' business suffered heavy losses. Similarly, Bates excised a large part of the traditional business in Calcutta and Mauritius when he found that the planters did not cover their bills by the crop for that season, and this saved the house from large losses in the Calcutta crisis of 1847.[34]

Joshua Bates was of course American-born, so it is not surprising that through the long period that he controlled Barings' commerce and banking, the main interest of the house was in the United States. Although Barings had a longstanding interest in North America which was strengthened by Alexander's personal interest and family connections (he married a daughter of Senator Bingham of Philadelphia), Bates undoubtedly brought a large volume of US business into the firm with him. When Samuel Williams, the great American banker of London, failed in 1825, Bates recognised that his bankruptcy had arisen from 'outside operations' rather than 'legitimate mercantile banking trade.' He wrote to Hopes's senior partner, P. C. Labouchère, with whom he had accidentally become acquainted in 1817, asking whether any Barings or Hopes were at liberty to seize the opportunity. The outcome was the partnership of Bates and Alexander's nephew, John Baring, which with a capital of only £15,000 took up the bills of Williams for houses in Boston and other towns on the Atlantic seaboard. The initiative was so successful that within fifteen months Bates & Baring 'were really a house to be considered in connection with the old house, which had become ... less

energetic in business.' Three years later Alexander retired in favour of
Bates, who was effectively the leading partner on the commercial side,
while Thomas Wren Ward, the US agent, was granted a share in the
business.[35] Soon after joining Barings, Bates recorded in his journal that
'American business will be safer than any other and should be cultivated
with the greatest care', and although there was some reining in before
the 1837 crisis, and again in 1857–61, the house remained true to his
resolution. The strength of the firm's connection with the USA was
steadily improved by the dedication of the partners in London, Liverpool
and Boston (Mass.) In London Bates himself spent a lot of time
entertaining American visitors, a stream that grew markedly from 1838,
when steamboats were able to cross the Atlantic in 14 days. In 1832 he
succeeded in opening a branch office in Liverpool, then the main gateway
to US trade, with S. S. Gair (an American) and Charles Baring Young as
partners. In the 1830s Liverpool merchants were still short of money and
the local banking system was yet undeveloped, so Barings were able to use
their capital to take a major stake in the cotton trade. In Boston Barings'
business was managed by Thomas Wren Ward, a lifelong friend of
Bates's, 'a slow thinker', but a man with an unrivalled knowledge of the
standing and operations of US merchants. Ward was succeeded by his
son, S. G. Ward, who moved his office to New York in 1869.[36]

Barings' other principal trading ventures were to the Far East, an interest
that can readily be traced back to Sir Francis Baring's membership of the
Court of the East India Co., but was also rejuvenated by Bates. In the early
1830s the partners bought new ships to carry manufactured goods to Calcutta, Colombo and Canton, returning with cargoes of tea, and agents were
posted in these centres. A large connection was also built up through
some of Bates's old friends in Boston, Russell & Co., who had branch
houses in Canton and Manila, and are said to have conducted more than
half the US trade with the Pacific coast and China between 1810 and
1840. Russell, Sturgis & Co. dominated the entire trade of Manila down
to 1875. In addition to loans and acceptance business, Russell & Co.
consigned tea and silk from China to the UK in return for cargoes of
manufactured goods, specie and occasionally opium. It seems that Bates's
policies were broadly maintained down to the 1870s, for after a short
interval he was succeeded as a senior partner by his protegé Russell
Sturgis who was born and trained in Boston and spent his early career
(1834–44) as a partner in Russell, Sturgis & Co. (of Canton) and Russell &
Sturgis (Manila). His period as senior partner in London (1873–82)
maintained Barings as the same dour puritan New England house that it
had been through Bates's long reign (1828–64).[37]

Despite the fact that Bates was primarily interested in Anglo-American
trade, as distinct from finance and investment, the roots of Barings'
transition to a finance house can be traced to the early years of his

leadership. During the two decades following Barings' famous negotiation of the postwar loan to France (1818), the firm showed little interest in foreign state issues, and their interest in railroad finance was very limited until the 1850s. Their stock-dealing issued rather from their position as a 'bankers' bank' for new-born American concerns. In 1828 Barings were selling $200,000 stock for the Bank of Pennsylvania, in 1830 making a loan to the Bank of New York, in 1832 selling $5.5m. stock (£1.03m.) for the Union Bank of Louisiana, and in 1834 advancing over £6,500 to the Planters' Association Bank of Louisiana. The correspondence with the Union Bank suggests that these sales arose out of the practice of depositing bonds with Barings as a security for advances. Consequently Barings' trade circulars for 1833 (the only ones extant) were advertising the sale of a limited group of US securities at the foot of the usual commodity lists. At this date the only ones on offer were those of four states (New York, Pennsylvania, Ohio and Alabama) and four banks, three of them in Louisiana. This limited connection was reined in in 1834 and not expanded again until Barings marketed the loan for the rebuilding of Charleston and the first Massachusetts Railroad loan in 1838.[38]

During these years, various members of the Baring family continued as partners, but showed a strong propensity to early retirement to landed estate. Bates's grip on the business strengthened as one after another withdrew. Sir Francis's son Alexander Baring (later Lord Ashburton) virtually retired on Bates's appointment, and John Baring, Bates's early partner, retired in 1837. Sir Thomas and Henry Baring died the following year, and the neurotic Mildmay finally withdrew in 1847. The only member of the family to stay for his entire career was Sir Francis's grandson Thomas III, who complemented Bates by taking charge of new issues and investments. Bates recorded his opinion that his most active partner 'has a very clever head and is just fitted for loan operations which require great effort for a short time and not a steady attention to business as commission and banking business requires.' On another occasion Bates complained in his journal that Baring 'works well at intervals but claims the right to be absent and in such a vast concern there remains but myself with proper experience.' Bertram Currie of Glyns, a friend of the Baring family, explained that Thomas III was 'a merchant prince, and worthy successor of the Medici or Fuggers. . . . He was certainly a proof, if any were wanting, that a merchant may be as good a gentleman as an acred Lord or squire and he was wisely content with and proud of his trade.' These personal details are reproduced to emphasise two points: first that in the middle decades of the century the Barings continued to live in a style no less magnificent than the Rothschilds, and secondly (much more significantly) that new issues were only of sporadic interest to them while acceptances were delegated to others. From the end of the

French Wars until the late 1850s, the firm sponsored very few issues; various opportunities were offered but declined. Mildmay lacked the nerve, Baring was involved in sumptuous living and 101 other interests, while Bates remained a merchant whose specific expertise was limited to the USA, a country whose public credit rating he was often ashamed of. 'There never was a country so disgraced in point of credits as the United States of America by the repudiation of some of the States and the inability of others to meet their engagements', he recorded in his journal in 1842.[39] The 'bread and butter' income of the house continued to be commissions and acceptances though this is not to say that it did not receive an occasional thick coating of 'jam' from a successful issue, especially from the late 1850s.[40]

Like Rothschilds, Barings were challenged by the rise of joint-stock banking, and more particularly by the development of the Crédit Mobilier type of industrial bank. But while Rothchilds eschewed the whole notion out of contempt for their upstart rivals in Paris, the Barings' thinking started with friends who were much in favour. Their principal connection in the French capital, Rudolphe Hottinger, enthusiastically recorded his response that 'The banker, who is becoming both economist and financier, from now onwards sees a field of activity opening before him vaster than that of any other period.' Barings' closest friends in the City, Glyn, Mills & Co., had raised themselves to a premier position among private banks by their commitment to railway finance, and were instrumental in the promotion of the Ottoman Bank (1856), the Bank of London and South America (1863) and the Anglo-Austrian Bank (1864). When the International Financial Society was formed by seven small London houses at the same period of passionate interest in joint-stock promotion, Geo Carr Glyn wanted to be involved, but again Barings prevaricated.[41] Thomas Baring said to Mallet, the Mobilier's envoy, 'such a combination must come sooner or later – that we would think about it ... we may have to join you sooner or later', while Bates responded, 'You see M. Mallet we consider ourselves a sort of Crédit Mobilier, ourselves alone.' Bates subsequently confessed to his journal that 'It appears to me that these sort of Banks will get all the Public Loans and that BB & Co. must content themselves with the Commission and Banking Business [that is merchanting and acceptances] for a time', but he did not believe their success would endure. Beyond the conservation of two elderly senior partners, these quotations reveal their commitment to the traditional forms of merchant banking; as soon as the American Civil War was over, Bates believed Barings would have all the acceptance business it wanted.[42]

Through this period, the principal value of Barings' connections with foreign governments appears to have been the deposits they left in London and the commercial prestige brought to the house by the patronage. In this respect, Alexander Baring followed his father's lead, and this was well known at Westminster at the time. According to *The Times*, Cobbett was accustomed in his coarse way to exclaim, 'There's Baring, now; he pretends to be a great Whig, but he is just as bad as any of the Tories. We all know that he married the daughter of old Bingham of Philadelphia, and that through the influence of his brother-in-law's connexions he ... contrived to keep up a close connection for the lucre's sake with a republican government.' Bingham induced the Washington government to transfer their banking account in Europe from Willinks of Amsterdam to Barings and this connection brought with it 'almost all the monetary agency, public and private, of the United States, together with a vast amount of mercantile business for individual citizens of America'. Consequently for many years Barings 'held such balances of American money that they were enabled to exercise great influence not only in New York, but even over the monetary affairs of Europe', *The Times* insisted in 1848. Ten years later Barings also held accounts for Russia, Norway, Austria, Chile, Buenos Aires and New Grenada, and the colonies of Canada, Nova Scotia, New Brunswick and Australia. Personal accounts were held by Napoleon III of France and King Leopold of Belgium, in addition to those of 1,200 correspondents round the world. Bates proudly confided to his journal that 'no House ever had such a business.'[43]

The Barings evidently collected further prestige from the eminence of a sequence of members of the family in public life. Two of Sir Francis Baring's sons spent some years in Parliament and his grandson (another Sir Francis) was Chancellor of the Exchequer for a short period (1839–41). The family was rewarded with several peerages: Ashburton (1848), Northbrook (1866), Revelstoke (1884) and Cromer (1892), more than any other City family, and at one time or another during the nineteenth century (1832–1918) had as many as a dozen MPs in the House of Commons, twice as many as Rothschilds, and three or more times the number of other merchant banking families prominent in politics.[44]   Barings' US connections obviously presented opportunities for issuing and dealing in federal, state and railroad securities, but for some years Bates restrained his partners from looking up capital in such risky ventures. George Peabody, Barings' principal rival in transatlantic finance in the 1840s, was dealing in US bonds through the decade, but Barings' and Rothschilds' aloofness prevented the development of any regular market in London until the 1850s and, even then, the two leading houses preferred to retail shares in 'safe' issues rather than taking the lead. It was not until after Bates' death that Barings became more bold, launching out into a sequence of US railroad issues, especially in Massachusetts. Other early ventures into railways were not particularly encouraging, but do not seem to have restrained Revelstoke's easy optimism.[45]

Though caution and restraint recurs in the annals of Barings' business, they were still sufficiently successful to excite the envy of smaller firms, and even some of the most successful houses. For many years the Browns struggled to keep up with the Barings, making up in number of clients and secured credits what they lacked in quality of their connections. At mid-century, Baron Alphonse Rothschild wrote to his London cousins from Cuba that 'Baring has immense connections everywhere in America and I have no doubt, my dear cousins, that should you enter business in this country with more confidence you will find opportunities to greatly extend our existing sphere of operations in America.' Unfortunately, Barings' enterprise sometimes transgressed the boundaries of discretion, resulting in serious losses to the partners.[46]

However, this envy of Barings' success should not persuade us that the partners were always rational entrepreneurs; on a few interesting occasions the leading partners speculated foolishly. Thomas Baring allowed himself to become involved in the Canadian Grand Trunk Railway, along with Glyn's Bank, an expensive enterprise that never paid a dividend. By September 1860 the Grand Trunk's debt to the two London banks amounted to £800,000 (equally divided), and it took a Canadian High Court case and special Act of Parliament to secure the repayment of the bondholders.[47] In the same decade Baring Bros were also lumbered with another heavy loser, the Weardale Iron Company, to which Bates committed £200,000, vainly hoping to profit from railway contracts abroad.[48] Despite this experience and the British public's hostility to the Imperial Russian government, Barings were active in a consortium led by the Crédit Mobilier and Steiglitz to raise loans for the Grand Russian Railway (1856–60), but the early history of the concern reflected little credit on either the Parisian management or its Moscow sponsors.[49]

Particular attention has been focused on the relative importance of the Baring family and the importance of 'outside' partners because far-reaching changes took place after Bates died in 1864 and Sturgis retired in 1882, neither of them with family successors in the business. Thomas Baring, who was a director of the Bank of England, tried to make good the lost professionalism by arranging a merger with the Scots firm Finlay, Hodgson & Co., as he admired the achievement of Kirkman Hodgson as Governor of the Bank during the financial crisis of 1866; but here again no new succession was established.[50] Consequently control reverted to the Baring dynasty, in particular E. C. Baring (soon to be first Lord Revelstoke) and H. B. Mildmay, a son of the family connection that was retired in 1847. At various times in the 1850s, Bates had recorded his opinion of them:

My impression is that neither of them will make a good merchant. Edward Baring is clever enough but very fond of pleasure and I doubt if his pleasure is of the right kind. He will not make business his main object. Mildmay is good and amiable but very slow and not of a strong mind [1853]. ... Mildmay is modest, willing, attentive and economical, but no marked ability, neither him or Edward Baring can ever become leading partners in the house [1856]. ... the present generation of young men appear to be educated superficially, there is a great desire to get rich without the study and labour necessary to qualify themselves for business [1857].[51]

When due allowance is made for the generation gap, and for the prejudice of a man who reached the first rank of business without inherited position or wealth, it must be allowed that this prognostication proved to be remarkably far-sighted.

Changes in the conditions of world trade in the last quarter of the nineteenth century made it impossible for the new leadership at Barings to maintain the old policies and connections, if they had wished to do so. The collapse of Russell, Sturgis & Co. of Manila in 1875 signalled the end of Barings' traditional connections in the Far East, while the obsolescence of the mercantile function in Liverpool eroded another prop of the firm's traditional interests. The intensification of competition in shipping created a situation in which only specialists were likely to survive; so early as 1859 Bates was advised the 'management of steamers is a business of itself and with which the less such houses as ours have to do the better ... competition is so great and commissions are so much reduced that it is not worth the attention of respectable houses.'[52]

Allusion to these economic developments must serve to demonstrate the context in which Barings were forced to shift from being merchants to being merchant bankers. Through the 1870s and 1880s the mercantile side of the business was gradually given up. In Liverpool some effort was made to get into new lines (for example, rubber, guano) but the area was already crowded by specialists. Revelstoke focused increasingly on acceptances and public issues, particularly for North American railroads. The issue business never quite caught up with that of Rothschilds, but acceptances climbed steadily until they were far above any competitors, in 1890 Barings reached some £15m. or one-sixth of the total acceptances issued in London on the eve of the crisis (Table 2.2).[53] Rothschilds were less than one-tenth of this, and the most pushing of Barings' new competitors (Kleinworts) scarcely reached £9m. or 10 per cent of the total. According to Revelstoke, both issues and acceptances became routinised in his firm at this period. 'Between the business of accepting bills on commission and the business of issuing loans on commission there is little difference; in the former case the issues are private while in the latter there is a strong element of publicity about them. Private bills mature of themselves and cease to exist, public loans are of more permanent nature.'[54] Convinced of this simple theory and no longer restrained by a prudent senior partner, in six years (1882–8) the house raised some £95m. by public issues, nearly all for foreign and colonial governments and public works. All might have been well if Revelstoke had covered himself by underwriting his public issues and feeding them on to the market a little at a time, and immense quantities of stock were disdained by a more prudent investing public.[55]

The consequent Baring crisis of 1890 will be dealt with more fully in Chapter 5. For the moment it is sufficient to notice that Barings' acceptances, so carefully built up for a generation, dropped from £15m. to £3m., while competitors moved into the void. The City was no longer dominated by two firms. Revelstoke was a broken man and the reconstruction of the house, which now became a public company, involved his resignation, along with that of Mildmay and J. S. Hodgson.[56]

The new public company was still dominated by the Baring family and the broad lines of policy continued as before. A push was made to re-establish leadership in acceptances which reached £6.6m. in 1913, nearly half the figure of 1890, but less than 5 per cent of the total London figure, and now trailing behind Kleinworts and Schröders.[57] Barings continued to issue stock for the parts of the world in which the house had specialised for most of the Victorian years. The second Lord Revelstoke, when he became senior partner in 1901, was just as autocratic as his father, but there were a number of policy departures that contributed to the re-establishment of Barings as a leading firm. 'Outside' directors were sought for, bringing in Gaspard Farrer, an expert on US and Canadian securities, from H. S. Lefevre & Co., but an attempt to merge with J. S. Morgan & Co. was repudiated by the US house. Revelstoke made annual visits to North America when he was younger but cut very little ice there; indeed a London director of Morgans maintained in 1901 that the old City house was by then 'a mere cipher' in the USA.[58]

Nevertheless, Barings maintained a foothold in Wall Street by building up reciprocal connections with US investment bankers. The advantages of a transatlantic connection, long demonstrated by Barings, became obvious to everyone after the American Civil War, when Morgans, Seligmans, Morton and other US firms opened offices in London, but the London firms were too proud or insular to open branch houses in US cities (see Chapter 3), and we have already seen how the Rothschilds retained their New York agent as a vassal rather than partner. In 1878 Kidder Peabody of Boston, a banking house that had risen rapidly during the railway boom of the 1870s, opened an account with Barings, and seven years later this had proved so mutually advantageous that Thomas Baring IV left Liverpool to become a partner in the US house. In the reorganisation that followed the Baring crisis, he moved to Kidder Peabody's New York City branch, which was now renamed Baring,

Magoun & Co. Cecil Baring went out to join the new partnership and the capital was augmented to $4m. (£0.625m.). The New York operation included both commercial credits and new issues of stock, particularly for US railroads. With the retirement of various partners, the name of Baring disappeared from the New York directories in 1908, but Kidder Peabody's links with London continued. The relationship broadly parallels that of the Rothschilds with Guggenheims of New York, but because of the interlocking partnership seems to have been more intimate.[59]

Looking through the share issues of the period, it appears that Barings were rather more involved in company business than Rothschilds, but closer inspection shows that all the industrial and commercial companies except the Mersey Docks & Harbour Board and the breweries were in the USA, and the issues made on the initiative of Kidder Peabody. In view of the fact that the Baring crisis was caused by Lord Revelstoke flooding the market with the stock of Argentine public utility company shares, it is not surprising that his successors needed to show restraint, but it seems that the crisis was not the only hard lesson of the period. Ernest Terah Hooley, the most notorious company promoter of the age, floated Trafford Park Estates Ltd in 1896 with the help of Barings, and the reformed house was fortunate that some of the odour of this convicted swindler did not attach itself (however unjustly) to them. Barings' records for this period are still private, but it is fair to discern in this episode yet another reason for their keeping out of the minefield of company promotion.[60]

Diverse Approaches to Merchant Banking

Although there are some obvious similarities between the nineteenth-century experience of Barings and Rothschilds (most notably that both rose quickly to the top during the French Wars, principally because of their ability to take advantage of the patronage of government and both continued to be dominated by family dynasties) the contrasts are at first sight more striking. While the English Rothschilds steadily increased their momentum along the well-marked groove of their founder, the Barings tried to concentrate on being general merchants and only when frustrated in this diverted towards pure finance. In the course of this book it will be seen that Barings' experience was much more typical than Rothschilds'; most merchant banks were directed towards acceptances, issues, arbitrage and other activities from having capital and connections yet suffering the curtailment of their traditional trading interests.

But taking a much closer view, it is possible to identify common elements of policy in both firms, elements that justify the accommodation of both in the category of merchant banks. Their policies had both negative and positive aspects; they were as much to do with what a merchant bank disdained as the opportunities it was likely to accept. For much of the century – at least from the 1830s to the 1880s – both Barings and Rothschilds conducted a highly restrained, highly selective kind of business, an élitism that appeared to be supported by their aristocratic life-styles and aloofness from lesser families. There was of course some pacemaking from 'external' members of the business – Thomas Wren Ward and Bates in Barings, and Baron Alphonse, Carl Meyer and Belmont in Rothschilds – but significantly these influences were not accepted as an integral part of the family policy. This conservatism produced both gains and losses. In periods of commercial crisis (most notably 1825, 1837, 1848, 1857 and 1867) both firms gained at the expense of more adventurous rivals, who were run into bankruptcy or laid low by heavy financial losses. At the same time, their policies left wide opportunities for more enterprising houses, particularly those that opened in London from a secure financial base abroad, or were more restrained in their personal expenditure. The ways in which such firms were able to establish a strong position in the London market are reviewed in Chapters 3 and 4. For the moment it is sufficient to note that it has been demonstrated that one of the closest rivals of the two houses reviewed in the present chapter, Brown Shipley & Co., succeeded with much less capital in making conspicuous gains in depression periods.[61]

Another feature of Rothschilds' and Barings' policies that left large opportunities for others was their disdain of joint-stock organisations. The general antipathy to this was commented on in the last chapter; the Rothschilds' personal hostility to the Crédit Mobilier and all that it stood for is well known. As we have seen, even before the Pereire brothers drew their contempt, the London Rothschilds had decided that they did not care for involvement in railways, let alone industrial investments. The Barings sniffed at joint-stock banking in 1863 at the time the International Financial Society (IFS) was formed but settled for a half-hearted commitment to the Anglo-Austrian Bank. In the City only Glyns showed continuous interest in transport and industrial concerns so that British economic historians have concluded a general lack of interest, the traditional prejudice finding support in the rash of joint-stock enterprises that led to the Overend Gurney crisis in 1867. But we shall see that this catastrophe did not deter the formation of limited liability banks abroad, not only by merchant banks of German and Greek origin, but also by East India merchants.[62]

However, one basic feature of Barings' and Rothschilds' policies evidently exercised a continuing influence. This was the pursuit of a package of interconnected financial and commodity business focused on two or three sectors of world trade in which they had come to specialise.

In other words, the essence of the leaders' practice through the period was to retain a diversified financial and commodity business, *within a specific geographical area* (or areas) shifting interest from one to another as opportunities changed. As we saw in the last chapter, specialisation in one or two of these areas was largely restricted to new firms finding their way into the market. The problem was of course that of maintaining expertise in diverse specialisms, and as we have seen both houses (like all their rivals) came unstuck at one time or another. The ways in which one branch of their activity could open up or support others are legion, but in concluding this chapter it is useful to offer a variety of illustrations to support this basic point.

It is interesting to notice that the Rothschilds' early policy, which reflected the long tradition of the Court Jews, started from the point that a princely connection must lead to a range of advantageous state and mercantile opportunities. 'Business transactions with royalties always end in a profitable way. Please do not let the smallest business go by', Amshel warned his brother in 1816, no doubt reflecting, as so often in his correspondence, his father's more insistent policy comments.[63] Soloman emphasised the same point when he wrote to Nathan and James that 'it is most important to remain in good relationship with a court such as the Austrian. A court is always a court and it always leads to something.'[64] For centuries Court Jews had been opportunists who were prepared to look at any business proposition that promised profit with integrity.

Though the Rothschilds stood in a long tradition of court patronage, they could teach little to the Barings about it. Sir Francis had climbed to the top aided by the patronage of Lord Shelburne, and his son Lord Ashburton through his connection with Senator Bingham, while their successors evidently benefited from their strong position in the two Houses of Parliament. The puritanical Bates might protest to his journal that 'we have never meddled with politics', but he was soon as gleefully counting the number of accounts of foreign states held by Barings as his partners had done.[65] The consequence of the recurrent crises of the century was to concentrate more business in the hands of the strongest and most prudent firms, and this process evidently included state accounts. Thus the 1847 failure of Harman & Co., the London bankers of the Russian government, brought the account (a deposit of 'many hundreds of thousands pounds') to Rothschilds, with a second account opened with Barings in 1857, and in course of the next few years, a sequence of issues to one or the other house.[66] There were other significant connections between one branch of a merchant bank's activities and other, and the conservative second and third generation Rothschilds certainly lost business through neglecting them. When George Peabody was trying to build up a merchant banking business in the late 1840s, it was reported to him that the Browns and the Barings granted credits only on condition that no credits were opened with others, and that in return for this privilege preference should be given to them in other business, such as consignments. These two houses, that is to say, used their positions as creditors to improve their own trading activities. A decade later Peabody had taken the point and it was Rothschilds who were learning from others' success. Belmont wrote, 'As long as the House [of Rothschild] will not enter upon the business of opening credits to our [US] importers of European and Chinese goods, we shall not be able to compete with houses like Brown & Co. and Peabody. Those gentlemen receive commisions and can send specie where we cannot do so, and they are realizing immense profits out of this commission business.' In the middle decades of the century, one of the liveliest branches of the British export trade was that of exporting rails to US and other overseas railway builders, and credits granted for this trade also opened up advantageous connections for dealing in railroad shares.[67]

Court Jews did not completely disappear from the royal entourages of European monarchies until the dynasties themselves were eliminated by the First World War. A few like Bleichroder in Berlin and Cassel in London continued to play significant roles on the political stage, moreover it is clear that the rise of London as the centre of international credit brought impecunious princes to that discreet market rather than descend into the nearest ghetto. In London there was choice and competition so that even small states might strike a bargain. As H. H. Gibbs (of Antony Gibbs & Sons) put it in 1863, 'Governments in fact like manufacturers don't think it unwise to have half-a-dozen correspondents if need be and see which does best.'[68] But while it was not so easy to win privileges and dispensations in the old way, it remained true that as always one thing could lead to another. The point can best be illustrated from the situation in the most open and competitive society, that of the United States. In 1869 dealing in Federal Bonds was largely in the hands of Brown Bros, Barings, and Fieldens of Manchester, while Rothschilds, who limited their agent to £300,000 a year, were in the second rank. Belmont complained to his principals that it was only by keeping in the front rank of *all* the financial connections between Britain and the USA that their house could retain good connections. 'One business brings another and by constantly having to refuse propositions of the most legitimate nature, people forget the road to our office.'[69]

While government patronage of financiers was a factor of declining importance in European commerce in the nineteenth century, it continued to be significant in more backward and autocratic states. Thus, to take just one example, Marcus Samuel, who rose into the ranks of merchant bankers through his dramatic success in the oil trade of the

Middle and Far East, and had extensive trading interests in Japan, negotiated the first Japanese loan in London at a time when the Japanese most needed friends abroad, and then, in 1909 offered the Persian government a vast loan in return for a place on the board of the Anglo-Persian Oil Company.[70] Further illustrations of this kind of connection are analysed in Chapter 6; for the present it is sufficient to make the point that almost all the merchant banks focused their activities on one or two countries with which they had a longstanding connection, and that this local eminence would often bring the opportunity of state, railway and other financial activities. In other words, the merchant banks that had evolved as merchants (as distinct from Court Jews) continued to regard government and public utility financing and trade credits as two sides of the same coin. In this sense at least, Rothschilds and Barings showed a strong lead in the City. And in so far as they neglected opportunities, they were always merchants with an A1 reputation ready to fill them, as the next two chapters will endeavour to show.

3 New Competitors

Fortunately it is possible to be more or less precise about the period at which a district group of specialists that were called merchant bankers came into existence. According to the *Circular to Bankers*, the decline of export merchants and manufacturers in the textile trade (explained in Chapter 1) was accompanied by the emergence of 'a few opulent firms of great resources' that changed their roles from 'commission merchants to commission bankers'. The transition occupied the decade from the crisis of 1825 to that of 1836. The bankruptcy of Samuel Williams & Co. in 1825 served to accelerate rather than retard the process, partly because 'every bill drawn upon him for the purchase of British manufacturers' goods was paid in full', and also because his acceptance business (£0.5m.) was quickly picked up by new firms, notably by Bates & Baring in Boston and other eastern towns of the USA and by Timothy Wiggin in Manchester. Shortly before the crisis there were seven prominent firms that were being recognised as merchant bankers: Barings, Browns, Morrison Cryder & Co., Lizardi & Co., and the so-called 'three Ws', Wiggin, Wilson and Wildes. 'Though they pass under the names of merchants, all their pecuniary affairs are of the nature or banking commissions charged for affording credit facilities', the *Circular* insisted, with some overstatement.[1] In point of fact, Barings commission account represented only half or two-thirds of the firm's profits in the mid-1830s, and no more than 75 per cent twenty years later. The position of other firms is not clear, except that Morrison Cryder retained its interest in textiles.[2]

The various investigations that followed the crisis of 1836–7 make it possible to assess the claim of early concentration of financial power. A very plausible contemporary estimate suggests that in 1836 the acceptances of the firms in the American trade at London and Liverpool was $100m. (£20m.). The *Circular* maintained that the principal Anglo-American merchant banks were responsible for £9m.–£12m. (or 45–60 per cent) of this.[3] The 'three Ws' that went bankrupt in 1837 were responsible for £5.5m. of this, or a little more than 25 per cent, and the four surviving firms for a further £6.5m. These figures do not take any account of Rothschilds, whose acceptances were high in the last years of NM's life, and who was also trying to push into the US market at this time, or of Frederick Huth & Co., who were pursuing a similar policy.[4] John Morrison of Morrison Cryder wrote to his New York agent after the storm had blown out that 'All who had not resources out of business like myself or opulent friends like Barings are gone. ... We shall of course lose and that I fear considerably but we shall soon make it up. A few of us must have all the business hereafter.' His estimate was that in the end only half-a-million pounds was lost through bankruptcies, which was probably about 2.5 and certainly not more than 5 per cent of US acceptances. It was no doubt for this reason that new entrants continued. Six years after the crisis, Barings drew up a list of no less than seventy London merchants 'that may be drawn on from the United States'.[5]

In view of the paucity of evidence on the subsequent numbers of merchant banks, particularly before Skinner's directories begin in 1880, it will come as no surprise that data on their capital, profits and other indicators of growth are quite meagre. From the end of the French Wars to the close of the American Civil War, the London market continued to be dominated by the two firms that made rapid fortunes in the Napoleonic period, Barings and Rothschilds. Towards the middle of the nineteenth century, £100,000 was considered a large capital for a British merchant, and by this standard the leading houses and their closest rival, Brown Shipley, were considered very rich (Table 3.1)[6] It should be added

Table 3.1   *Assembled data on the capital of the leading London and Liverpool merchant banks 1815–75*

	1815–16	1825–30	1870–5
N. M. Rothschild & Sons	£1.05m.	£1.14	£6.51
Baring Bros	£0.7–1.1m.	£0.49	£2.10
Brown Shipley & Co.	£0.12m.	£0.35	£1.02

Sources: B. Gille, *Histoire de la maison Rothschild*, I (1965) p. 458, II (1967) p. 571. R. Hidy, *House of Baring* (Harvard, Mass., 1949) pp. 40, 129, and Barings' ledgers (1870). E. J. Perkins, *Financing Anglo-American Trade* (Harvard, Mass., 1975) pp. 237–9 and Brown Shipley archives at London office.

that in the boom period in Anglo-American trade in the early 1830s, several young houses grew very rapidly, easily outpacing the usual kind of merchant house (Table 3.2). Other more respectable merchant houses that were beginning to assume the role of merchant banks were evidently trading on much less capital. Peabody, the most distinguished survivor of the small Anglo-American houses, had only £65,000 at this time, while Rothschilds' competitors in the continental trade included Frederick Huth with £312,000 (1845) and Frühling & Goschen with as little as £40,000.[7] In the middle decades of the nineteenth century, many of the names that subsequently won distinction in the City were still winning their fortunes, often in some remote parts of the globe, while, as we shall see in Chapter 4, others were yet to arrive from the continent, the USA, South Africa and further afield. It was not until the late 1860s and 1870s that capital began to mount rapidly among a range of houses (Table 3.3).

Table 3.2 *Capital and acceptances of some leading Anglo-American houses in 1836*

	capital	US acceptances
Baring Bros	£0.78m.	£0.39m.
Brown Shipley & Co.	1.35m.	0.62m.
Wiggin & Co.	0.38m.	0.42m.
Wilson & Co.	0.30m.	0.72m.
Wildes & Co.	0.27m.	0.53m.
Morrison, Cryder & Co.	1.00m.+	0.56m.
Lizardi & Co.	n.d.	0.15m.

Sources: Bank of England archives, 'American Accounts 1836–42', ADV/B521. The figure for 'acceptances and discounts' refers to 8 Dec. 1836. The capital of Morrison Cryder is a contemporary estimate from *Circular to Bankers*, 10 Oct. 1834. Lizardis, the other Anglo-American house, was much smaller than the others.

The early success of Barings and Rothschilds had the inevitable consequence that younger rising firms tried to emulate them, at any rate in those sectors of their activities that were deemed to be most profitable. It is an easy generalisation that Barings were copied by British merchants evolving towards pure finance, while Rothschilds were the model for several German-Jewish and American-Jewish families, particularly for those originating in their home town of Frankfurt.

However, during these years Barings' closest and most persistent rivals were undoubtedly Brown Brothers, the Baltimore family of linen merchants that moved into cotton and opened branches in New York, Boston, Philadelphia and Liverpool. Like the Rothschilds and the Barings, Brown Shipley retained their traditional mercantile functions for many years. A letter book of 1825–7 shows the US partners ordering a variety of textiles from more than fifty correspondents in Britain, but mostly from connections in familiar localities of Glasgow and Belfast.[8] At the same period the Liverpool partner (William) was beginning to develop a banking business in a way explained by the Bank of England Agent in the port: 'they act as agents for some of the American banks in that a considerable portion of the exchange business between the two countries is effected through their house, and they are ... in the habit of giving credits to different agents of American houses who travel through the manufacturing districts and order goods at Manchester, Birmingham, Sheffield and other places, and who pay for such goods by bills drawn upon their house on which they receive a commission for which they get repaid by consignments of American produce.' William Brown, the Liverpool partner, would have liked to diversify into insurance, cotton mills and land speculation but was restrained by his father. 'If we look around here [Baltimore] we find that those persons who have steadily kept to one pursuit are far the richest men and those who are interested with one and another in different pursuits, no matter how profitable they may be or appear to be at first, are always ruined sooner or later', he insisted to his son.[9]

However the founder, Alexander Brown, was not entirely true to his own precept, for in 1811 he had started building a shipping line, though perhaps he would have argued that this was the means to make him the leading exporter of raw cotton to Liverpool, a position he attained by 1827. Importing into the USA was also conducted with characteristic rigour, undercutting other Liverpool exporters, and channelling the increasing trade into Browns' ships. But in the 1830s, when the cotton and 'dry goods' trade became increasingly competitive, the most anxious of the brothers was reminding his partners that they 'were doing too much business involving risk and [generating] a great deal of anxiety' and already in 1834 it was resolved to concentrate on the provision of financial services for international trade, though in fact this ambition was not completely fulfilled for another generation.[10]

The Browns' opportunity came after the crisis of 1837 when Barings, their principal competitors in transatlantic finance, did not attempt to retake the acceptance business they had declined after 1834. Barings granted credits almost exclusively to established, wealthy merchants whose accounts were little trouble to administer, and insisted that they had the whole of a house's account. This simplification of administration allowed them to maintain the largest acceptance business and diversify further into foreign issues. Browns' policy of opening numerous small credits for men of 'ability and integrity' can easily be recognised as a formula for growth, but it involved more labour, anxiety and risk than the two leading houses were willing to give.[11] During the 1840s Browns' assumed the leadership of their chosen field; in the USA 'no other banking house could provide such broad and comprehensive service to the international trader'. In 1849 Baron Alphonse Rothschild wrote from New York, 'There is only one banking house here, and that sole concern is that of the Browns', and the next year they opened a branch in San Francisco. In the years after the American Civil War, a new generation of Barings and Rothschilds belatedly revised their policy and regained some ground but it was too late to displace the Browns. In 1870 August Belmont, Rothschilds' agent in New York, wrote that Browns had 'such large credit settlements that they monopolise the bill market'; in the 1870s and 1880s their acceptances of sterling bills fluctuated between £6m. and £12m. a year. In the years after the American Civil War Browns also became large dealers in US Federal bonds, competing with Barings and Fieldens (of Manchester) for market domination. Rothschilds were (in Belmont's words) placed 'quite in the background' for want of initiative.[12]

The only question that arises about this apparent success story was that of the profit margins on this kind of business. The point was succinctly explained by Belmont in 1884:

> Brown Bros. & Co. and Kidder Peabody in joint account with Barings do an immense exchange business by drawing commercial bills which they pick up all over the country [but] I am sure that their average profit does not exceed one-eighth to three-sixteenth per cent to be divided between here and London and for that they have to run the risk of bad bills among their remittances which even with the greatest caution from time to time sweep away some of the profits.[13]

In other words, the profit margins were small, which is probably one reason why, despite this huge business, Browns' capital was smaller than some of the much younger US banks who specialised on the issues side, particularly the marketing of railroad shares (Table 3.3).

Despite the reverses of 1836–7, Barings' business in Spanish America continued to attract emulation. The early history of Alexander Kleinwort & Sons (now Kleinwort Benson) offers an illuminating example of this. Kleinwort left Hamburg for Havana (Cuba) as a young man where he became clerk and eventually junior partner in Drake Brothers, an English merchant house that had been exporting cane sugar to Europe since the late eighteenth century and had now attained a premier position. As he gained seniority in Drakes' family business, the ambitious young Kleinwort no doubt came to recognise the implications of the basic point made by Baron Alphonse Rothschild when he visited Cuba in 1849:

> The sugar business here is a monopoly of the exporters, Drake, Burnham, Picard and Albert. However they are not doing the most important or weighty business; this is being done by Baring, Coutts, and Fruhling & Goschen in London, who are making all of the profit from commission, credits and consignments. The credits are mostly given for the account of Continental houses.[14]

Kleinwort was too clever for his Havana partners so in 1858 it was agreed that he should open a London house (initially Drake, Kleinwort & Cohen) specialising in accepting house business for Cuban and continental account. The partners started with a capital of £200,000, but by 1914 this had grown to £4m., probably the largest private bank in the City apart from Rothschilds and almost certainly the fastest-growing accepting house, easily outstripping both Barings and Browns with £1.25m. and £0.775m. capital respectively. There was no magic formula behind this apparently dramatic. achievement; it was simply that Kleinwort and his partners were more willing than the old-established houses to accept less conventional business and take more risk, so in the

Table 3.3   *Capital of some leading merchant banks in the 1870s (target date 1875)*

Jewish group of international houses			*Source* ₁
Baron Maurice de Hirsch	1878	c.£10m.	*Statist*, xxxvii (1896) p. 570.
N. M. Rothschild & Sons	1875	£6.51m.	B. Gille, p. 571.
Stern Bros	1887	£5m.	*BM* 1887 p. 1047.
R. Raphael & Sons	1876	£2.01m.	Raphael MSS
Seligman Bros	1873	£1.35m.	Hellman
Speyer Bros	1872	£0.6–£1.0m	R. G. Dun
Lazard Bros, Paris	1876	£0.6–£0.8m.	R. G. Dun
Kuhn, Loeb & Co, New York	1878	£0.16m.	Brandt Circulars 1878, p. 40.
Anglo-American group of international houses			
Baring Bros	1870	£2.1m.	BBAB
J. S. Morgan	1871	£1.6m.–£2m.	R. G. Dun
Brown Shipley & Co.	1875	£1.2m	BS MSS
Morton, Bliss & Co.	1871	£0.7m.	R. G. Dun
Dennistoun Cross & Co.	1870	£0.4–£0.6m.	R. G. Dun
J. & J. Stuart	1875	£0.2m.	R. G. Dun
Robert Benson & Sons	1870	£0.11m.	BBAB
Anglo-German group of international houses			
Alex Kleinwort & Sons	1875	£0.84m.	KB MSS
Schuster, Son & Co.	1873	£0.70m.	BBAB HC16
C. J. Hambro & Son.	1875	£0.63m.	CJH MSS
Frederick Huth & Co.	c.1870	c.£0.5m.	Murray and Hughes
Ludwig Knoop & Co.	1877	£0.6m.–£0.7m.	BBAB HC10.28/7
William Brandt's Sons & Co.	1877	£0.176m.	Amburger

Abbreviations used in the sources column:

B. Gille, *Histoire de la maison Rothschild*, t. II (1848–70) p. 571. The figure given here refers only to the capital of the London house; that of all the Rothschild banks totalled £34.3m.

R. G. Dun Credit Registers, Baker Library, Harvard University USA

Raphael MSS refer to records of Raphael Raphael & Sons at the firm, London EC

BS MSS: Brown Shipley & Co's records at the bank, London EC2

BBAB: Baring Bros records at the bank, London EC2

KB MSS: Kleinwort Benson records at the bank, London EC3, and at Newbury

CJH MSS: Hambros records at Guildhall Library

BM: Banker's Magazine (London)

Murray and Hughes; a figure estimated from A. J. Murray, *Home from the Hill* (1970) p. 182. (1850 = £0.498m.) and Appendix 1, 1896 = £0.6m.

Amburger: C. Amburger, *William Brandt and the Story of his Enterprises* (typescript, 1937), pp. 52–3. Brandt MSS

Hellman: G. T. Hellman, 'Sorting out the Seligmans', *New Yorker*, 30 Oct. 1954, p. 46

long run earning better profits. They lived modestly and left their capital in the business, while third and fourth-generation Barings and Browns withdrew much of theirs, so that total partners' capital contracted rather than grew. Barings' prestige was lost in the crisis of 1890, while Browns' London partners failed to keep in personal contact with US conditions and were then restrained by their limited capital. In other words, it was not so much the brilliance of Kleinworts' partners as a classic case of entrepreneurial failure in the third generation of both the old-established family firms.[15]

Rothschilds were initially the model for several other Frankfurt Jewish families that, responding to the rapidly growing opportunities of international trade and government loans, dispersed their sons to the financial centres of Europe and the USA. Jakob Stern, son of the earliest great Jewish wine merchant, brother-in-law of N. M. Rothschild and banker, sent two of his eight sons to London, two to Paris and one to Berlin. The London partners, who became Baron David Stern and Baron Herman Stern, made fortunes out of such diverse speculations as company promotions in the boom of the early 1860s, the first Turkish State loan (1864), Portugese bonds and Argentine *cedulas* (guaranteed land bonds).[16] One of N. M. Rothschild's sisters married Benedikt Moses Worms, whose three sons all moved to London to open a merchant bank. Ralph von Erlanger was a Frankfurt employee and then agent of the Rothschilds in the period after the French Wars; launching his own concern, he sent three of his sons to London, Paris and Vienna.[17] The richest Frankfurt Jew at the close of the eighteenth century was not Rothschild but the Speyer brothers, and the family intermarried with the next richest family in the *Judengasse*, the Ellisens. In the next generation we find them active as bankers in Frankfurt (as Lazard–Speyer–Ellisen), from 1861 in London (as Speyer Bros) and from 1837 in New York (as Speyer & Co.). They were largely concerned in marketing railroad and other securities in Europe but were also involved in foreign exchange dealing and, in a residual way, in exporting textiles to the USA.[18] Speyers were also intermarried with the Schuster family of Frankfurt, who were not only bankers but also one of the earliest and most successful firms to open a branch house in Manchester to develop their textile interests. Extending their interests, they opened more branches in Liverpool, Bradford and London, but in later years the banking interest seems to have focused on the Union Bank of London, which in the 1860s was already one of a dozen major bill drawers in New York.[19] Bischoffsheim & Goldschmidt, yet another Jewish firm originating in Frankfurt and having a marriage connection with Rothschilds, opened in Antwerp in 1820 and soon had offices in Brussels, Amsterdam, Paris and Frankfurt and then, from 1846, in London. Between 1866 and 1875 the London house placed a sequence of loans for South American states and became heavily involved in US railway and Swedish mining affairs, though not with uniform success.[20]

Seligman Brothers followed a similar course to Speyers, repudiating their US textile trading activities in the early 1860s when the Civil War created unprecedented opportunities for marketing Federal bonds in Europe. In a burst of feverish activity the eight brothers opened offices in New York, New Orleans, London, Paris, Frankfurt and San Francisco. After the war they were largely involved in selling US railroad, municipal and state securities, but especially railroads. 'We have made a fortune these past 6 years and made it principally out of new R. Roads', Joseph Seligman reminded one of his brothers in 1872. The usual commission for marketing these stocks was 3.5–4 per cent and at this time the writer was making $5,000–$10,000 *a day.* By the middle 1870s Seligmans were one of five big investment houses serving the European market, the others being Rothschilds, Raphaels, Speyers and Morgans. They made their debut as an independent issuing house in 1872 offering $4m. of City of Washington bonds and in 1874 entered the first division by compelling Rothschilds to share the issue of the $55m. US government loan with them.[21]

It seems that the one opportunity that all these new banking families shared, in greater or lesser degree, was the rapidly developing market for US securities on the continent. The Low Countries and perhaps France were adequately prepared for this, but in the German centres the sudden popularity of Federal bonds during the Civil War offered a quick ladder to wealth. Saemy Japhet, then a young banker in Frankfurt, recalled this period vividly:

> There was hardly an investor in South Germany who did not buy United States bonds. ... They all believed in the ultimate victory of those who identified themselves with the cause of liberty. ... At the same time the export houses arranged for credits, shipped their goods to the States and left the dollars in America, financing themselves elsewhere. ... The profits made in American securities and American trade were one of the stepping stones on which the newly enriched world of Germany could tread. ... It tended to educate the German investor to buy bonds of overseas countries.

US government securities were for some years the 'backbone' of the Frankfurt Stock Exchange. The old Anglo-German banks in London that had developed close connections with Liverpool and hence with the South (that is the Confederate States) withheld their support from Lincoln, so giving even more latitude to the Germans.[22] The counterpart of the prosperity of the Frankfurt houses was of course that of their New York correspondents, among whom Seligmans and Speyers were particularly prominent, and probably also Bischoffsheim & Goldschmidt.

Lazard Brothers were slightly different from the other houses placed in this category because they came of a French-Jewish background, but they were later linked to the Frankfurt cousinhood in the Lazard–Speyer–Ellisen group. Having accumulated a large capital in the textile industry and trade (mostly importing wool from San Francisco and manufacturing for export in France), in 1876–7 they repudiated commerce to open a chain of banking offices in San Francisco, New York, Paris and London. Their banking business largely consisted in buying and selling British and foreign securities and financing trade to the USA from Europe, Australia and the Far East; it differed from the Frankfurt Jews only in the emphasis on oriental acceptances.[23]

Down to the 1870s the leading merchant bankers met twice a week on the Royal Exchange to settle among themselves the rates which ruled the exchanges of bills and currencies between the various centres. But from this period the leading firms, notably Rothschilds and Barings, found that foreign investments were 'more alluring than the comparatively moderate profits to be obtained from exchange operations'. 'Natty' Rothschild and E. C. Baring (later the first Lord Rothschild and Lord Revelstoke) ceased to attend the meetings on the Exchange, and the dwindling interest of the traditional leaders in the market left a great opening, which was largely occupied by the foreign banks and their agents which were opening offices in the City in the 1860s and 1870s. However a number of British firms also moved into the gap, the most successful of whom were two Jewish houses, Samuel Montagu & Co. and Raphael Raphael & Sons. These firms were strictly bill and exchange merchants rather than bankers in the conventional sense; technically speaking, they were specialists in arbitrage or trafficking bills of exchange and currencies so as to take advantage of the daily quotations of rates in the several world centres (London, New York, Paris, Berlin and so on). Montagu and his original partner Ellis Franklin organised the office on lines which made it easy for them to assemble data from all the world's financial centres, a development no doubt stimulated by the spread of international cables from the late 1860s onwards.[24]

Samuel Montagu & Co. are the most familiar firm in this development, probably because the principal was also prominent in politics through the period, but it is not to be assumed that they were always the most profitable, for Raphaels were operating on a much greater capital in the 1870s and 1880s. Raphael Raphael came to London from Amsterdam towards the end of the eighteenth century and had early business connections with the Rothschilds. He established offices run by his sons in Amsterdam and Hamburg, and a grandson opened another branch in Paris. According to a newspaper report in 1893, the firm was one of the first importance on the stock exchange, but 'Unlike any other firm on the

Exchange, it transacts a bullion and banking business and has taken quite the leading place in the arbitrage business between London and New York.'[25] Another more shadowy firm operating in this sector of the market and also closely connected with the Rothschilds was Lewis Cohen & Sons. The partnership was formed from the descendants of Levi Barent Cohen, the Dutch-Jewish merchant who settled in London and whose daughter married N. M. Rothschild. It seems probable that their business originated with Rothschilds, or perhaps with Samuel Montagu who was also connected with the Cohens by marriage. The Cohens all retired from business in 1901, but Jewish hegemony in this sector of the market was maintained when A. Keyser & Co., originally launched as a kind of 'second eleven' for the overcrowded flanks of Montagus and Franklins became independent in 1908.[26]

In addition, the Rothschilds had a number of protégées that originally dealt in stock for them and in course of time followed a similar path of development. The best-known surviving firms are Warburgs (originally Hamburg bill brokers) and Hambros, but there was also Helbert Wagg (now incorporated in Schröder Wagg). On the Warburgs' centenary in 1898, Moritz Warburg wrote to Lord Rothschild that 'above all praise is due to the founders of our house who set about a hundred years ago and who already then had the highly valued privilege of acceptance in business negotiations with the House of Rothschild.' The Rothschild patronage had been 'vital' to the three generations of Warburgs, he said, and he was glad to think that his son (the fourth generation) had improved his mercantile knowledge at New Court.[27] Hambro & Son of Copenhagen conducted their London business through Rothschilds for fifteen years from 1826 before the principal settled in London. Helbert Wagg & Co. were Rothschilds' principal brokers at the Stock Exchange for most of the nineteenth century (1823–1912), being related to them through the Cohens. From time to time they also appeared as brokers on new company issues. When Rothschilds' patronage began to fall away in favour of their rivals, Panmure Gordon & Co., they launched out on their own as merchant bankers.[28]

It is easy to assume that the common origins and marriage connections between the Jewish houses led to close business connections, or at any rate an easy-going give-and-take between them, but in fact there is no real evidence for this. In the last chapter we noticed that N. M. Rothschild and his brothers, though frequently suspicious of Gentile houses (sometimes with good reason), nevertheless entered into a series of syndicates with several of them. In the next generation they had raised themselves so far above their Jewish cousinhood in Britain that they felt little need or inclination to partner them, and such British connections as were maintained were nearer to patronage than partnership. The second and third generation preferred to maintain an independent connection with their imperial and royal clients, and accepted other firms (whether Jew or Gentile) on equal terms only when forced by circumstances to do so.[29]

Two examples will serve to illustrate the point well enough. The rapid rise of Raphael Raphael & Sons in the 1870s was clearly connected with Baron Rothschild's desultory interest in US opportunities and frequent disdain of Belmont's advice. At the end of 1869 Belmont tried in vain to persuade his masters to offer a loan to Vanderbilt on the security of his $80m. fortune for 5 per cent plus the opportunity of securing the business of the extensive system of railroads under the Vanderbilt control, both in placing their bonds and in supplying them with iron rails and other materials. Raphaels moved to occupy the gap, and consequently secured a £2m. issue for the New York Central Rail Road on which they made a 'handsome profit' as the bonds moved up from 80 or 90 (1873) to 130 in six years (1879). When the Baron showed little interest in the First National Bank, Raphaels were able to forge the strongest links with Washington. In Belmont's opinion, an early Rothschild interest 'would have prevented the intimate relations and immense transactions between that institution and the Raphaels in London and their agents here von Hoffman, which I fear will now be insisted on by the Bank as a necessity for them to let these two houses have a share in the Syndicate'. Rothschilds, it should be added, were members of syndicates for the Funded Loans of 1871 and 1873 totalling $500m., but their partners were Morgans, Barings and other Gentile houses.[30]

Another instructive example is provided in the story of the rise of the Seligman brothers. The Rothschilds' decided policy in relation to the US government funding operations was that they were not willing to join any American Syndicate 'and be at their mercy or command'. On his side, Joseph Seligman, the head of the house, was only too well aware of 'the difficulty of dealing with so purse-proud and haughty people as the Rothschilds'. Nevertheless, a determined Seligman assault finally compelled Baron Rothschild to capitulate and to share the $45m. loan of 1874. The issue brought no profit to either contractor but Seligmans was more than satisfied, for the joint issue signalled their arrival in 'division one' of the league of international financiers. Moreover, Belmont, who had hitherto been cool, declared 'this would pave the way for greater intimacy between our house and the Rothschilds and would lead to more transactions', while in London Isaac Seligman was shortly referring to Baron Rothschild as 'his warm friend' and Rothschild introduced Isaac as 'the most honest merchant in London'. Despite this epithet, Seligmans generally worked with Morton Bliss & Co., while Belmont and Rothschilds preferred to deal with Morgans when forced into syndicated issues.[31] By the 1870s prestige and personality preferences were far more significant then ethnic connections.

It might also be assumed that the Rothschild kind of international network imitated by the Seligmans, Speyers and Lazards was another key to success, but specific evidence questions this. In Chapter 9 it will be shown that, in the age of the telegraph, the dispersed family proved less flexible than the individual operator who could shift his connections to meet particular needs. For the moment, it is sufficient to note that all US commentators are agreed that the significant feature of the 'Rothschildesque' structure after 1866 was direct access to European capital. Of course, New York–London partnership links were by no means limited to Jewish houses. [32]

The Rothschild cousinhood and its protégées, and the group of continental Jews who came to London via the USA, were by no means the last of their type to settle in the City. In the 1880s and 1890s a further contingent arrived from Frankfurt, this time for rather different reasons. Until 1876 Frankfurt was the principal banking centre of the numerous German states, much of the business consisting in changing the currencies of the imperial cities, electorates, bishoprics, dukedoms and other small states that constituted Germany down to that time. One of the new arrivals, Saemy Japhet, later recalled how Hamburg had banco mark, which existed only as paper money covered by gold and silver, while North Germany had thaler and silver standard while South Germany had gulden. But this was only the beginning of the problem, for no official gold coins existed, neither in thaler, not gulden, banco mark nor Bremen thaler. But from the foundation of the German Empire in 1871 there was a strong movement to adopt the gold standard and a uniform currency supported by a central bank in place of the many issuing banks. On 1 January 1876 the Reichsbank opened its doors and the whole of Germany recognised the gold Deutschmark as their only legal tender and currency. The consequence was that the traditional money-exchange firms (*Wechselstube*) which proliferated in Frankfurt and other commercial towns suddenly had no business. From the point of view of the present study, the most important point is that such firms had capital and unrivalled experience in international money exchanges, but little familiarity with traditional British expertise in acceptances.

Inevitably competition in Frankfurt intensified, and many of the old firms declined or left the town. Berlin quickly outstripped Frankfurt, which after the introduction of the new currency even lost its influence in the South German market. Frankfurt's plight was all the worse because the demand for US government securities, which had become very popular during the Civil War, as much for political as financial reasons, now fell away. Some old houses went into liquidation, others withdrew from business, while others again were absorbed by the rapidly rising joint-stock banks. A few, more boldly, made the decision to migrate to other financial centres, Berlin, Paris and London. Around eight German firms migrated to London between 1880 and 1910, but unfortunately less is known of them than almost any other category included in this study, no doubt because most of them disappeared from the City as a result of the First World War. Indeed we know so little about them that it seems impossible to make any generalisation beyond that they brought impressive expertise and considerable capital with them which strengthened the international position of the City in this period.[33]

Rüffer & Sons, the earliest of this group to arrive in London, were originally a Lyons and Leipzig house in the silk trade, but after Baron Joseph Rüffer opened a London office in 1872 they specialised more widely in the financing of imports into Europe of goods from all over the world. Ladenbergs were first a Mannheim and then a Frankfurt bankhouse that developed out of a jewel and money exchange business and became involved in the international trade in metals. Saemy Japhet, as we noted above, graduated from money-changing and general financial agency work to arbitrage. Leopold Hirsch & Co. were the most influential firm engaged in the mining share market, and probably became merchant bankers because one of the partners was a brother of the Rand financier Sigismund Neumann.[34] Baron von der Heydt & Co. (1910) originated with the son of a Prussian minister of finance who was said to be very rich. In 1866 it was reported from Berlin that he did 'a large business in metals and enjoys the highest credit'. The connection with London appears to have began in 1873 when he became one of the two directors of the Berlin office of the Russian Bank for Foreign Trade, a concern which had an even larger operation in London.[35]

The financial expertise of the later German migrants was, however, very modest compared with that of the Americans, or at any rate a small but powerful group of American pacemakers. The most successful and best-known of this group was undoubtedly J. S. Morgan & Co. Morgan and his son have been the subject of so many US studies that it hardly seems necessary to repeat any details here beyond a few salient points.[36] In the last chapter we mentioned George Peabody's pioneering contribution to the development of a market for US securities in London. Peabody had no heirs and so in 1854 took Junius Spencer Morgan into partnership. When the senior partner retired a decade later the firm changed its name but maintained the style and policy of the parent company; Peabody had avoided dealing with Rothschilds because he believed they spoiled the market for US bonds by undercutting. Overend, Gurney & Co. had been early purchasers of Peabody's US bonds, and in 1852 they appear as Morgan's 'confidential correspondent', backing his bid for the Pennsylvania Central Rail Road issue. Such powerful support was the best testimonial of Morgan's ability. J. S. Morgan confirmed his position in the first division of European finance in 1870 when he issued the French government war loan of £10m. despite the furious adverse publicity generated by Bismarck. Rothschilds' strong connections with Prussia no doubt restrained any interest they might have felt, but in any case the issue was no doubt too risky for them, the bonds slipping from 85 at issue to 55 at France's defeat.[37]

Following this coup, J. S. Morgan strengthened his transatlantic connections by uniting his son's house in New York (Pierpont Morgan & Co.) with the London house's principal US correspondents, Drexel & Co. of Philadelphia, with a united capital of somewhere between £3m. and £4m. However, perhaps Morgan's most profitable years were the middle 1870s, for after the collapse of Jay Cooke & Co. in 1873 it became almost impossible to float railway issues in New York, and a large quantity of 'first-class' US railroad securities were consequently offered in London at prices calculated to yield large capital gains. The investment boom of the 1880s also brought some easy profits; for instance, in 1885 Drexel Morgan & Co. reaped $2m. (£400,000) as agents for the New York West Shore Railroad.

A decade after the Paris loan, Belmont reported the strong competition of Drexel, Morgan & Co. saying they 'seem determined to monopolise everything', while another acute American commentator remarked that they 'sometimes make losses but their profits are heavy and their losses are not at all serious with them.' They remained largely in railroad issues, but were also large dealers in sterling loans, and in both areas left the old firms (Rothschild and Baring) some way behind. In the 1880s they were much involved in South American issues, in the 1890s in the Philippines and in Chinese railways (notably the Hankow and Canton), and in the early years of this century in Russian railways. Their ubiquitous enterprise echoed that of Barings before 1890 and set a hot pace for competitors in London and New York alike.[38]

Morgans' closest connections were a firm known in London as Morton, Rose & Co. Like Seligman and Lazard, Levi P. Morton began his business career in what was called 'dry goods', taking his earliest lessons in international finance as an importer of British textiles, then repudiating trade for finance when he had accumulated sufficient capital. And like these Anglo-American rivals, the bulk of his fortune was built up in the reconstruction years following the Civil War. In 1865 he was reckoned to be worth half a million dollars (say £100,000), but by 1871 the sale of US securities made him a millionaire in the USA (say £200,000) and he was able to draw in George Bliss and his $2.5m. (£500,000), also from 'dry goods'. The London house was opened in 1869, for which Morton drew in Sir John Rose with a capital of $250,000, but worth much more to the business from his reputation in government circles in Ottawa, London and Washington. Morton also acquired advantages in London from his 'intimacy' with J. S. Morgan (who had been a partner for a brief period in their days in the dry goods trade), and from his Republican Party connections, which enabled him to acquire the US fiscal agency in London from 1873 to 1884 and again from 1889-93. Morton's American critics considered him to be 'a rash and risky speculator', only restrained by Bliss and his London partners, an opinion that easily could be dismissed but for the fact that the firm was permanently damaged at the time of the Baring crisis by locking up too much capital in Argentina. But in the previous twenty years it was one of the leading houses in US and Canadian railroad financing, selling large quantities of bonds and shares in London. Its near-uniform success in an area in which failures were common may well have been a direct consequence of Morton and Bliss using their economic and political power to obtain representation on the boards of the various railroad companies.[39]

Morgan, Morton Rose, Seligmans and Speyers were only the most prominent of a string of US houses that opened in London after the Civil War. At the period the most celebrated was undoubtedly that of Jay Cooke & Co., the financier of the war. When he came to grief in 1873 his London house, Jay Cooke, McCulloch & Co., was reformed as Melville, Evans & Co., with R. L. Melville (later eleventh Earl of Melville) as senior partner.[40] Another US house, McCalmont Bros, appears to have moved into investment banking shortly after the crisis of 1837 by buying up American stocks at panic prices. Twenty years later at the crisis of 1857, they still had some £700,000 locked up in US securities, principally those of the Philadelphia & Reading Railroad. The house gradually submerged as the P. & R. R. sank, and finally disappeared in 1884. This misfortune did not however prevent Hugh McCalmont from leaving over £3m. at his death in 1887. Other firms were less fortunate, disappearing at the time of the Jay Cooke crisis, or soon afterwards.[41]

Barings and Rothschilds were enervated by the Baring crisis (1890) while the later 1890s saw Morgans increasingly involved in US industrial issues. Both the crisis and industrial issues are considered in some detail in later chapters; for the moment it is enough to notice that by the turn of the century the US house was spurting past the traditional British leaders. Neither Morgans nor Rothschilds are willing to reveal the size of their partners' capital at this period but the testimony of Sir Clinton Dawkins, Morgan's London partner, is sufficient to substantiate the point:

Old Pierpont Morgan and the house in the U.S. occupy a position immensely more predominanant than Rothschilds in Europe. In London J. S. Morgan & Co. now come undoubtedly second to Rothschilds only. Taken together the Morgan combination of the U.S. and London probably do not fall very far short of the Rothschilds in capital, are immensely more expansive and active, and are in with the great progressive undertakings of the world.

Old P. Morgan is well over 60, and no human machine can resist the work he is doing much longer. Behind him he has young Morgan, under 40 with the makings of a biggish man, and myself. The Rothschilds have nothing now but the experience and prestige of old Nattie [first Lord Rothschild]. The coming generation of the Rothschilds *est à faire pleurer* [is enough to make you weep]. Therefore provided we can go on and bring in one or two good men to assist the next twenty years [1901–21] ought to see the Rothschilds thrown into the background, and the Morgan group supreme.

In London, the resuscitated Barings are the only people nearly in the same rank with us. In the U.S. they are nowhere now, a mere cipher, and the U.S. is going to dominate in most ways. The Barings have nobody but [the second Lord] Revelstoke, a man commonly reported to be strong, but a strange mixture of occasional strength and sheer timidity. He has no nerve to fall back upon. ... He has greatly irritated the Morgans once or twice by want of tact and by talking loosely (after they helped Barings largely in 1891) and it cost me a good deal of difficulty this summer to patch up the old alliance between the two houses, which was on the point of dissolution.[42]

Dawkins was trying to persuade his friend Sir Alfred Milner to join Morgans and certainly did not understate the standing of his own house, but we leave refinement of the position to later chapters of this book. For the moment, the important point to add is that the other Anglo-American houses did not keep up with Morgans. Seligmans' early success with US railroads was not sustained; their capital tumbled from £5m. or £6m. in 1881 to £1.6m. at Joseph's death in 1897. Morton, Rose & Co. never recovered from the Baring crisis and, though reconstituted as Chaplin, Milne & Co., was wound up in 1914.[43]

What Dawkins failed to mention was that the real pacemaker of the City, so far as issues and new ventures were concerned, was now Sir Ernest Cassel. He came of a family of German Court Jews, but came to England in 1869 with little or no capital. He won his spurs with the loan contractors Bischoffsheim & Goldschmidt as 'an ambitious and able troubleshooter', but his real break was winning the confidence and patronage of Baron Maurice de Hirsch, who had no direct heirs to whom he could confide his £10m. or so capital, the largest in London at the time. Cassel destroyed his personal papers and business records, but from other sources it is known that he was closely associated with Jacob Schiff of Kuhn, Loeb & Co. of New York in their numerous ventures in railroad finance, and in the development of Swedish iron-ore reserves and the Aswan Dam in Egypt. We shall catch glimpses of him regularly through the pages of this book, but he remains an enigmatic figure.[44]

Precise information on the capital of the leading accepting houses is

Table 3.4 *The Accepting Houses' Committee at its formation on 5 August 1914 (alphabetical order)*

		origins	date in London	capital c. 1914(£m)
1.	Arbuthnot, Latham & Co.	Agency house	1833	0.44
2.	Baring Bros & Co. Ltd	German (via Exeter)	1763	1.125
3.	Arthur H. Brandt & Co.	German	1899	(small)
4.	Wm Brandt, Sons & Co.	German	1805	c.1.0
5.	Brown Shipley & Co.	US	1810	0.775
6.	Cunliffe Bros	English	1890	0.50+
7.	Frühling & Goschen	German	1814	
8.	Antony Gibbs & Sons	S. America merchants	1808	1.215
9.	C. J. Hambro & Son	German (via Copenhagen)	1840	c.1.00
10.	Horstman & Co.	German	1802	
11.	F. Huth & Co.	German (via Spain)	1808	0.750
12.	Kleinwort, Sons & Co.	German (via Cuba)	1855	4.431
13.	König Bros	German	1899	0.750?
14.	Lazard Bros & Co.	French	1870	1.0
15.	Morgan, Grenfell & Co.	US	1838	c.1.0
16.	Neumann, Luebeck & Co.	S. African	c.1900	
17.	N. M. Rothschild & Sons	German (via Manchester)	1805	c.1.0
18.	A. Rüffer & Sons	German (via Lyons)	1872	1.0
19.	J. Henry Schröder & Co.	German	1804	c.3.00
20.	Seligman Bros	US	1864	
21.	Wallace Bros & Co. Ltd	Agency house (Scots)	1862	0.8m.

Sources:

List: Minutes of Accepting Houses' Committee, London EC3. Origins and dates: T. Skinner, *The London Banks* (various dates), with revisions and additions (see text).

Capital: R. J. Truptil, *British Banks* (1936) pp. 151, 155, (1, 18). Both these figures are late (1930, 1923) but not misleading.

T. Skinner, *The London Banks* (2, 21).

Kleinworts' 'Information Books' (6, 11, 13) and 'Analysis Book' (12).

Amburger, *Wm. Brandt and the Story of his Enterprises* (typescript, c.1950) (3, 4).

Guildhall Lib., Brown Shipley MSS, 'Partners' File' 1914 (5).

Guildhall Lib., Antony Gibbs MSS, 11,064/2 (8).

History of Lazard Bros & Co. (typescript with the firm).

Stock Exchange Year Book, 1922. The figure is that registered at incorporation as a private company in 1917. (15) US capital is excluded here.

Where the capital is not known but data is available on acceptances (4, 9, 17, 19) an approximate figure has been calculated on the basis of the convention that acceptances were 3–4 times the capital.

In the case of Rothschilds, this figure must be understood as that fraction of a much larger capital which may be thought of as committed to the firm's interest in accepting house business.

almost as difficult to assemble as that for issuing houses, but there is sufficient to confirm that Kleinworts' and Schröders' single-minded dedication to the growth of their two houses was sustained down to 1914 (Table 3.4). The crisis faced by the accepting houses on the declaration of war produced the only official attempt to assess their capital. A conference with the Chancellor of the Exchequer discussed an estimate of £20m. for the twenty-one houses initially composing the committee,[45] which harmonises well with the material in Table 3.4 in the sense that material from the firms suggests a median figure of about a million pounds capital for the twenty-one firms. But the most striking point about the list of accepting houses is that it underlines the importance of the Anglo-German firms as a whole, eleven out of the twenty-one belonging to this category. Of course, a few of these had now been in London for two or three generations, but there is clearly an important cause to be identified here. The problem will be considered in Chapter 5 and subsequent thematic chapters. The immediate need is to measure the economic structure of the City merchant bankers at the pinnacle they reached in the late Victorian and Edwardian periods, and to this we turn in the next chapter.

4 The Structure of Merchant Banking at its Nineteenth-Century Pinnacle

In earlier chapters several references have been made to the amorphous nature of merchant banking. Merchants moved in and out of commission banking, issues, foreign exchange, arbitrage, insurance and other related activities according to changing circumstances and the dispositions of the senior partners. As so often happens in the evolution of an industry, a period of opportunity led to multiplication of numbers until an economic crisis or recession pitched some newcomers and a few unwary older firms into bankruptcy, or perhaps some safer line of enterprise. The French Wars, as explained in Chapter 1, generated unprecedented opportunities for loan contractors but the recurrent crises led to a high mortality among the bold entrepreneurs who had leaped to the front of the new City specialism. The rapid expansion of Anglo-American accepting houses in 1825–36 was terminated by the well-documented crisis of 1836–7, again with heavy losses.[1] The crises of 1847–8, 1857–8, 1866 and 1875 also had their victims, though losses among firms that can be connected with merchant banking were light.[2] The big expansion of foreign loans in the period from 1875 to 1890 had severe repercussions as the Baring crisis but failed to deter the expansion of exchange and accepting house business. Consequently numbers again multiplied in the thirty years before the First World War.

Numerical definition of merchant banks is only possible with the appearance of Thomas Skinner's annual directories *The London Banks* from 1880, but the numbers and categories cited in Table 4.1 are not so precise as tidy-minded scholars would like them to be. In the early 1880s the small numbers are more evidence of the compilers' limited knowledge than of any dramatic growth in the next decade, and omissions are evident to the end of the period.[3] Until recent years almost all the merchant banks preferred to style themselves 'merchants', so the first line of the table represents the main group under consideration. 'Agency houses' was the traditional name given to merchants trading to India and the Far East; their historical roots followed a different course to merchants in other sectors of world trade but by the later decades of the nineteenth century they had much the same functions so we shall include

Table 4.1   *Numbers and types of private banks in London 1885–1915*

type	1885	1895	1904–5	1914–15
'Merchants'	25	55 (1)	56 (4)	68 (5)
Agency houses	6	17	20 (2)	17 (6)
merchant banks (umbra)	**31**	**72** (1)	**76** (6)	**85** (11)
Army and navy agents	4	7	6	5 (1)
Foreign bankers	10	15 (2)	17	15(1)
merchant banks (inc. penumbra)	**45**	**94** (3)	**99** (6)	**105** (13)
Discount agents	17	18	23 (1)	20
Deposit banks	23 (1)	14 (2)	7 (2)	6 (1)
Miscellaneous	8	11	5	6 (1)
Closed down	0	0	2	2
	93 (1)	137 (5)	136 (9)	139 (15)

Private banks that had been incorporated are recorded in parentheses.
Source: Thomas Skinner, *The London Banks and Kindred Companies and Firms*, 1885, 1895, 1904–5 and 1914–15. Minor adjustments to the classifications have been made in the light of more complete evidence; in particular 'Agency houses' also includes several 'Merchants' known to have been specialising in trade to India and the Far East, notably Edward Boustead, Mathesons, Dent Palmer & Co., David Sassoon and E. D. Sassoon & Co.

them as merchant banks.[4] 'Army and navy agents' found their origins in the British government's practice of employing private contractors to supply and pay the armed services, but by the period of our table the credit activities of some of them had extended to private trade, particularly in the British Empire.[5] Foreign bankers were dealers in foreign exchange; most of them were small firms of continental origin who moved to London in the 1870s as the traditional leaders of this sector, Rothschilds and Barings, abandoned the Royal Exchange to concentrate on less exacting and more rewarding activites.[6] However, some of the more successful of them (notably Raphaels and Montagus) acquired interests in public issues, so that we may consider this group and the last as the penumbra of merchant banking, a concept that harmonises with the notion of specialisation and irregular or occasional activity in the last paragraph. 'Discount agents' (otherwise known as bill brokers) were the specialists who discounted inland bills of exchange, while 'Deposit banks' refers to the retail banks, neither of which were normally involved in public issues, accepting house business, or (until the early years of this century) in foreign exchange. However, there are two or three important exceptions to this general position; in particular the old private bank of Glyn Mills & Co. was prominent in both.[7] These two groups are included in the table mainly for comparative purposes. The decline of numbers in the last two groups is evidence of the amalgamation movement rather than any decline in strength.

Down to the First World War the merchant banks largely maintained the geographical specialisation that was central to their long mercantile tradition. Some of the bigger and older firms began to diversify as continental Europe and the USA presented stiffer competition, but in 1914 the typical merchant bank remained a family firm that was still largely committed to the sector in which it had won its reputation before graduating to pure finance. Though there was inevitably some shift away from Europe, when war broke out there were as many as twenty-one firms with considerable commitments in central Europe, a dozen of them of German origin. At the same period there were at least eighteen firms with major interests in India and the Far East, eleven in South America, eight in Russia and four in South Africa. Small firms retained their position in the market by specialisation in a small country, for instance Blyth, Greene & Jourdain in Mauritius, Blyderstein in the Netherlands, Ladenburg in Romania, and Le Lacheur & Son in Costa Rica.[8] Similarly, firms that entered accepting house business or investment banking in the period covered by the table had opportunity to develop expertise only in one area. Again to take just a few examples, Cox & Co., the army agents established in 1758, did not begin to take an interest in the finance of India's external trade until after 1905, so their later connections with Egypt were not initiated until the close of the First World War.[9] Balfour, Williamson & Co., which began in a small way as a firm of forwarding agents in Liverpool in 1851, was only just beginning to be involved in investments in Chile in the 1880s, and did not look elsewhere until after the founder's death in 1903.[10] Erlangers, one of the old Frankfurt Jewish houses, opened in London in 1870, but acceptance business was not started until 1910, and scarcely got under way before the war broke out.[11] Robert Fleming, the so-called 'father of the Investment Trust Movement', had few interests outside the United States before the First World War.[12]

Side-by-side with this specialisation, it is possible to identify some shifts of interest and diversification during the longer period in which the major firms were established. Information is too scarce to be sure of any overall patterns, but some interesting tendencies can be discerned. Barings are often thought of as Anglo-American merchant bankers, perhaps because Hidy's study of them deals only with this branch of their activities, but from the 1830s they were moving into the finance of Indian and Far Eastern trade, followed by that with Russia, and later with South America, and a number of other firms can be seen to have evolved in such diverse ways. Cropper Benson and Rathbones of Liverpool and Peabody both shifted from the USA towards India and China, while at various dates Kleinworts and Schröders transferred some of their activities from

Cuba-American trade towards Russia and South America. Lazards and Brown Shipley also shifted towards Russia in the early years of this century. Rothschilds nourished an early interest in Brazil and from the 1870s Barings committed themselves heavily in South America, competing with the local specialists, Antony Gibbs and Balfour Williamson (Chile), Knowles & Foster and Pinto Leite (Brazil). A similar track was followed by Brandts (Argentina), Louis Dreyfus & Co. (grain trade) and Huths. Meantime, Ralli Bros were moving the focus of their interest from the Black Sea and Mediterranean trade to India, along with fellow-Greeks Schillizzi & Co. Matheson & Co. and some of the older agency houses, and the Persian-Jewish Sassoons steadily shifted the weight of their interest from India to the 'treaty ports' of China while the Liverpool branch of Antony Gibbs (Gibbs, Bright & Co.) focused first on the West Indies then Australia. From the middle of the nineteenth century the reputation of US bonds steadily increased, so that not only firms with an old connection there revived and strengthened their interest (notably Browns, Barings, and Rothschilds), but also new houses started investing there: Hambros from a background of specialisation in Scandinavia and Italy, Raphaels, Bischoffshein & Goldschmidt and Cohen from the German-Jewish connection, and Thomson Bonar from Russian trade and finance. Some of the economic developments and personal dispositions that prompted such departures from more familiar territory will be noticed in later chapters; for the moment it is sufficient to make the point that there is ample evidence of an outward emigration of interest from the old centres of financial activity in European and Anglo-American trade to the new continents, with the consequence that by 1914 the vanguard of the merchant banks had interest that, geographically speaking at least, were far more diversified than their original connections.[13]

Table 4.1 fails to disclose a further thread of the background and tradition of the merchant banks, that of stockbroking. Present-day City bankers will often insist that in England Stock Exchange regulations and historical tradition have always kept banking and stockbroking as quite distinct professions, without realising that the present prudent demarcation took a long time to evolve, and that in this sector of finance, as in so many others, functions were ill-defined for generations. Raphael Raphael & Sons was a stockbroker of the first importance who from 1870 conducted a banking business, and Samuel Montagu pursued similar type of business. L. B. Cohen, Helbert Wagg and Saemy Japhet all moved into merchant banking from stockbroking while Robert Kindersley, for fifty years the presiding genius of Lazards, was recruited from the same background.[14] To judge from the success of all these firms, the experience was valuable training for a merchant banker.

Despite the existence of the great financial houses and a preponderance of hereditary leadership, it continued to be possible for small specialists with sober reputations to push their way into the system. A few examples chosen from firms that were leaders in 1914 will illustrate the point. John Horstman was a clerk with Hope & Co. of Amsterdam and started in the City in 1802 on an annuity of £300 pa given to some of the old firm's faithful servants. His extensive connections with the Netherlands brought him, according to a report of 1830, 'a fair share of banking business with some of the most respectable houses' as well as 'large insurances at Lloyds on Dutch account'. Frühling & Goschen, who opened in London in 1814 as commission agents exporting colonial produce and cotton to Germany, began modestly, but from their 'economical habits' accumulated some £15,000 by 1830. Brandts, an old German mercantile family trading to Archangel, Riga and St Petersburg, opened a London office in 1805, but in 1861 became insolvent. Augustus Brandt scraped together £10,000 and with the help of old connections steadily built up a concern whose capital reached a million pounds in 1904.[15] But his success story fades alongside that of some of the firms in the foreign exchange and arbitrage business. Samuel Montagu began his City career with £5,000 lent by his father in 1853, while Saemy Japhet came to London from Berlin in 1896 with a mere £15,000. When Montagu retired in 1909 he had £600,000 in his firm, and Japhet incorporated his business with a capital of £750,000 in 1920.[16] The earlier success stories are not irrelevant to this chapter for they helped to sustain the legend of 'self-help' that feature so prominently in the business ideology of the period.

While successive crises of the nineteenth century produced a heavy mortality of firms, the expansion of trade and investment opportunities offered a more or less continuous flow of new entrants. A high turnover of firms and the migration of profits into gracious living maintained a situation in which numerous new entrants, often ephemeral firms, competed for new business or that left by the handful of big names. It is difficult to make any very precise calculations, but it may help to note that in 1914–15 at least 20 firms out of 105 had been set up in the previous quarter-century, though a few had evidently transferred from other branches of business, such as Helbert Wagg and Cazenove from stockbroking.[17] Bonn & Co., founded in 1910 and occupying the first floor of 62½ Old Broad Street, was described as 'a typical small banking business' of the period. 'The business of the firm was very good, if small, and its contacts were of the highest class', a former clerk insisted. 'Its functions were in the usual banking fields – current accounts, borrowing and lending money in the Discount market, Stock Exchange transactions for the firms and for clients, financing industrial projects, mostly overseas, and investments.' The capital was said to be £0.5m. in 1911 but the active labour force was only three partners (one English, one French, one German) and about ten clerks.[18] At the turn of the century the best-known firms still employed well under 100 clerks – Brandts 80, Barings 71, Kleinworts 58, Hambros 48 and Schröders 36, to mention just a few. Morgans, probably the wealthiest firm, had a staff of no more than 150 in New York in 1914.[19]

For the end of the nineteenth century it is possible to assemble information on the capital of 41 of the 106 merchant banks (Table 4.2). The list does not pretend to be a sample of the whole; except in a few instances the firms identified are the more prominent ones. The firms on which we have no information are generally the smaller and more ephemeral ones, and it is difficult to suppose that an average figure for their capital would exceed £0.25m. each. If this is a reasonable 'guesstimate', the total capital of the large unknown sector would be 65 × £0.25m. or £16.25m. The total capital of the merchant banking sector would therefore be of the order of £50m., only 12.5 per cent of the capital of the London joint-stock banks, £400m. in 1904–5 (Table 9.2) and rather less than that of the eight great German investment banks (73m. in 1908). Given this inferiority, one of the main tasks of this book will be to assess how the London merchant banks managed to retain their reputation and influence through the nineteenth century and beyond.

Table 4.2   *Capital of the London merchant banks c. 1900*

Size of partners' capital	nos.	total capital
£5m. +	1	6.0
£1m.–£2m.	11	14.9
£0.5m–£0.99m.	10	6.4
£0.1m.–£0.49m.	19	4.9
total of known firms	41	32.2
estimate for unknown firms	65	16.25
estimated total capital	106	48.45

Source: Appendix 1

However, an initial word of explanation can be offered. It is that the merchant banks' most important assets were their reputation and connections, which enabled them to recruit large sums at short notice, even in crisis years. In the nature of things, it is practically impossible to put a figure on the value of such kinds of business assets, and the most that can be done is to illustrate the inadequacy of partners' capital as an index of their economic standing. Wernher, Beit & Co., who had made their fortunes in South Africa, opened in London as an investment house in 1890 with a nominal capital of £2m. but the two principal partners were evidently worth much more; between them they left some £18m.[20]

Matheson & Co. were incorporated in 1909 with an issued capital of £200,000 but this sum could not have been a tithe of the capital that Jardine Matheson & Co. controlled in the Far East as they spawned joint-stocking companies for shipping, industry and railway development. The only figure disclosed in the recent official history of the oriental enterprise is a capital of £1.72m. in 1891.[21] However, not all figures were gross understatements. A case study of Antony Gibbs & Sons examined in Chapter 9 shows that for some years before 1914 the net worth of the partnership was less than its reputation in the market would have led creditors to suppose.[22] Another factor in this complex situation is that the standing of the international houses invariably benefited from wealthy partners abroad, sometimes a branch of the London house but more often a parent or sister concern on the continent or in the USA. Clearly it is impossible to put a figure on this kind of connection, or indeed to deduct one when some branch of the dispersed family interest went bankrupt, as it did, for instance, in the case of the Schröders, Rallis, and Rodocanachis.[23]

The great preponderance of firms covered in this study remained family businesses, and most continued to be so for another generation after 1914. Of course, able men from outside the ruling family sometimes succeeded in obtaining partnerships, but they usually married into the founding family and in this way were incorporated into it. Experience showed that there could be problems recruiting men of ability from outside. In the few instances that we have detailed correspondence of partners appointed on merit with numbers of the 'ruling' family, conflict is much in evidence. Bates regularly complained that he was not accepted by his partners at Barings. 'The return of Lord Ashburton [from the USA] has renewed the mortification and pain I have always felt in consequence of my social position', he wrote in 1844. 'On joining the house of B B & Co. when Lord A. was a partner [in 1827], I found that he and Mr Mildmay did not consider that by forming a co-partnership with me they had incurred the so-called necessity for and intercourse with me and my family in our social relations.'[24] Similar tensions developed at Brown Shipley & Co., which during much of the second half of the nineteenth century was run by two 'outsiders', Mark Wilks Collet (later Sir Mark Collet) and F. A. Hamilton. When William Brown died in 1865 a major crisis broke out between the Browns as owners of much of the partnership capital and the 'outsiders' which brought the firm to the verge of break-up at a time when the house was reaching the pinnacle of its influence in Anglo-American trade.[25] It does not seem overbold to venture the generalisation that outside partners were only drawn in when this was absolutely necessary to maintain the continuity of the firm or (more rarely) to inject some expertise that was unknown to the founding family; under this second heading we may instance J. A. Bryce, the explorer of Upper Burma, becoming a partner in Wallace Bros in 1885, and Saemy Japhet taking Gottfried Loewenstein, a German arbitragist, as his London partner in 1900. Also at the turn of the century, the London house of J. S. Morgan & Co. drew in Clinton Dawkins from the Colonial Service to exploit his expertise in Egyptian and Indian finance. The notion of a meritocracy recruited from the universities evidently did not occur to anyone in the City until much later; the only business history to record the idea, that of Wallace Bros, notes that the policy was accepted when an Oxford classical scholar recruited in 1905 won a place on the board twenty years later, but this was only because of a dearth of younger Wallace sons interested in a business career.[26]

Most firms sought to protect their futures by selecting the next generation of leaders from the most industrious sons or nephews.[27] The point can be strikingly illustrated with an extract from a letter written from Vicary Gibbs of Antony Gibbs & Sons to one of his more indolent young nephews in 1891

> there is no way for anyone to get on in Anty Gibbs & Sons except by following in the same lines as [others] have done to the complete satisfaction of all who had to deal with them, namely working steadily and regularly in London or Liverpool like any other clerk till such time as a vacancy occurred in the colonies or West Coast for which they were considered to have qualified themselves, and then going to one or the other country for an indefinite period until such time as an opening should occur which would allow of their being employed as principals in England.[28]

In other words, the senior partners contrived to maintain a meritocracy *within* the family by following traditional mercantile precepts, resorting to talented outsiders only when internal supply gave out. Large families were the favourite Victorian solution to the succession problem. Less able sons could be put out to farming, the services, the church or some other occupation combining security with minimal risk to the family name and fortune.

The earliest case on record of an attempt to constitute a whole board of directors as a meritocracy came from the history of Lazards. In the decade before the First World War, the Lazard family rejuvenated their London operation by appointing a sequence of specialist directors: Robert Kindersley from the Stock Exchange in 1905, G. S. Hein with experience of German banking in 1908, Emile Pusch, who came of a Russian background, in 1912, and the Hon. R. H. Brand, who had spent some years in South Africa as a member of Lord Milner's 'kindergarten', the same year, and Hugo Schirer, who had been a private banker in Mexico City for some years, in 1913. The firm's capital was almost doubled by drawing in part of the fortune of Weatman Pearson, a Yorkshire contractor who had become one of the legendary figures of British industrial history, and who was now deeply involved in Mexican oil. This formidable combination of talent and experience, united under Kindersley's leadership, lifted Lazards into the first rank of merchant banking. In the 1920s and 1930s Lord Kindersley and Lord Brand were probably the best-known figures in City merchant banking, regularly appearing as spokesmen for the whole group. However, this meritocracy, despite its undoubted achievements and eminence, was not emulated in other family firms until after 1945, and in 1914 was practically unique.[29]

Though the loyalties of the merchant bank focused on the founding family (or families) and its (or their) traditions, there were some interesting external connections. Most of the banks were, as we have seen, of foreign extraction or, if they were British, of Scots or North of England origin, and it is easy to suppose that the 'exiles' clung together and intermarried. Consequently we might expect to find Huguenot, Jewish, Scottish, Quaker, Greek, Lutheran and other ethnic or religious groupings. In practice such loyalties often proved weak or ineffective, at any rate after the alien group had acclimatised itself to the City, for the need for co-operation quickly overwhelmed ethnic loyalties. The quality of surviving records seldom allows us to get close to the family and social as well as business life of bankers of the period, but in the few instances where this is possible, the range of contacts is a revelation. The most interesting case is that of the Rothschilds, already examined in Chapter 2. Though raised in the Frankfurt ghetto on strict Rabbinic teaching and initially suspicious of richer and often hostile Christian rivals, they were conducting operations with them from their formative period as European bankers (1814–18).[30] Gille's monumental work on the French branch of the family reveals the extent of their association with the Huguenot banks, and their Manchester clients included former Huguenot families like Gontard and Du Fay. Apart from the Jews, the racial and religious minority that appeared most clannish is the Greeks. Though Greek merchants began to settle in London and Manchester in numbers in the 1820s, there was still a lot of prejudice against them and their 'clan' solidarity forty years later. The author of the popular *Bubbles of Finance* (1865) maintained that 'the Greeks are the only people of the world that could carry on that extraordinary trade [in Levant trade bills] because they form the only nation the natives of which have implicit confidence in one another. Whatever a Greek may be to the foreigner, he is always true to his countrymen.'[31] However, in this case as with the Jews, business exigencies regularly conquered social prejudice. At the same period that Meason's work was the gossip of the City, leading Greek firms were being drawn into the various financial companies that were inspired by the Crédit Mobilier.[32]

Another religious grouping whose members were said to have worked hand in glove with one another were the Quakers. Nolte's reminiscences of the transatlantic cotton trade in the 1820s contains several references to 'the Quaker Confederation', in which he included such merchant houses as Cropper Benson & Co. and Rathbones in Liverpool and Isaac Cooke and the Thompsons (Francis and Jeremiah) in New York.[33] Nolte maintained that Dennistoun of Glasgow routed this group, but in 1837 Henry Burgess (the distinguished writer of the *Circular to Bankers*) was referring to 'that powerful money-sect, the Society of Friends, who may be said to be the leading operators and most constant and extensive dealers in credit in both countries' (that is in Britain and the USA).[34] He was apparently thinking of Nicholas Biddle of the United States Bank and his London correspondent Samuel Gurney, the bill broker 'who virtually directs the course of investment for one half of the surplus floating banking capital of the country', but whatever the truth of this, Biddle collapsed in 1839 and Gurney's successors disappeared in the notorious crisis of 1867. The Bensons, Croppers and Rathbones managed to survive the devastation of 1867, and kept on good terms, but the Bensons family records show that their social connections now blossomed elsewhere – with the Barings, Rallis (Greeks), Arbuthnots (Scots), and Sassoons (Jews) rather than their old connections.[35] In merchant banking the Quaker cousinhood scarcely survived into the second half of the century, with members drifting into more orthodox religious loyalties.

The stronger and more enduring links were between firms at the main and satellite financial centres of the world. The earliest and best-documented case is that of Barings of London and Hopes of Amsterdam. M. G. Buist's history of eighteenth-century Hopes sees the long association between the two firms beginning with state loans, but in fact Hopes first used Barings as local (London) agents to collect and take care of the small bills they could not discount in Amsterdam. When London superseded Amsterdam as a financial centre during the French Wars the roles were reversed.[36] Rothschilds built up a comparable structure with firms at other satellite cities such as Hambros (Copenhagen), Behrens (Hamburg), and Bleichroders (Berlin).[37] George Peabody, the leading Anglo-American house, was earlier a Baltimore house that received credit facilities from Brown Bros[38] and Overend, Gurney & Co., but Peabody's London successors (J. S. Morgan & Co.) forged strong links with satellite European and US houses.

The third and least important kind of link between the banks was that of the interlocking partnership. The idea was evidently very familiar from the common practice of the 'international houses' mentioned above, but in that case the system was essentially one of main and branch houses governed by dispersed partners, while we are now focusing on integration between autonomous firms. An interesting early example is that of a cluster of Liverpool-Scottish families engaged in trade to India and the Middle East. Ogilvy, Gillanders & Co. started in Calcutta in 1824 with a capital of £10,000 lent by John Gladstone (father of W. E. Gladstone) to two of his nephews, but in 1833 G. C. Arbuthnot joined adding £20,000 to the partners' capital and eventually becoming senior partner. Arbuthnot simultaneously started another firm called Arbuthnot, Ewart & Co., also trading through Liverpool to India. At the same time, the two Gladstone brothers who came into Ogilvy, Gillanders were concerned in Thomson Bonar, an old Russian mercantile house that was graduating into pure finance and in 1859 joined with Bischoffsheim & Goldschmidt of Brussels, Paris and Frankfurt to form a bank of industrial and commercial credit at Paris.[39] Another interesting case is that of Gaspard Farrer, a director of H. S. Lefevre & Co. and a specialist in Canadian railway finance, who about the turn of the century became a director of Barings.[40] But these instances are in no way typical or representative; they were mutations in the accelerating process of evolution, soon to be discarded. It seems that in the later decades of the nineteenth century, the City of London became more focused on the individual entrepreneur of talent, rather than the international family or the ethnic cousinhood. The exemplars of the new age were all 'loners' – Baron Maurice de Hirsch, Sir Ernest Cassel, Saemy Japhet and Jacob Schiff in New York – rather than families like the Rothschilds, Seligmans, Sterns and the rest. The reasons are not far to seek. Before the telegraph and transatlantic cable inaugurated instant communications, ties of blood and religion were the most enduring guarantee of mutual trust and harmony, but in the 1880s this was becoming old-fashioned. By moving as a unit, the family group moved relatively slowly and sometimes not at all, while the individualists could select their alliances to suit the occasion, and make instant decisions. Despite reiterated appeals for the old family unity, the third-generation Rothschilds in Vienna and Frankfurt were torn away from London and Paris, whose interests now diverged, while Belmont went his own way. The Seligman family 'was forever having to stop what it was doing to assist some brother who had made an expensive error, or to buy out a brother-in-law, or to help William in Paris buy his wife a diamond necklace', and it was only Joseph's autocracy that kept the brothers together. After his death the remaining brothers drafted a 'Family Liquidation Agreement' to separate the New York, London, Paris and Frankfurt branches and divide their assets.[41] Other international houses had gone the same way; Baron Schröder drifted away from his Hamburg cousins, Ralli Brothers broke up in 1860 and the Brandts the next year. Morton Rose was dissolved in 1899 to separate London from New York while the London partners of Brown Bros are said to have lost the old contact with their US partners. Lazards finally separated in 1920.[42] In other words, the 'international house' was now only a historical phenomenon, but for the time being at least, there were few institutional links to connect London houses with overseas banks.

Some reference is made in Table 4.1 to a small but increasing number of incorporations among the various categories of banks listed and, in concluding this chapter, we must mention the role of the joint-stock company in City merchant banking in the period. There can be no doubt that business opinion continued to prefer the traditional family partnership, not merely because it preferred the familiar form, but because the record of the early joint-stock banks, especially in the provinces, left much to be desired. The generally perceived advantages of the private banker were fairly summarised by *The Statist* in 1885:

> The private banker can act with a promptitude and decision which cannot be exercised by the manager of a joint-stock bank. For he is part owner of the concern, and can act for his partners. Moreover, he has a skill and training, has accumulated special knowledge, and is possessed of the traditions of the business, in a way and to an extent the directors of a joint-stock bank [who were generally part-time] cannot pretend to; while in addition he is a specialist no more likely to abuse the secrets of his customers than their doctor or solicitor, whereas the joint-stock director may be a competitor in their own trade. And, lastly, the private bank has this great advantage over the joint-stock bank, as the latter is now constituted, – that the liability of the partners is unlimited. If, then, the partners are wealthy, the security offered is larger than that offered by any except the very greatest of the joint-stock banks.

The last point was by no means an academic one, for there was a sequence of bankruptcies of inexperienced joint-stock banks from the 1830s.[43]

However, the pressing need for more and more capital to meet the growing dimensions of international trade and public finance prompted some of the old private banks to reconsider the position, and in 1885 Glyn Mills took the plunge, but with the provision the current partners remained the only directors of the business, and that their liability continued to be unlimited. *The Statist* applauded this initiative as uniting the best features of the old and new systems, and was so enthusiastic as to prophesy that Glyn Mills' enterprise would prove to be 'the death-knell of the small private banks', for 'when the greatest of the private banks has taken this step, the others cannot refuse to move'. The long-term consequences were therefore all too clear:

> The strong private banks may be expected to follow the example of Messrs. Glyn, Mills, Currie, and Co., and the weak ones to amalgamate with the enterprising and powerful Scotch and provincial banks that desire to open offices in London, or to gain admission to the Clearing

House. Amalgamation between themselves is hardly probable. A doubling, trebling, or quadrupling of the partners would make the proprietary too numerous for a private bank, while it would render harmonious co-operation extremely difficult. Then, again, the amalgamating banks would have different traditions, which would be likely to conflict unless one institution were to give the law to the others – a result that would naturally follow absorption by a powerful joint-stock company, but not easy to attain when equals combine their resources. And, lastly, the partnership arrangements offer many obstacles. It is probable, therefore, that one consequence of the new departure will be a speedier extinction of the small private banks of the City, and a fresh introduction of provincial joint-stock banks.[44]

Evidently the writer was thinking primarily of the small private deposit banks which (as Table 4.1 illustrates) continued to be absorbed in larger concerns through the period. But, as we have already noticed, Glyns also conducted some merchant banking functions (issues and acceptances), so that its initiative could not have passed unnoticed in that sector of the City. In fact, however, almost the only other incorporations before 1914 were Barings and Morton Rose (both casualties of the crisis of 1890) and a group of five Scottish houses with interests in Indian trade and finance.[45] Chapter 8 of this book shows how the 'East India houses' moved strongly into real estate (tea and rubber plantations, cotton mills, and so on) in the Edwardian period, and it can be inferred that the partners were avoiding locking up their personal fortunes in the manner of the old 'agency houses' that collapsed in 1830–3. A sixth Indian house that incorporated (David Sassoon & Co.) is known to have been receiving large deposits for investment in India, and with the Scottish passion for overseas investment, it is easy to suppose they were doing much the same kind of thing.[46] On this limited evidence it seems that the company merchant banks were those that, in one way or another, were deviating from the traditional merchant bank activities.

Of course, this does not explain how all the other firms met the growing demand for capital. This is a large subject which will be examined in some detail in a later chapter. For the moment it is sufficient to observe that they appear to have encountered few problems in raising adequate capital to maintain their traditional activities, and so felt that the gains of incorporation weighed little compared with the acknowledged merits of the private partnership.

5 Qualification: 'Indubitable Credit'

The one essential qualification for the merchant bank in all these diverse forms of business and phases of development was that it should enjoy an impeccable financial record. The partners' collective fortunes must be large enough to take the strain of all conceivable circumstances in the money market, including the recurrent financial crises of the century. All the members of the firm must abstain from anything that could be called speculation, and the partners must have a personal reputation for regularity and probity in all their dealings. Such at any rate was the ideal, the yardstick by which the various firms constantly monitored each others' standing in the money market. Since accounts were never published, most of the assessment was of individual competence and estimates of capital, and regular attempts were made to ascertain that firms were not likely to be drawn upon for total amounts beyond which they were perfectly safe. Firms that passed this test were conventionally classified as A1 in the private business reports that were common through the century. A2 firms were usually those with smaller capitals, while classes 3 and 4 might stand for other firms and those that could not be trusted. Those who won the coveted accolade of A1 were frequently accepting houses, but A2 houses are not infrequently found providing extensive credit for smaller or less experienced firms.[1] The standing of any firms could easily be ascertained by the amount by which its bills were discounted for sale: the smaller the discount the higher the standing of the firm. Obviously all firms took the closest possible interest in the standing of their bills in the market, noting with pleasure how some favourable event could increase their discount value, or with chagrin the consequences of some business or political setback. Thus in 1814 when it became known that N. M. Rothschild was being employed by the British Commissory-in-Chief (J. C. Herries), he wrote in delight to his brothers, 'My bill in London is better than Bethmann [the leading banker] in Frankfurt because everybody feels honoured to speak to me.'[2] Similarly, when Joshua Bates was firmly in the saddle at Barings and the *Edinburgh Review* had identified him as 'perhaps the most extensive, and certainly one of the best informed merchants in the country', he was able to boast his firm's premier credit rating. 'We have hitherto considered ourselves at the top in point of credit amongst Merchant and Bankers here [London], of this we have daily proofs in our negotiations and we think that not unconnected with our not pushing our business to the extent to which our Capital would warrant', he proudly noted.[3]

For any given group of merchants the A1 accolade was a rare distinction but consolation might be found in the common experience that estimates of credit rating could shift quite sharply over short periods of time. We have only space here to take one example to illustrate this point. As we saw in the last chapter, the East India houses were a group that produced several merchant bankers during the century. The rating of the various firms by the Bank of England in 1844–7 shows only five out of twenty as first class in the earlier year, but as many as eighteen out of twenty-six at the second count. Clearly the early part of 1847 found Liverpool optimistic about prospects in the Far East, but the bankruptcy of Reid Irving & Co. shortly afterwards changed the mood. The next year the Bank's Liverpool agent was writing that there were now only two houses in the East India trade which at the time he considered 'first class and perfectly undoubted'.[4] One of the two Gladstones presently rose to the status of a merchant bank, but so did some houses for the time being placed in the second rank, Arbuthnot, Ewart & Co., Finlay & Co., and Ogilvy, Gillanders & Co. The kind of feelings that prompted removal to the second category are reflected in remarks on Far Eastern traders in the Preston Bank's 'Character Book'. Thus on Fletcher, Alexander & Co. of London in 1845 it was noted: 'I think the parties perfectly safe and there would not be the slightest reservation in speaking of them, but that all the old East India houses, having to enter into competition with younger blood, are hardly able to keep up with them, and at the same time saddled with expensive Establishments.' But neither could the younger, smaller firms qualify as A1; thus on Lysaght, Smithil & Co. it was recorded: 'A young East India House of limited means in a trade which requires large capital ... (1846). Failed ... 1847.'[5]

The difficulty in practice was one of striking a balance between conducting a safe business and trying to expand. As one of Barings' partners succinctly expressed the point, 'by being too liberal we lose our money and not being sufficiently liberal we lose our business.' The compensation for sacrifice of some new risky business for the conservative houses was that they emerged from the periods of commercial crisis stronger than ever. In 1837 Barings was the only large Anglo-American accepting house to live through the crisis without recourse to the Bank of England, and the firm consequently reached a new pinnacle of prestige. Following the crisis of 1847–8 Bates wrote, 'Amid the convulsions of the past year it is a matter of great thankfulness that the interests of my House have not suffered, on the contrary they have rather benefited. Perhaps the House never made greater profits in one year than in 1848.' Then again after the crisis of 1857: 'It was a remarkable fact that nearly all the firms that stopped payment proved to be insolvent, all were more or less engaged in accepting [bills] uncovered for Americans, Swedes, Hamburgers. ... Our business has very much increased, and the state of commercial credits is so much reduced that everybody runs to us.'[6] John Killick has demonstrated a similar phenomenon in the growth of Brown Shipley & Co., but by calculation of their relative importance as cotton importers rather than by quotations from the partners. In the boom of the 1830s the firm fell from second largest importer in Liverpool to sixth, but after the crash of 1837 it reverted to first place. In the mid-1850s M. W. Collet, still a junior partner in Brown Shipley, was fighting his seniors to maintain the firm's liquidity against the inevitable day of crisis. He could not 'call to mind a single large House in England or New York that had departed from its legitimate business to enter into large lock-ups and has not thereby been ruined sooner or later.' The restraint that he exercised over William Brown probably saved the house in the crisis of 1857, and the firm's record during this period, in the words of its most recent historian, 'elevated the house to a position of unquestioned pre-eminence among financiers of the international trade of the United States.'[7]

In this matter they showed more responsibility than the rising US investment bankers, several of whom were opening offices in London in the early 1860s. Seligmans will serve as an apt illustration of this point. In 1867 Joseph Seligman, the founder and supreme autocrat of the firm instructed his younger brothers on his precepts:

> You are, of course, green yet in the banking business, as we were a few years ago, and it is only through extraordinary caution and knowledge, trusting no-one except we knew from our own knowledge that he was safe beyond all doubt, that we got along without making heavy losses.... The main thing in a banker is safety, with ability to reach his money at a moment's call. ... The subject of taking deposits is rather a risky one, inasmuch as depositors can (and will in times of panics) call for all their deposits, which is enough to break any but the very strongest banks. You will at first not take any deposits on call from anyone. ... Never lend money without a security, which you can sell at any time. Never endorse or go security for a living man.

Despite these stern instructions, only six years later Seligmans had some $2m. locked up in railroad securities and only $1m. available in liquid capital. Seligmans tried to lift their spirits with the thought that 'Drexel [Morgan] and Morton [Rose & Co.] are both in much deeper than we are with the Mo., Kans. & Texas' railroad bonds, but the firm continued to be heavily committed to a form of security that was often far from liquid.[8]

However these US-based firms were by no means the only ones vulnerable to criticism. Frederick Huth & Co. were regarded as one of the more 'solid' German houses in the City; in the 1830s their policy was explained by the principal's faithful son-in-law:

In such a world-wide business as ours there are many accidental circumstances which would bring about unforeseen losses and disasters unless each one of the chiefs faithfully and industriously sticks to his post. It is not the greater or smaller profits that matter as much as the safety and regularity with which the concern is conducted.

Nevertheless, Huths lost £10,000 (10 per cent of their capital) in the crisis of 1836–7, a large sum for a firm whose main interests were reckoned to be in Spain and Germany. Six years later they were still assessed cautiously: 'Means are overrated and hardly equal to the amount of their business, nevertheless we consider them safe and likely to continue so.'[9]

Large capital was in itself no guarantee of a high credit rating, for it was all too easy to lock up a fortune in unsaleable property or bonds. Examples abound; only three or four can be mentioned here. James Holford ran a trading and accepting house with branches in Liverpool, New Orleans and New York and a capital of some £300,000, but much became 'locked up' in the Russian trade and a further £100,000 in Arkansas bonds. Not surprisingly his rating in 1843 read: 'must have the greater part of his capital locked up or lost, avoid bills on him', and he shortly relinquished business.[10] At the same period, another prominent Anglo-American house, Francis de Lizardi & Co. (Paris, London, Liverpool and New Orleans) locked up much of their capital (£0.4m.+) in Mexican bonds and real estate in the USA. The last we hear of them (in 1843) is an injunction in Barings' reports: 'Don't touch any of their paper [bills] in any shape.'[11] Forty years later, Lazard Brothers, a French-Jewish house with offices in Paris, London, New York and San Francisco came under suspicion simply because they were trying to keep pace with ambitious US rivals like Drexel Morgan and Seligman. 'Considered good for what they undertake, and wealthy, but speculative and wide-spread. Their acceptances would not be taken at the finest rates and their credit must therefore be considered 2nd class.'[12]

In practice, of course, the real culprits were not always spotted until it was too late. Dennistoun of Glasgow, a leading Scottish-American house, offers an instructive case study. The firm began in Glasgow in 1790 and by the middle 1820s were major cotton importers. They ran into trouble in the crisis of 1825 when Dennistoun senior was in partnership with two firms that failed. He reconstituted his business with a New York partner who had had to compound with his creditors in the same disastrous year. In 1829 it was estimated that they 'can have very little capital' but were doing a good business 'shipping goods abroad for different manufacturers at a charge of 2s 6d [£0.125] per package.' However, twenty years later they were said to be 'very rich', worth £300,000, and had opened branch houses in Liverpool, London, New York and New Orleans. They had lost £50,000 in the crisis of 1848, but one might suppose that experience and wealth would have brought prudence; certainly Barings thought the firm enjoyed 'unlimited credit'. By the next crisis, that of 1857, the partners had accumulated a capital of £560,000, but they nevertheless ended in the bankruptcy court. At the creditors' meeting in London it was claimed that 'All the transactions of the firm have been on a sound and legitimate basis, and no discreditable act can in any way be imputed to them', but this view was not universally held. Belmont wrote from New York: 'In order to give you one instance of many of the reckless manner with which business has been done here by some of our leading houses, I will only name Dennistoun Wood & Co., the well-known Scotch house, who lose by one failure of an importing house the enormous sum of $900,000 [£186,000].' However, the London end of the business managed to pay off its debts, continuing as the leading merchant bank of Dennistoun, Cross & Co. for another generation. The records of this ambitious firm have disappeared, but the details assembled here suggest that the partners were willing to take large risks to grow quickly, and that they learned discretion only at the third and most damaging of three crises in which they were involved.[13]

Other leading firms can be seen to have skated on thin ice at periods and to have been more lucky than Dennistoun. Sir Robert Kindersley explained to the Macmillan Committee on Finance and Industry in 1931 that there was a sort of unwritten rule among acceptance houses that a firm should not accept bills for more than three to four times the value of its capital and reserve; this convention was evidently inherited from nineteenth-century practice.[14] However in boom periods in trade there was often a great temptation to rise above the conventional ratio, though this might provoke criticism from rival houses as soon as it was spotted. Thus in 1901 Herman Kleinwort of Alexander Kleinwort & Sons wrote of their rivals J. Henry Schröder & Co.:

> Capital is £1,500,000 and there is no doubt about [the A1 position of] them – at same time they certainly are fond of big deals in some of which they make large profits and they do a lot of speculation. . . . They financed for Lewissohn of N[ew]York (a wealthy man) on a/c American Sugar Co. and although this is an undoubted concern their acceptances on this account surprised me as they were more than their capital.[15]

In fact Schröders' acceptances were only just topping £6m. a year at this date, so the deviation from the path of City orthodoxy can have been only minor and temporary. Surviving records reveal that deviations from the golden rule could be much bolder than this; thus in the middle 1870s, when Browns' total capital was £1.8m. (£1.2m. in London and £0.6m. in the USA), acceptances were fluctuating between £6m. and £9m. a year.[16]

Alexander Kleinwort's stated policy certainly did not transgress the banker's orthodoxy:

> We hope to continue to do a large and increasing business, but it is more important to do a profitable safe business – to avoid reckless speculation and all parties who do not deserve and inspire confidence. We would at all times rather increase the number of our correspondents than the transactions with a few of them – large credits are desirable only when the position of the parties concerned is thoroughly known to us.[17]

Consistent with this policy, Kleinwort maintained a sequence of 'information books' in which he recorded endless details and reports on all his clients, country by country. No City banker was more meticulous, orthodox and (in the long period) successful than Kleinwort, but his sons were less conventional. On assuming control of the firm in 1886 they raised the capital/acceptance ratio above 1:5 and it remained at this level until 1905; the partners saw their problems as simply that of disposing of a steadily increasing volume of bills on the London and New York markets. The discount houses and other purchasers of 'first class paper' liked to spread their holdings, and at any given time there was an unspoken limit to what the market would freely absorb of any one name.[18] The bold challenge to convention in raising the ratio was soon noticed by Brown Shipley, who wrote to their US partners that 'the amount and unwieldiness of their acceptances as compared with their means is beginning to excite unfavourable comment.' In 1897-9, Brown Shipley again tried to interpret the response of the City in advice to their US partners:

> It will be as well not to send for a while blank endorsed bills of Kleinwort Sons & Co. They are of course perfectly good, but just now the market is very full of the name and for some time past indications have come to us from the discount houses that their lines are full. ... Of course we do not want to shut down the name altogether, but to suggest that you send us for a while more moderate accounts and ... some other names.

Evidently Kleinwort brothers chose to ignore these signals, for two years later Brown Shipley were writing:

> You will notice that Kleinworts' bills do not command such good rates as those of other drawers by 1/16th of one per cent.... It may be of interest to you to learn that the two largest acceptors in London at the present time are Kleinwort, Sons & Co. and J. Henry Schröder &

Co., both of whose acceptances we should estimate at two or three times the total of ours, but the discrimination against the former's bills is not due so much to this fact as that our bill broker ... has a limit of course to the number of firms with whom he deals, and that these particular institutions happen to be rather full up of Kleinwort & Co.'s paper.

The 'institutions' referred to were the National Discount Co., the Union Discount Co., Alexanders and Cunliffes – in fact the principal discount houses – but it was left to the Manager of the London & Westminster's City office to remind Kleinworts of opinion in the City.[19] The partners were again in trouble with the discount houses in 1907, but by this date they had clearly established themselves as the largest house in the acceptance business, and so began to assume a more orthodox posture.[20] This important case shows that it was possible for determined entrepreneurs to defy convention to outpace more orthodox firms, but their unique growth-rate confirms the impression that few were prepared to do so.

For the vigilant observer, even minor transgressions of business orthodoxy and personal moral rectitude of the partners was reason enough for suspicion and consequent warnings to their correspondents. Two final examples, deliberately chosen from among the smaller firms, will serve to illustrate the point. Pinto Leite & Nephews originated with a merchant house at Oporto (Portugal) known as Joaquim Pinto Leite & Son. By 1868 they had branches in Liverpool, Manchester and London, and seem to have largely been involved in shipping textiles to Brazil. The senior partner, Sebastian Pinto Leite (the Count de Penha Longa), who had evidently built up the business, died in 1892, and he was succeeded by three Portugese nephews and H. J. Glanville, an English manager who was now offered a partnership. One supposes that they became involved in the acceptance house business during their halcyon years, the 1870s and 1880s, but the firm did not find an entry in Skinner's *London Banks* until 1900. Early in 1914 Brown Shipley & Co. confided to their New York partners:

We are told in Paris that, of the four partners in this firm, the three members of the Portugese family do not understand or pay any real attention to the firm's business, which is chiefly controlled by the one English partner resident in London.... They [the three] are apparently conducting themselves with some considerable degree of imprudence, and it seems to be a mystery to those who know them how the firm's credit stands so high in London. We therefore think that, in view of the present position of affairs in Brazil, where they give considerable credit, it would be advisable to go very slowly with regard to the name, and perhaps to purchase bills on them only from those Drawers whom you consider quite undoubted.

The firm were bought out by Knowles & Foster, another Brazilian house, in 1928.[21]

Benjamin Newgass was one of those adventuring entrepreneurs commonly encountered in the industrial annals of Lancashire and Yorkshire, and had a career, as Brown Shipley gently put it, 'full of ups and downs'. He first appeared in Liverpool as a commission merchant (Newgass, Rosenheim & Co.) in 1873 with a capital of £100,000, in partnership with Lehman Bros in New York, when Barings reported he was doing a 'dangerous and unprofitable business'. Moving to London and dissolving his partnership, he became connected with one of the railroads in the American South, but this proved disastrous, though he eventually managed to put it on a sound footing. On the basis of his intimate knowledge of America, he focused his interest on the Stock Exchange where he was 'known as a keen operator', no doubt buying and selling US railway bonds and other foreign securities. In the Stock Exchange boom of 1886 he was reported to be 'coining money'. Soon after he became the largest shareholder in the International Bank of London Ltd, an ambitious accepting house, but must have lost money when it got into a mess and was wound up in 1905. In 1914 Brown Shipley advised that he was 'a very shrewd old man, somewhat rough as you will see', and that the inherent merits of any of his propositions had to be scrutinised closely. Newgass was still advertising himself as a 'general merchant' in 1897, but appears in Skinner from 1911, no doubt because he was primarily functioning as a foreign investment banker.[22]

These last two examples serve as a reminder that, although the concept of 'indubitable credit' was the aim of all private (and other) banks, there continued to be numbers of smaller firms through the period that did not consistently make the grade. Most of these were probably the one-man or family enterprises that disappeared within a generation or two. The image of the City was, very fortunately, built up round the vanguard firms whose record was (apart from a few notorious cases) exemplary, but an adequate historical record must recognise these more erratic concerns as a continuing part of the merchant banking scene.

The deviations from financial orthodoxy described in the last few pages were of course only minor ripples compared with the storm that blew up over the Baring crisis of 1890. The full story of the crisis is still not known because neither Barings nor the Bank of England have opened the relevant papers to scholarly analysis, but even if the papers were available this is not the place to embark on the task, which might constitute a major study in itself. Comment here is confined to consideration of the practices and image of City merchant bankers at the period.

The basic facts of the Baring policy that led to the crisis are not disputed and easy to relate. An American correspondent of Barings called Sanford became acquainted with the President of Argentina and established such confidence that he induced the Head of State to entrust him with a large number of concessions for harbours, docks, railways and other public works, the stock to be guaranteed by the government. He lost no time in sailing to London and winning the confidence of Barings' senior partner, Lord Revelstoke. Forty years earlier, as a young man, Revelstoke had spent two years touring Latin America and the USA, staying for some months in Buenos Aires, so apparently he did not feel the need to look further for information. He saw such possibilities in these concessions that he resolved to keep them all for his own firm, no doubt for the profits of promotion, but also to overtake Rothschilds as the premier issue house. The long-established practice of syndicating state loans suggests that this was incautious, but it was followed by two fatal errors. Revelstoke was too proud to share the risks by underwriting them with lesser houses, a system which (as we shall see in Chapter 6) was already well-established for public utilities. But the chief fault was to make the issues so rapidly that the investing public had inadequate time to absorb them, so that Barings had to lock up an increasing proportion of their own capital in unsold Argentine stock. As always, rumours soon got about the City, which made the stock even more unsaleable.[23]

The Baring crisis differed from earlier crises in that there was now a strong financial press to restrain adventurous houses and warn the public. In general, this press was far too gentlemanly to mention the names of any firms, but *The Statist* parted from convention at the end of 1888 in two articles on Barings' issues. By twentieth-century standards the criticism seems restrained, but at the time it was almost unprecedented. *The Statist* declared that

in old times Messrs. Baring Brothers had conducted their business so well that they had not only amassed a vast fortune, but that they had acquired a reputation which gave a prestige to any issue brought out by them; that consequently they had it in their power to assure themselves of the goodness or badness, as the case might be, of an issue offered to them; and, further, that they could, if they so pleased, compel borrowers to be moderate. Instead of enforcing moderation and ensuring good business to the public, the Messrs. Baring Brothers have of late been growing more speculative; they have taken up business which they ought to have rejected, and they have enabled borrowers in many cases to obtain more money than ought to have been given to them.[24]

Forebodings of trouble ahead, especially in relation to Argentine and Uruguay issues, were now confided among the City houses,[25] and the rumours fed the growing crisis. As *The Statist* remarked in July 1889, 'It is notorious that most of the issues made since the late Autumn [1888] were not placed. A large proportion of these had to be kept by the great houses that brought them out, and another portion was taken by syndicates, but the investing public took up scarcely any.' Consequently, the journal added a few weeks later, 'The truth is that even the most sanguine [City houses] can no longer shut their eyes to the fact that a crash is inevitable.'[26]

Though Barings were obviously exposed to criticism for almost two years before the crash, the extent of the mismanagement was as yet inadequately recognised. In 1891 William Lidderdale, the Governor of the Bank of England at the crisis, confided that even without its Argentine involvement Barings would have run into trouble 'because the business was entirely managed by [Lord] Revelstoke and he did not seem the least to know how he stood: it was haphazard management, certain to bring any firm to grief.'[27] Consequently there was little sympathy for the stricken house; in contributing to the guarantee fund to save Barings, the other merchant banks were only trying to save themselves from even more disastrous losses. Until the crisis Barings were, as Baron Alphonse Rothschild put it, 'the keystone of English commercial credit ... all over the world',[28] and in forestalling the calamity of Barings' fall they were primarily protesting their own international reputation. Probably the general opinion of the City houses was reflected in a letter that Raphaels wrote to their New York agents, Van Hoffman & Co.:

The Bank of England in conjunction with Bertam Currie (Glyn & Co.) has during the week been organising Barings' affairs. They resolved last night [14 Nov.1890] to make the announcement at once that they would assume all Barings' engagements provided firms would guarantee 4 millions payable at the end of 3 years if there were any loss. Probably we were known to be large holders of their bills and we were applied to. It appeared to us that it was to the interest of our Joint Account to come forward, not only to diminish our loss on Barings' bills but to avoid the danger of losing by other firms stopping. ... The Bank people think there will be no loss, we are not so sanguine, but of course the crucial point will be the future of Argentine securities. It appears that the capital of the firm [Barings] on 1 Jan [1890] was *only* 2¼ million and there is 1 million in real estate. If decisive steps had not been taken and the firm allowed to go our loss we are convinced would have been much greater than it is likely to be now.[29]

I have italicised *only* £2.25m. to emphasise the point that Raphaels obviously thought such a capital small in relation to the size of Barings' operations. Leaving the problem of unsold issues aside, Barings' acceptances were £15m., 6.5 times the partners' capital, a figure well above that for which Schröders and Kleinworts were criticised.

The final point to make is that, despite the guarantee fund, two other merchant banks disappeared in the wake of the crisis. C. de Murrieta & Co., an old Anglo-Spanish house that had got itself involved in Argentine issues, slipped into bankruptcy early in 1892, while Morton, Rose & Co. were crippled and forced to give up their commercial credit business. They spent the 1890s realising large stocks of Argentine, Brazil, US and Canadian bonds, and were then reconstituted as Chaplin, Milne, Grenfell & Co. in 1898. By 1914 the business was 'small', and became bankrupt when Grenfell locked up too much of the firm's capital in real estate in the Canadian Prairies. Barings of course survived, and is still a major merchant bank in the City, but inevitably its reputation suffered, and its former leadership in acceptance business gave way to Kleinworts, Schröders and Hambros.[30]

The Baring crisis shook the City and, though the situation was retrieved without the catastrophic losses of some earlier crises (most notable the Overend Gurney crash of 1866), the lessons were well marked. Overseas investment was restrained for more than a decade and, perhaps more significantly, the old principles of financial rectitude pursued with even more single-minded dedication. Two examples must suffice to express the mind of leading merchant bankers of the period. Bertram Currie was the distinguished senior partner of Glyn Mills & Co., 'the Railway Bank', and (as we saw in Raphaels' letter) an active figure in resolving the crisis. In 1897 Mr Gladstone insisted that Currie was 'so entirely first among the men of the City that it is hard to measure the distance between him and the second place', so that his opinions and judgements were obviously of real consequence for his contemporaries. His verdict on the Baring crisis is therefore worth quoting in full:

For once my principles [in urging Barings' soundness] were at fault; and although, in common with most discerning people, I deplored the departure from sound traditions which was manifest to all observers, and disapproved the intimacy with Mr Sanford and the close identification of the firm with the needy republics of the River Plate, I could not bring myself to believe that the resources and credit of the house of Baring were not equal to any strain. Let this example be a warning to my successors. If such colossal houses as those of Overend and Baring, the two greatest probably that I had known, paid the penalty of their imprudence, what man of business can with impunity depart from the beaten track? In both cases the evil probably began from a plethora of money attracted by the high credit which each house enjoyed. In the case of Messrs. Baring, it was aggravated by a taste for extravagant expenditure, and by the marvellous success which had attended some of their ventures.[31]

Perhaps the more characteristic response, delivered by the head of a merchant bank to his staff, is represented by that of Alexander Wallace of Wallace Bros, the East India merchants. In his own words, written in 1891, he wished

> to impress upon all that the sun does not always shine, that the best ships have to face storms and that credit which has taken fifty years to create may disappear in a night; it is such a delicate thing. All our businesses must continue to be surrounded by the reserve power which has gradually been built up and we must be as careful of our credit now as if we were still creating it.[32]

Barings' problem was clearly connected with their issuing house policies, and had nothing to do with their continued growth as an accepting house. Nevertheless, as we explained in Chapter 4, the two were closely connected so that a failure in confidence in one quickly led to the evaporation of business in the other. Acceptances plummeted from £15m. in 1890 to little over £3m. the next year. The merchant bank *as a whole* stood or fell on its A1 credit rating.

6 The Work of Issue Houses

In earlier chapters it was recognised that for much of the nineteenth century the emergent merchant banks earned their bread and butter from merchanting and accepting house activities, and that issues offered more speculative income for those who were prepared to take the often quite considerable risks. A number of successful houses seldom if ever made issues, and the small number of specialised investment houses earned most of their income from retailing a share of issues passed on to them by the big names rather than making their own issues. The experience of the French Wars showed all too clearly that realistic assessment of the price and market for an issue could be a life-or-death calculation for a house, and the mortality rates among eminent firms was enough to deter all but the strongest and boldest, or most foolhardy. The ultimate irony of the British merchant banking scene was that a number of houses that, functioning as merchants and acceptors, were so meticulously careful in mutual assessment of credit-worthiness, while in state and public utility issues they became gamblers.

It is of course impossible to prepare any calculations of the risks involved, but a few statistics and a handful of case studies where detailed inside information is available offer some feel for the considerations weighed by the issuers, the ways in which they were able to reduce risks, and the ultimate benefits to them. In the early 1880s it was reckoned that about 54 per cent of the entire amount of foreign government obligations listed in London were in default, despite the pressures exerted at different times by the issue houses, the Foreign Bondholders' Association, and the British government. By 1927 discretion had taught some hard lessons, and the percentage was reduced to 24, a fifth of which was due to defaulted Russian bonds.[1]

The Prussian loan of 1818 was the first important landmark in the history of international loans in London in the nineteenth century. The *Gentlemen's Magazine* explained that

Rothschild may be said to have been the first introducer of foreign loans into this country; for, though such securities did at all times circulate here, the payment of the dividends abroad, which was the Universal practice before this time, made them too inconvenient an investment for the great majority [of men] of property to deal with. He not only formed arrangements for the payment of the dividends on his foreign loans in London, but made them still more attractive by fixing the rate in sterling money, and doing away with all the effects of fluctuations in the exchanges.

The problem was solved by the appointment of an independent commission of seven trustees for the loan, three of them Prussian dignitaries and four foreign merchants and bankers, and the floating of a sinking fund so that the debt should be repaid in thirty-six years. Five per cent interest was to be paid by way of interest and 2.5 per cent to the sinking fund. In the course of the following fifteen years or so nearly all of the loan stocks of the continental powers launched in Europe returned to the countries that generated them at 20 or 30 per cent or more above the issue price, with consequent gain to the prestige of Rothschilds, Barings and their clients.

However, it is not to be assumed that the Prussian loan was immediately profitable to the Rothschilds; indeed all the indications are to the contrary. According to an account in the Baring manuscripts the Prussian loan was originally negotiated by a Prussian coffee and sugar merchant living in London called Barandon (or Baranton) who possessed 'first rate connections in that country ... but finding his credit would not enable him to succeed in it as he had anticipated, Mr. Rothschild took it off his hands giving him it is said £30,000 for the transfer.' In the postwar anti-Semitic reaction, Rothschilds were evicted from the Russian court and had to promise a blank credit for £75,000 to stay in the Berlin court. The Rothschilds triumphed over the local (Berlin) bankers only after a long struggle because the government needed to call on external (that is London) funding, and they took the most competitive offer. In the end the Rothschild brothers kept only £0.5m out of the £5m loan for themselves, 90 per cent being distributed among other bankers and connections across Europe, but particularly in Paris and Frankfurt. In all these circumstances, it is difficult to suppose that they made much profit on the issue despite all the effort they put into it. The significance of the deal is rather that it established their claim to membership of the élite of European bankers. Attaining this position, the profits were to be made elsewhere.[2]

On the investor side, the nature of the risk actually taken by Rothschild can be assessed from unusually detailed subscription books. A little over a quarter of the £5m. loan was taken by four major London merchants, Haldimand (£423,000) Isaac Solly & Sons (£423,000), Samuel & John Ward (£282,000) and Barandon (£250,000). Fifteen other City firms raised a further 10 per cent. Apart from a score of relatively small private subscribers (largely continental aristocrats), the remainder was bought by financiers in Paris, Frankfurt, Amsterdam, Berlin, Munich, Hamburg and other places, many with familiar names – Mendelsohn, Hecksher,

Parish, Lafitte, Wertheimer, Gontard, Bethmann, and so on. Thus almost two-thirds was sold abroad directly, while it is easy to suppose that the large bond-holdings of Baltic merchants Haldimand and Barandon were destined for early repatriation.[3] The secret of success evidently lay in finding major backers in London and having good connections on the continent. It seldom happens that so much detail is available as in this instance, but more fragmentary material suggests that this pattern became fairly representative. In other words, a pattern had been established in which London houses acted as a kind of sanctioning and distribution centre for major loan flotations.[4]

Rothschild's determination to take loans, even if immediate sale involved him in considerable loss, appears to have set a precedent for other ambitious firms set on attaining the pinnacle of European banking system in the nineteenth century. It is easy to observe that the heavy mortality of loan contractors during the French Wars created a situation in which Rothschilds were only one of three or four loan contractors in London, but British historians have been too parochial about this; the fact is that the newcomers to London still faced the stiffest competition from old rivals in Frankfurt, Berlin and other financial centres, and won the contracts because they were willing to take them at lower cost and (in the case of the Prussian loan) with better service to the British investors. In much the same way, Hambros broke into Division I by winning the Sardinian loan of 1852 despite strong competition from Rothschilds, who shortly afterwards returned to Italy in strength.[5] Hambros were lucky in the sense that so much business was on offer at the time that Rothschilds did not care to lose money in Italy; as Baron Alphonse wrote in June 1852,

> business was never as prolific as at this time, with propositions coming in from everywhere. After having just concluded the Austrian loan we can already turn to other prospects. For some months Belmont has not stopped drawing our attention to various bonds issued in turn in the States, not all are equally good, but some are first rate ... Belmont suggests a loan of £1.3m. for the Pennsylvania Railroad, the Erie bonds (first mortgage) are at present at 116 and can be easily disposed of in Germany.[6]

Clearly there was room for more firms in the first division, and in the next quarter-century several others forced their way to the top.

J. S. Morgan, the American financier, won a central place on the European stage by wresting the French War loan of 1870 from the powerful interest of Barings and Rothschilds. The £10m. bonds were issued without a contractor's commission at 85 but at first were regarded as so risky that they fell to 55 despite Morgan's heavy purchases. Even before the French defeat in 1871, *The Economist* maintained that 'French securities have never been very profitable here ... it is a commodity which no Englishman appreciates, and which no English banker (to whom ready saleability without loss is essential) would under any circumstances ever touch'. Meanwhile, the London agent of the Crédit Lyonnais reported to his principals that while Morgans were 'excellent', they had hitherto done almost nothing with the continent.[7] But Morgan, no doubt through his French family connection, had observed that, despite the numerous changes in the regime in Paris, whether empire, monarchy or republic, France had never repudiated its debts and, supported by his son-in-law who was living in France at the time, continued to back his faith. Within three years of the Peace of Versailles the French government repaid the loan at par and the gamble paid off handsomely, bringing Morgan both £400,000 profit and international prestige.[8] Shortly after Morgan's triumph, Seligmans were challenging the leadership of the Rothschilds and forcing them to share the US government loan of 1874. The loan was a financial failure but the ice had been broken with Rothschilds for future collaboration.[9]

Perhaps the most audaciously successful loan of the century was that of Erlangers to the Confederate States during the American Civil War. According to Charles Kuhn Prioleau, the Liverpool partner of Fraser Trenholm & Co., the Confederate bankers in Europe, Emile d'Erlanger was still based in Paris at this time and operated in London only through J. H. Schröder. Prioleau wrote in 1863 that

This man Erlanger is a dangerous one; he has the quickest intelligence I have ever been thrown in contact with and he is well calculated to exercise great influence over other minds not so active, but I judge him to be ambitious, selfish, daring and unscrupulous, and he is a Jew with an enormous connexion and entanglement with others of his persuasion all over the world. It is apparent to me that he desires to become the general agent of the [Confederate] Government to keep them always in debt to him and to secure to himself the benefit of all future loans.[10]

Erlanger managed to convince the Confederate commissioner in Paris that his connections there and in London would help to bring the Confederate states the badly-needed support of Napoleon III and of Britain, and so won the loan on the most attractive terms. After some haggling in Congress a £3m. issue of 7 per cent bonds at 77 per cent secured by cotton was agreed to, but by issue day Erlanger had managed to puff the bonds above par. The subsequent progress of the issue was vividly described by Prioleau in May 1863:

The Confederate Cotton Loan is I regret to say, so far a failure as a source of revenue although nominally keeping at a small premium. In order to prevent it going to 10 or 20% discount in the first month of its existence which would have resulted in the non-payment of the May instalments and in public disgrace it was necessary for the friends & agents of the [Confederate] Government to buy it up largely for Government account which was done to such an extent that I do not believe there are £100,000 actually held by the general public [in Britain] ... which is extremely embarrassing in view of the large Government operations now in progress and wanting funds for their completion.[11]

In fact, half the £3m. loan was spent in a vain attempt to maintain the market price of the bonds at par, but a year later (May 1864) they stood at 61 or 62.[12] But in the mean time, Erlanger had done very well out of the issue, and it is instructive to calculate his gross profit

Purchase discount, 23% of £1.5m.	£345,000
Commission, 5%	50.000
Collection fee, 1%	10,000
	£405,000

Some of this profit was lost on resale; Fraser Trenholm were allowed 5 per cent (£20,000) on the £400,000 stock they took, two London stockbrokers shared £1,000 for their services 'and for the respectability of their name', and £12,000 was lost on the Confederate defeat. But when these costs are allowed for, Erlanger seems to have made over £390,000 on the issue. He went on to make the first issues for Hungary (1871–3), this time using Raphael as his London agent.[13]

Apart from wars and the emptying of national treasuries as a result of wars, the most characteristic state clients of the merchant banks were new countries. Here again Rothschilds showed the way, carefully nursing the credit of Brazil in a loan of 1824–5 and then for most of the nineteenth century. According to the authoritative *Circular to Bankers* in 1835, Brazilian bonds 'have been sustained in the money market principally by Mr. Rothschild and one or two of his powerful coadjutors whose stake was too great to permit any other consequence than that of maintaining a high state of credit for the Brazilian government.' A new loan in 1829 was issued as low as 54, but Rothschilds nursed the bonds so well that an 1839 issue was contracted at 78, an 1843 at 85, and an 1852 loan at 95, notwithstanding the bankruptcy of one of the 'powerful coadjutors' (Thomas Wilson & Co.) in 1837. The profit margins look large on paper, but there were hidden costs, in particular the burden of greasing the palms of foreign agents. In the case of Brazil, Rothschilds' agent admitted receiving some £200,000 in commissions over the years 1855–89. Rothschilds also nursed the credit of the new state of Belgium (from 1832), of Chile (from 1886), and of the Transvaal Republic (from 1892).[14] Meanwhile, Barings supported Buenos Aires from 1824, then its successor, Argentina, then Canada (1835 onwards), and Cape Colony (1882).[15] It is well known that several of these loans, particularly those of the 1820s, brought heavy losses to the issuing houses.[16] The predicament of an issuing house that backed a loser is painfully described in a Baring letter about their South Carolina loan of 1838. They had induced 'their friends and those with whom their opinions had weight to take largely of the loan' but twenty years later still held large quantities despite the fact that they had 'always stood by the credit of the loan and of the state in the midst of an almost universal prejudice.'[17] Nevertheless there was seldom a shortage of London houses ready to 'take on' new states. The prejudice of the investing public was largely directed against the autocracies of central Europe – Tsarist Russia, the Ottoman Empire and the Habsburg Empire – whose bonds received only sporadic support in Britain.[18]

By mid-century Rothschilds, Barings, and a small number of other élite firms could pick and chose their clients as their reputation was sufficient to give prestige to any issue to which they lent their names. They underlined their proud position by declining to support a particular issue unless they alone took 'the lead', or at least shared it with one or two partners of comparable standing. As late as 1879 Sir Nathan Rothschild acknowledged an offer of participation in United States funding operations with the cool comment that 'we were ready to go into the matter, and would willingly take hold of it, but on one condition only, that we were not willing to join any American syndicate and be at their mercy or command, and would only take it up if we were given the lead to work it our own way with a group of friends [that is with a syndicate] around us, as in my father's time.'[19] One of Brown Shipley & Co.'s partners concurred with this view, insisting that they either led themselves or partnered Rothschilds. Barings' spokesman to the British government's inquiry (Select Committee) on loans to foreign states of 1875 displayed comparable arrogance by insisting that the role of such a house was limited to granting its imprimatur to suitable issues and distributing the foreign bonds, an operation it was able to undertake because of its reputation with the investing public and familiarity with the money market.[20] This pride suffered permanent damage in 1890, but even after that time the status of the leading houses was evidently different from that of the numbers of peripheral operators in the loan contract business.

The motives and practices of the less reputable issuers, which suddenly became notorious following the publication of the report of the Select Committee on Foreign Loans in 1876, only make sense in the light of the record of the leaders and those who broke into the first rank. States seeking external financial support were by definition a credit risk, and the art of the successful merchant was to ingratiate himself with a government that was a safe bet for recovery or growth. The merchant backed his personal experience of the debtor state (though he might also commission representatives or send emissaries to secure further information), but in the final analysis he was dealing with forces beyond his control.[21] The high interest rates on such bonds – in some instances as much as three or four times those paid on the established European securities and five times those on Consols – simply reflected the high degree of risk incurred in lending to new states.[22] It was well known that the leaders of the issue business had suffered several disastrous losses, and lesser houses were aware that they were by no means immune from loss.

The published data on issues suggest that down to the crisis of 1890 Rothschilds and Barings were able to maintain their early lead, though now closely trailed by Morgans and Hambros. Jenks shows the existence of forty-six loan contractors in the peak period 1860–76, with Rothschilds taking nearly a quarter of the value of all issues and Barings 15 per cent. In the following period, 1877–90, only twenty-eight firms appear in the lists. Rothschilds' share exceeded a third of the total and Barings 10 per cent, though the latter were just overtaken by Hambros, with three US houses (Morton Rose, Morgan, and Seligman) close behind.[23] The whole business fell away for some years after the Baring crisis, and when it was cautiously resumed, it was often on the basis of the mutual insurance system known as underwriting loans. Now not even the leaders could pretend to act independently, though the tradition of associating a single City name with an issue was often retained.

The origin and principal of the system of underwriting is best summarised in the words of H. O. O'Hagan who claimed to have originated it. In his attractive autobiography he explained that

> the principle of insurance was almost as old as the hills, but originally was confined to life, fire and marine risks, and then these were extended to sickness, burglary, plate glass, licences, weather, and other things. Why should insurance not be extended to the guaranteeing of the subscription of issues of shares and debentures of public companies? It should always pay the financier engaged in floating a concern to give up some portion of his profit to secure a successful flotation. Having come to this conclusion [in the 1880s] I began by approaching some of the larger trust and investment companies, and when I found them inclined to take shares or debentures in an undertaking I offered them, I persuaded them to risk having to take three or four times the amount they were contemplating if the capital was not fully subscribed, I paying them a commis-

sion for so doing. ... At first it was difficult to get the banks and the big financial houses to go into this under-writing, but it was soon found to be so profitable to participate in the formation of well-launched concerns that my list of underwriters became a very substantial one, and in a short time underwriting became almost universal.[24]

In fact, the merchant banks were rather slower to adopt the simple technique than O'Hagan implies. According to his obituary in *The Times*, Lord Rothschild 'was a strong opponent of the system' as he believed underwriting 'made it fatally easy to bring out almost any loan'. However, in 1907 Rothschilds had obtained underwriting support for their Japanese Loan, though they still kept aloof from other merchant banks by assembling their list from the South African group (Wernher Beit & Co., Barnato Bros), and from stockbrokers and private wealth.[25] Barings' stock ledgers suggest that the firm did not begin to adopt the system until around the turn of the century, and then at first only for US industrial issues, most probably at the behest of their New York agents. The earliest state loan underwritten by the firm appears to have been the Imperial Russian Government's 5 per cent loan of 1906, which was intended to raise £13.1m. The underwriting list contained 370 names, including 22 merchant banks, but only 2 of these were for large sums – Sir Ernest Cassel for £3m. and Speyer Bros for £0.5m. As so often seemed to happen in the City, the belated response suddenly collected very rapid momentum; what had been disdained for years suddenly became a passion, and Lord Rothschild's apparently reactionary view should be understood against that background. Thus Schröders, who for years had made their numerous issues for Cuba, Chile and Peru alone, began to share them after 1909. In 1872 they had raised £15m. for the Peruvian government alone, but now turned to friends for much smaller loans.[26] Perhaps this change of mood was encouraged by the menace of competition from the chartered and imperial banks but, in any event, underwriting was adopted too late to save the merchant banks from losing a large part of the state loan business to other forms of City enterprise.

Railway Finance

The transition from government to railway finance, which began in the mid-1830s, was a fairly easy one in the sense that outside Britain almost all railways were built under state control, so that the kind of financial diplomacy and negotiation with prospective partners that was necessary to secure state issues was relevant here. In the early years several British railways proved to be very profitable, and the disappointment with defaulting states was sufficient to draw attention to the new public utility enterprise. Costs of railway building under state control were lower than the pioneer enterprises in Britain had been, and so promised to be even more profitable. Some of the earliest foreign railways were in fact financed by state loans, as for instance the Belgian loans of 1836, 1837 and 1840 raised by Rothschilds, or the Massachusetts loan of 1838–9 issued by Barings, or the Russian loan of 1850 jointly floated by Steiglitz of St Petersburg, Hopes, Barings, Hottinguer of Paris, and others.[27]

Aside from these earmarked state loans, a good deal of early railway financing was undertaken by a specialist group of railway bankers who worked in close association with the contractors. In the early years the best-known names were Edward Blount, a Paris-based banker whose partners were Brassey, the railway contractor, and Buddicom, the engine builder, and Samuel Laing, a railway magnate who became Chairman of the Railway Share Trust and the Railway Debenture Trust.[28] The London financial interests were relatively slow off the mark for two or three reasons. While Baron James de Rothschild was the foremost name in railway financial promotion in France and Belgium, his brother Nathan died too early to become involved while his nephew in London, Baron Lionel, was simply not interested. The dispatches of Lionel's younger brother Nathan II from Paris in the 1840s did little to reassure the new head of New Court. In 1846 the reports were emphasising that, despite the high profits from railways and associated concerns, 'I don't like things which are entirely dependent on others and of which we understand nothing at all', and then the next year, with even more emphasis, 'You have no idea how plagued we are by the different railroad concerns; first the Northern fall (frs. 300), then Marseille–Avignon, and now St. Germain. I cannot recommend you enough to keep out of all sorts of concerns and affairs in which you risk money and where you have the entire management. I am sick of all railroads and coal companies.' Of course, Rothschilds' lack of interest did not prevent other London houses taking an initiative, and instances of investors are not wanting – Reid Irving in Belgium in 1838, Tastett in 1840, Baring, Thomson Bonar and Devaux in various syndicates in France in 1843, and so on – but they lacked the necessary local representation to challenge the leadership of Baron James, and their interest was evidently sporadic.[29]

Another reason for the slow initial response of London was that in the pioneer years the railway interest centred in the North of England, and many of the early investors came from Manchester and Liverpool.[30] In the mid-1840s, according to the Bank of England's agent in Manchester, the Manchester commercial community's obsession with railways was so great that it diverted capital from the regional industries and international trade; indeed exporters were unable 'to get their long dated paper [bills of exchange] reasonably converted into cash' with the result that at one period spinners and manufacturers were so crippled that they had to suspend production. An interesting example of this diversion of capital was Sir William Fielden & Son of Blackburn, who had a total capital of £360,000 in 1847, £200,000 in mills and land, £30,000 in stocks, and all the remainder – no doubt the more liquid part in earlier years – locked up in railways. Another well-known Manchester merchant who became heavily committed to railways at this time was Leo Schuster; his firm were shortly describing themselves as 'merchants and bankers', perhaps drawing capital from their native Frankfurt to feed the voracious appetite of the early railways.[31] When Liverpool became the principal exporting port of rails to the United States, numerous merchants of the port were drawn into investment in US railway bonds, either for an investment or because the companies lacked other means of paying them. In 1853 it was estimated that half the European investment of £70m. in US railway bonds and state bonds to aid railways represented securities obtained in return for purchases of British rails.[32]

But having identified the company and geographical factors, it must be conceded that the main reason for the tardy and intermittent response to the opportunities for investment in overseas railways was the erratic credit of the governments of the debtor countries. The largest recipient of European investment capital was the United States where, as elsewhere, railroad borrowing started via state loans; something like a quarter of the $172m. issued by nineteen debtor states of the Union in the late 1830s (mainly 1834–7) was intended for this form of development, and a great part of these bonds – perhaps as much as three-quarters – eventually found their way to Europe. When nine of these nineteen states defaulted in the early 1840s, European investors responded with a boycott of all US bonds. Three Americans who were influential in London investment circles, George Peabody, Joshua Bates (of Baring Bros), and August Belmont (Rothschilds' New York agent) managed to generate some interest in the later 1840s and (encouraged by the European revolutions of 1848) in the early 1850s, but the panic of 1857, the American Civil War (1861–5) and the Overend Gurney Crisis (1866) restrained British interest. London did not become receptive to new issues until the early 1870s, and it was not until the overseas investment boom of the 1880s that US railroad securities gained substantial popularity.[33]

In the earlier decades London merchant banks' interest in foreign railroads was more evident on the accepting house side than among the issuing houses, with which so much of the literature is concerned. From 1848 – and perhaps earlier – several firms were financing the export of rails from Welsh ironworks to the USA. The main firms involved were the London houses with branches or agents in Liverpool, notably Barings, Huths, Palmer, McKillop & Dent and Peabody, and the Liverpool merchants that had survived the crises of the 1840s and were already functioning as accepting houses, notably Cropper Benson & Co. and Rathbones. In the 1850s Barings, Rothschilds and Huths became so intensely interested in rail production that they each locked up considerable capital in ironworks. Barings became involved in the Weardale Company through the enthusiasm of Joshua Bates, in the firms long history a unique instance of industrial investment that can only reflect the senior partner's dedication to the new trade. However, in each case the involvement in this trade appears to have encouraged their interest in railroad issues.[34]

Nevertheless, the cautiously growing interest in US securities was largely the work of the three Americans already mentioned, and initially of Peabody. He was a major dealer in US securities from 1843 and became the major London specialist through the period in which all US stocks had a bad image owing to the default of Pennsylvania and Maryland. He was convinced of the ultimate integrity of the issuing states, perhaps because he had more and better first-hand information than anyone else in the City. He managed to secure the co-operation of Barings, which in itself gave a lift to lifeless bonds, but even in the 1850s the premier house in US finance was still proceeding very cautiously, only taking a share in US loans rather than a 'lead'. Barings finally plunged into US railroad issues in 1852, the transition being the profitable acceptance of Baltimore & Ohio bonds in exchange for rails exported.[35]

The most vociferous promoter of US stocks of all kinds was Belmont. He was constantly pressing his London masters to take up portions of the most profitable US issues, but having burned their fingers on Maryland bonds they held off for a long time.[36] Rothschilds began to revise their views in 1852, partly from the growing prosperity of the USA following the Californian gold rush, and partly through the discovery that US bonds sold well in Germany because intending emigrants found them an ideal means of transferring their capital, but above all because they combined high returns with growing security. Belmont's lucid advocacy of the advantages of investing in his adopted country is still a pleasure to read, but we must confine ourselves to one example here, written from New York in 1853:

> I have for my own part, as mentioned to you in my last, not the slightest doubt but that all the maintrunks of railways, uniting the far and fertile West with the Atlantic, will pay very handsome dividends and that the first mortgages are not only as good a security as Gvmt. stock or English Consols, but that 7/8 of them will be converted into stocks that will pay from 8 to 10% before we are two years older. ... The Central line of railroads in this State connecting the lakes with our City is now worth from *140 to 180*% having paid regularly 10% and laid over besides handsome surplus and I do not see why the Penn[sylvani]a

Central railroad connecting the lakes with Philadelphia, and running through the most thickly populated and most fertile portion of Penn^a, should not within a short time yield the same results. Penn^a is nearly as rich in agricultural production as New York and her mineral wealth in coal and iron is determined at no late period to make her the wealthiest State of the Union. I have sent you under separate cover a railroad map of the U.S. where I marked the chain formed by the Parkersburgh (N.W. Virginia railroad as it is now named) Baltimore and Ohio and Ohio and Mississipi roads, the bonds of the latter of which have just been negotiated by Peabody & Co. and connecting St. Louis with Baltimore – farther the Penn^a chain between the lakes and Philada and the Illinois Central connecting the lakes with the Mississipi. Since 1842 I have urged you earnestly and repeatedly to the investment and negotiation of numbers of Gvmt, State, City and railway securities – in *not one* of them have I been mistaken and not one of them, which since then has not improved from 5 to 30% and in some instances more, besides paying in the meanwhile 6 to 7% while money was with the exception of 1847 a drug at 2 to 2½% in England.[37]

The young Baron Alphonse Rothschild was converted to the promise of American economic growth during a tour of the country in 1849 and from that time was a regular supporter of Belmont's causes.[38] In the final analysis, it was probably a report that Overend, Gurney & Go., advised by their confidential correspondent Morgan, were ready to take the whole issue of the Pennsylvania Central Railroad Company that forced their hand for (as Baron Alphonse emphasised) they did not want 'to let other houses enjoy the monopoly of this line of business.'[39]

The response to opportunities in other parts of the globe was even more hesitant. As an instance of the kind of considerations that governed the minds of investors, the Grand Russian Railway offers a useful case study. In the aftermath of the Crimean War, some dramatic changes took place in Russian foreign policy, and the Grand Russian Railway scheme brought the first invitation to foreign capitalists to make major investments in Russia.[40] The Russo-French treaty of 1857 improved the legal position of foreign merchants resident in the country, and the Crédit Mobilier, seeing a chance to outflank Rothschilds, took the initiative. They were supported by a number of other Parisian houses, notably Hottinguer, who approached Barings and Hopes in June 1856. Barings also had a direct line to Russia through their old correspondent Steiglitz, the premier Leningrad merchant of the day. The conservative Bates at first thought that the project was not likely to succeed as the Russians wanted to make it a national affair while foreign capitalists were 'not likely to place confidence in Russian management'. However, in September Steiglitz was assuring them that the scheme was likely to go ahead, and in

November Hottinguer had decided to 'mettre l'affaire en syndicat, après la première distribution fait avec discernement au public des capitalistes et des diverses bourses.'[41] In Moscow Thomas Baring caught some of the excitement of lucrative gain and finally managed to convey his mood to Bates, who wrote

> if it does not prove a brilliant affair I shall be much disappointed. The Russian Government guarantees 4% on £16,500 per mile also ½% for sinking fund, now if it can be constructed as many suppose it can be at £8,000 per mile, of course the guarantee is 9%. The press has attacked it most violently but of late there has appeared no new attack and the *Economist*, *Daily News* and *Chronicle* are in favour of the undertaking.[42]

The concessionaires were to be allowed ten years to build the 2,500 miles and all the iron could be imported free of charge. Nevertheless, *The Times* continued to make the most vociferous attacks on this and all other Russian projects, and the newspaper was followed by such eminent public figures as Sir Robert Peel and Horseley Palmer, a director of the Bank of England.[43]

The outcome of what became a public debate is unfortunately more difficult to discern. Early in May 1857 *The Times* gleefully reported that 'there have been scarcely any English applications for the shares of the Russian railway', but added a sinister comment that the Russians' own allotment of £3m. would be taken 'sooner or later, by hook or by crook'. Bates sadly recorded that 'it seems probable that BB & Co may have to hold for their own account for a time 100,000 shares of £20, say £2,000,000, of which 30% [that is BB's immediate liability] will be £600,000 ... it may be possible that we must sell them at 10% disct. which would yield a loss of £200,000.' B.W. Currie of Glyns was sure that the 'Russian railways will do well after a time', adding that the 'tirades in *The Times* are ridiculous and repudiated by all reasonable people.' But the commercial crisis of 1857–8 further evaporated confidence and in 1861 Barings still held large stocks of Russian bonds.[44]

Meanwhile, Barings and Glyns had also become encumbered with heavy credits to the Canadian Grand Trunk Railway. The story of this troublesome and profitless venture has been related at length elsewhere so need not occupy much space here.[45] In 1856 the venture was represented as a public scandal in which the contractors were accused in the press of duping both the investing public and the City financiers involved.[46] Fortunately for Barings, the generation of investors that followed these disasters (1860–90) proved much more sanguine, and their connectors produced a sequence of large and profitable loans, nine each to Russia and Canada. But it is noticeable that they avoided further involvements in grandiose railway ventures as such, concentrating rather on much more limited ventures in the USA. Rothschilds pursued much the same policy and so, too, did the 'second division' firms. With few exceptions, the Indian railways were left to the specialist railway contractors and financiers, and central Europe to the local interests.[47] Clearly Russia and Canada taught some well-marked lessons: that press and public opinion, whether militarist or imperialist, was a dangerous factor in the equation, and more neutral investments were to be preferred.

The experiences of the 1850s cast a long shadow and kept British firms away from some of the more profitable continental schemes. While British adventurers ranged North America in search of 5 per cent, the most spectacular success of the later Victorian age was won on a calculated gamble in Europe. Maurice de Hirsch (Baron Hirsch) was a German Jew who spent much of his life on the continent, but most of his accumulated wealth was held in London and used to sponsor Sir Ernest Cassel, so that he is entitled to be included in this study. He was trained in the service of Bischoffsheim & Goldschmidt of Antwerp and Paris, and married one of the partner's daughters, but from about 1862 ran his own firm, Bischoffsheim & de Hirsch in Brussels. The parent firm was active in railway flotations in France, Italy and the United States, and less successfully in loans to small Latin American states and Swedish mining ventures, so it was to railways that young Hirsch was drawn. Most of his initial capital appears to have been derived from his wife's dowry (£0.8m. in 1855) and is supposed to have reached about a million pounds fourteen years later when he commenced his connection with the Turkish railway (Vienna–Istanbul) project. The concession for the 1,000km *Orientbahn* was originally awarded to a syndicate, but when the other members got cold feet Hirsch boldly decided to go on alone. The construction was estimated at a cost of £8,000 per km (including all buildings) but Hirsch managed to keep average costs down to half that, and further increased his profit margin by selling the shares at a premium, so that his fortune is supposed to have reached £10m. in 1878. This colossal profit – far outstripping anything realised by Rothschilds or Barings – was multiplied by successful speculation in international securities, notably Italian Rentes and 'Unified' Egyptian bonds, so that at his death in 1896 he was supposed to be worth between £20m. and £25m., a fortune that made even Rothschilds' capital look modest.[48]

As often happens in finance, what started slowly and reluctantly suddenly became a matter of almost obsessive interest. US railway issues were easily the most continuous preoccupation of London and the New York investment houses from the end of the Civil War (1865) until the Baring crisis (1890), and interest did not end there. The London houses involved and the relative size of their interests are set out in Table 6.1. To the leading British houses (Barings, Brown Shipley, Rothschilds) was

Table 6.1   *City firms responsible for United States and Canadian Railroad Issues 1865–90*

	No. of firms	Value of issues (£m.)	percentage of total issues
Merchant banks	19	120.86	65.2
Other banks and discount houses	14	12.38	6.7
Stockbrokers, trusts, etc.	35	52.16	28.1
	68	185.40	100.0

A small number of railroad companies issued their own shares.

added a clutch of US firms with a London base (Morgan, Morton Rose, Jay Cooke, Seligman, Speyer) and the leading continental house involved in railway finance (Bischoffsheim & Goldschmidt). Liverpool interest was represented by Bensons, the arbitrage houses by Cohens and Raphaels, and the diversifying interests of the old Anglo-German houses by Schuster, Schröder and Hambros. US issues were now fair game for anyone: Thomson Bonar & Co were an old Russian house, Murrieta was a Spanish firm with interests in South America, while Henry S. King & Co. still called themselves 'East India Agents'. However, despite this diversity, two firms were predominant: between them Barings and Morgans took 50 per cent of all the issues in the period.

City interest in US and Canadian railroad issues was by no means confined to the merchant banks; indeed they took no more than two-thirds of all the issues. Other types of banks (joint-stock, international and imperial) and discount houses also moved in, competing with stockbrokers, trusts and a medley of other firms, while a few railroad companies continued to market their own stocks and bonds.[49] It has been claimed that the major transatlantic houses had the edge because, from the early years of this quarter-century, they were represented on the boards of US railroad companies. As early as 1870 the Illinois Central directors included J. P. Morgan and George Bliss of Morton Rose & Co. (Morton Bliss & Co. in New York), and in 1873 no less than forty-three such connections between bankers and railroad boards have been identified, including Seligman, Rothschild (that is Belmont) and Benson. In this way the leading houses maintained a close and continuous relationship with the lines they sponsored, for the benefit of the shareholders and general credit-worthiness of the company. The snag of this argument is that it fails to weigh the experience of railroads as a drain on banks' capital and periodic threat to their liquidity.[50]

In this instance, it is possible to place the contribution of the merchant

Table 6.2 *United States and Canadian Railroad Stocks issued through London merchant banks 1865–90*

	Value of issues (£m.)	% of total issues made by these banks
Baring Bros	34.68	28.7
J. S. Morgan (US house)	26.09	21.6
Bischoffsheim & Goldschmidt	10.17	8.4
Morton, Rose & Co. (US house)	9.48	7.8
Speyer Bros (US house)	9.16	7.6
Brown, Shipley & Co.	6.39	5.2
Robert Benson & Co.	6.07	5.0
Jay Cooke, McCulloch & Co. (US house)	5.12	4.2
L. Cohen & Sons	2.31	1.9
Union Bank of London (Schuster)	2.24	1.9
Thomson, Bonar & Co.	2.00	1.7
J. H. Schröder & Co.	1.85	1.5
R. Raphael & Sons	1.50	1.2
Seligman & Co. (US house)	1.40	1.2
N. M. Rothschild & Sons	0.80	0.7
C. de Murrieta & Co.	0.55	0.5
C. J. Hambro & Sons	0.50	0.4
Henry S. King & Co.	0.45	0.4
Jay & Co. (US house)	0.10	0.1
Total, 19 firms	120.86	100.0

Sources:
1865–80: D. R. Adler, *British Investment in American Railways 1834–98* (Charlottesville, Virginia, 1970), Appendix I.
1881–8: *The Statist*, XXII (1888), p. 685.
1889–90: *The Statist*, XXIII–XXV, weekly reports of new issues.

banks in an international perspective. At the end of the period reviewed, in 1890, the capital stock of the entire US rail network was reckoned at around £1,000m., of which as much as £300m. (or 30 percent) is estimated to have been held in Britain. The year 1890 appears to have been the high-water mark of British interest in US railroads; in 1860 it was about 17 per cent, in 1880 perhaps 15 per cent, and in 1914 the same. At least £100m. of the US railroad stocks admitted to quotations on the London Stock Exchange were not issued in the City. That leaves some £200m. issued in London, perhaps two-thirds of which came out of the merchant banks. In other words, so far as can be estimated, no more than one-eighth of US railroads were financed from the City. This figure of course stands for the US alone and the finance of other developing countries was very different; in 1914 the British are supposed to have owned about three-quarters of the railway capital in Argentina and over 90 per cent of that in India.[51] But the figures serve to restrain the wild notion that one still sometimes hears in City bars, that '*we* built the world's railways.'

Finance of Industry

Most economic historians have agreed that the London capital market was biased towards overseas investment, neglecting the opportunities of domestic industry, and Professor Saville and others have seen clear evidence of lack of entrepreneurial spirit in the situation. Their charges are made in the context of a long-running debate on the performance of the British economy in the last quarter of the nineteenth century.[52] The wider issues cannot detain us here, but our study of the evolution and characteristics of London-based merchant banks can help to explain their limited interest in industrial development.

Examination of the family origins and connections of the merchant banks serves to emphasise that for the most part their traditions and loyalties were no means British; they came to London (or Liverpool, or Manchester) because of the opportunities for free trade, because these towns were the emergent world centres of rising trade in textiles, and perhaps also because they were seeking an escape from religious or ethnic discrimination. They settled in English cities, but that did not always make them English. Their immediate environment (social circle, church and principal employees) often remained foreign, and their loyalties continued to be *international* in their scope. In a word, they had little more interest in British industry than they had in the industry of any other country, and that interest was inevitably minimal, for their training and experience directed them towards trade and government finance, and not to manufacturing.[53]

There was, of course, a small group of merchant banks of English and Scots origins whose interests might have been expected to be more focused on the home country. We lack authoritative case studies of such firms, so generalisations are hazardous, but it seems that the general outlook was reflected in the Scottish disposition to 'face almost any risk for the sake of the difference between four per cent at home and 4½ per cent across the Atlantic.'[54] Of course, Edinburgh was not London, and it is well known that the Scots revelled in foreign investment, but it should be added that the investment trust movement in London was predominantly in Scots hands. The doyen of the movement was of course Robert Fleming, who moved from his native Dundee to London in 1888.

His 'syndicate books' survive from 1900 onwards, showing that until the First World War his main interest remained with US railroads and public utilities. Only four industrial issues appear among the sixty accounts in the first volume (1900-3), and two out of them were for British subsidiaries of American companies (British Westinghouse Co. and British Thomson Houston Co.). In the next decade US industrial shares became more numerous, but it is difficult to spot British names; indeed the only ones appear to be Imperial Tobacco (1902), Wemyss Collieries (1902), Lever Bros (1911), Portland Cement (1912) and Lancashire Power Construction Co. (1911), though holdings were also taken in three shipping lines. Of 445 accounts opened in the years 1900-12, only 8 appear to be for British Companies. It was not until the eve of the First World War that Fleming began to take a serious interest in British industrial shares.[55]

However, it is fair to add that investment houses were influenced by other criteria than maximisation of profit and secure investment. The industrial shares on offer were issued by limited liability companies, a form of business organisation that was pushed through Parliament against the tide of business opinion, which continued to believe that *unlimited* liability offered the only real security for creditors. From 1856 English company law became the most permissive in Europe, a situation that did little to attract merchant bankers whose orientation was international, while the early experience of the legislation was anything but reassuring. The freedom granted to company promoters created a situation in which *all* companies were under suspicion, and for some years 'reputable' industrialists avoided them.[56]

In the 1880s, incorporation became more popular with industry itself, but in the City - or at any rate the more 'respectable' part of it - British industrial shares fell under suspicion because they were one of the casualties of the speculative investment boom of that decade. *The Statist* (15 Nov. 1890) explained that

> For some years past there has been a constant fixing of capital in the thousand and one industrial enterprises floated in 1885-9. The mischief here is that maximum prices have been paid for business, old-established or new, with, in a great many cases, dividend-earning power quite inadequate to remunerate the subscriber to the company formed, and no ability on the part of the investor to sell the shares he has acquired. A business worth £50,000 to two or three vigilant private partners is sought to be made into a limited company by a group of promoters. The partners sell it under temptation of an offer of £100,000. The promoters fix up contracts, and the limited company that comes out pays some intermediary £150,000. Where vigilant private partners succeed with £50,000, a loosely managed company with £150,000 paid for the business makes a lamentable show. Very

much of this kind of thing has been going on, and the public has the shares of loosely managed companies with often no marketable value.

The villains of the piece, according to this account, were the 'promoters', a shadowy group whose precise identity has eluded the searching eye of some of the most dedicated historians.[57]

The earliest promoters were a heterodox group of City specialists that took advantage of a gap that first appeared in the company boom of the early 1860s. The best-known names at this period were Adamson, Collier & Chadwick, a Manchester-based firm that took a leading role in incorporating coal and iron companies in the 1860s, and Baron Albert Gotheimer (or Grant), who began his long career in the City in 1873 by retailing railway and tramway shares in small denominations. The Manchester firm seemed to fade after a brilliant start, probably because its entrepreneur (Chadwick) went into Parliament. According to O'Hagan, for 'several years' Grant was the one 'shining light in company flotation'. But in the tradition of the railway promoters of the early 1860s, he 'had a very great following of people who wanted to get rich quickly', and his heavy commitment to speculative mining shares in the USA eventually brought him down, leaving his new profession in some disrepute.[58]

The field was for a time left largely to O'Hagan, whose autobiography is consequently almost the only guide to developments in the 1880s. We may certainly accept his comment that at this time 'it had not occurred to our great banking houses that promotion of companies was too good a business to ignore.' O'Hagan built up a lucrative business very quickly by choosing his clients with very great care, being prepared to spend 'many thousands of pounds' investigating potential clients which he might have to reject. By degrees he appears to have secured acceptance of the promoter, or at any rate assured his own personal reputation. Some of his early competitors, such as the stockbrokers Foster & Braithwaite, had standards of integrity to maintain.[59]

Apart from the image of the company and of the company promoter, the main barrier to merchant bank entry to company promotion was their professional fees. Charges were high because there were at least four elements: the bank's commission (which varied enormously, but could be as much as 5 per cent), underwriting (say 2.5–4 per cent), broker's commission (perhaps 0.25–0.5 per cent), and advertising, often the highest cost of all. Then there were charges for solicitors, printers, stamp duty, registration fees, postage and sometimes others besides. The consequence was that, even as late as the 1930s, any issue below £200,000 or £250,000 was reckoned to be uneconomic.[60] Before the First World War, companies of this size were still exceptional.[61]

It was the practice of underwriting company issues that introduced the merchant banks (among others) to corporate finance, but it was an area in which they soon found themselves competing with a host of other bankers, trust companies, stockbrokers, lawyers, accountants 'and all the loose ends of the City'. Most of the merchant bankers, like Rothschilds, 'just took a bite or two at the cherry and retired, finding the morsel not so tasty as they expected', while others, like Morton Rose, actually lost money on their early speculative encounters. Moreover, the image of the system was soon dented by what the financial press castigated as 'manipulating cliques' of underwriters, who 'nursed' some less reputable companies until they could be publicly floated. The partners in merchant banks had little of the specialised expertise needed in this area, and were reluctant to compromise their proud position by stooping to participate in underwriting 'cliques'.[62] Instead, they preferred to adapt the underwriting techique to secure them against loss on foreign issues, particularly after the Baring crisis, which might have been prevented if Barings had not been too proud to underwrite their diverse Argentine issues. British investment abroad is supposed to have increased from some £479m. in 1885-9 to £784m. in 1910–14 so there was clearly ample scope for the merchant banks within their traditional area of expertise.[63]

The brewery issues made by Barings, Hambros, Gibbs and other houses around 1888 are sometimes cited as an exception to the inhibitions of the system, but in any event this new interest evaporated quickly in 1890. The pace-setting was largely taken over by a group of Anglo-German banks (Schröders, Kleinworts, Speyers and others) who however never made an industrial issue before the First World War. Morgans were of course prominent in industrial issues, but until after the First World War saw more enticing opportunities in the USA, and in this matter they were followed by the much smaller investment houses like Helbert Wagg, Bensons and Flemings. In the 1920s Morgan Grenfell & Co. were probably the first merchant bank to become heavily involved both in advising and in financing industry but that happened only when their traditional interests in railway finance and foreign loans fell away, and this was a whole generation after the industrial securities market soared in the 1880s (in Britain) and 1890s (in the USA). Several British merchant banks were in close contact with the US developments at the time. The US investment banks most closely associated with this were August Belmont & Co. (Rothschilds' New York agents), Baring, Magoun & Co. (Barings' New York operation), and two of the London firms' correspondents, Lee Higginson & Co. and Kidder Peabody & Co. The traditional British leaders, that is to say, were early in the field. But in the middle 1890s Morgans moved up from a slow start to take the lead. As the largest of the railroad banks, they were able to take a $2m. bond issue for Studebaker Wagons in 1896, then headed the syndicate that forged Federal Steel. It is said that nearly all the railroad investment houses participated in the merger boom, 'but only Morgan with any zest.'[64]

In assessing the merchant banks' role in the promotion of industrial shares, it must be borne in mind that the ultimate arbiters were the investing public, and they were advised, if by anyone, by stockbrokers and by the financial press. A recent survey of the late-Victorian and Edwardian London stockbroker as investment adviser concludes the 'few stockbrokers were possessed of any unusual degree of prescience, above all long-term prescience.'[65] Most were highly conservative; a textbook writer of the Edwardian period wrote that 'I have heard myself old-fashioned stockbrokers maintain that, after all, there was no investment like Home Rails, because investors could always go and look at their property, which could not run away'! After the turn of the century, when British industrials might have found more favour, Lloyd George's budget aroused resentment and fear among the investing public, while the Tariff Reform politicians were laying much stress on Britain's 'dying industries'. Consequently the prices of home securities declined in favour of foreign and colonial stocks.[66]

However, stockbrokers were not entirely an homogeneous group and one exception to the general position points to a future line of development for merchant banks. Sir Arthur Wheeler began his career in Leicester in 1899 as an 'outside' broker, which meant that he was not subject to Stock Exchange rules and so free to advertise. From the first he offered shares in sound local companies, and shortly came to be a specialist in retailing them to private investors throughout the country. He built up a mailing list which by 1928 totalled some 750,000 names, and there were 50,000 regular clients, many of whom came to trust Wheeler's firms implicitly. 'If they were prepared to recommend an issue ... its success was virtually assured', one of Wheeler's executives recalled. 'By the 1920s it was by far the largest, and easily the best business of its kind, and during the first 30 years of this century it was a pioneer in making a fundamental contribution to financing small businesses by maintaining a market in this type of share – something which the Stock Exchange was not able to do, even in those days before some of the excellent local exchanges were closed', he explained. In 1931 Wheeler, by then aged 70, went bankrupt, but two arms of his organisation survived to evolve into merchant banks. One of his London enterprises, the Charterhouse Investment Trust, which was formed in 1925 as an issuing house sponsoring good industrial issues of £200,000 upwards, survived and (as Charterhouse Japhet) maintains an important place in the City. Naturally its chief executive, Nutcombe Hume, maintained Wheeler's successful policy of financing medium-sized businesses. The other important connection was with Philip Hill & Partners, for whom Wheeler made issues before they became a private company in 1932. The history of this interesting house (now Hill Samuel) has never been written, but enough is known of its issue business to recognise it as having similar interests to Charterhouse.

These details are carrying us too far beyond the limits of this book, but they serve to underline a basic point, that the London merchant banks did not become seriously interested in industrial issues until their traditional business fell away to nothing and the average size of companies rose to meet their ceiling. Case studies show that, even then, there were major problems in directing thinking towards new opportunities. It has been said that until 1945, when the government-sponsored Industrial and Commercial Finance Corporation was launched, 'the small businessman had absolutely no organisation to which he could turn for his long-term capital needs.' So far as the private sector of the City was concerned, it was another newcomer, Sir Siegmund Warburg, a member of an old Hamburg Jewish banking family who had been correspondents of the Rothschilds for three generations, that made an explicit policy of closing the gap pointed out by the Macmillan Committee in 1931. When all allowances are made, the British merchant banks were incredibly slow to take this opportunity, for it is almost a truism that the best small and medium-sized firms are the real growth points of the economy, and hence the best long-term investment.[67]

7 The Work of Accepting Houses

The precise relationship between issues and acceptances is, on present evidence, impossible to define; indeed it seems likely there is no precise or invariable connection between the two. In Chapter 3 we noticed Barings striving to win the official recognition of foreign governments, apparently as one means of obtaining commercial connections, but their willingness to make issues was irregular, ruled by the overriding need to maintain their liquidity. Rothschilds were cultivating foreign governments and potentates in much the same way, but evidently much less interested in acceptances. In 1866 James Rothschild maintained, in evidence to a French government commission, that 'seven-eighths or fifteen-sixteenths of any loan issued are employed in buying goods', and he instanced locomotives and other railway fixed capital, but did not suggest that his firm handled such orders.[1] Certainly the English Rothschilds had few if any direct connections with railway contractors. In the case of Rothschilds, it is possible to plot the course of their annual acceptances and issues over the whole century 1815–1914, but the two sets of data do not suggest any direct or inverse correlations. In terms of value, their issues peak in the mid-1870s and decline to 1914 while acceptances follow a much more erratic course, with peaks in the 1860s, 1895 and 1910. Barings' acceptances are not disclosed to historians before 1890, but are believed to have followed a rising curve to the crisis year before crashing to the low levels of the 1890s. The fevered period of the 1880s also saw numerous loan issues, but the biggest loans made by Barings came out in the 1870s. The interest of other English (as opposed to Anglo-American) firms was evidently sporadic, and data on their acceptances available at best for only short runs, so that general correlations would be of no real value. The most that can be done is to notice the attempts of the newer firms to link loans with export trade and finance, for instance Gibbs with Chilean railways and Hambros with loans to Norway in 1851 and Denmark in 1860, both intended for railway development and involving English contractors.[2] But later in the century the financial needs of railways became too large for such small houses to handle, and the most that they could hope for was to head an 'anonymous' syndicate in the way that Gibbs did in Argentina (Table 9.4). However, as we shall see in Chapter 9, such consortium arrangements evidently gave only limited leverage in export finance, and new kinds of financial connections, such as those between merchant banks and railway contractors, were slow to develop and, taking the merchant banks as a whole, only in their infancy on the eve of the First World War.

The Total Volume of Acceptances

A key problem in tracing the evolution of the British merchant banks is obtaining some measure of their overall growth in the most important and continuous sector of their activities, that is, in accepting house business. A sequence of dedicated scholars has been frustrated by lack of data and after a long search offered an odd figure or two, with no very great confidence in them.[3] Such information as is usefully available from these and other sources is assembled in Table 7.1. Clearly there is not sufficient data here to form the basis of any very far-reaching conclusions, but two or three significant points can be made.

In Chapter 3 we saw that the earliest development of merchant banking was in connection with the United States, and the various estimates collected for 1836 complement that interpretation by suggesting that on the eve of the crisis of 1837 something like half the acceptances were for the transatlantic trade. In the 1830s, according to a leading merchant banker, London credits were used to a much greater extent in carrying on all commercial transactions than at any former period. Of course, this branch of finance contracted sharply as a result of the crisis but, as we noticed above, the extent of the ultimate losses were exaggerated at the time and other houses quickly moved in to fill the vacant ranks. Scattered estimates suggest that within twenty years acceptances to the USA were up 50 per cent on 1836 (to £30m.) and doubled within forty years, to £40m. about 1876.[4] This momentum was evidently more than adequate to maintain the USA as the principal recipient of commercial credits.

Precisely what happened after that is obscure, but it looks as if the imposition of the highly protective US tariff of 1864 not only served to cut back Anglo-American trade, but also restrained credit.[5] In the later decades of the century all the merchant banks on which we have any information were diversifying, not least those like Barings and Browns that had earlier dominated trade with the USA. Clearly this diversification was a painless process due to the continually increasing volume of international and, until shortly before the First World War, lack of significant competition from other quarters. Data are available on the acceptances of seven leading acceptance houses (Rothschilds, Barings, Kleinworts, Schröders, Hambros, Brandts and Gibbs) and these show quite clearly that much of the increase took place in the ten years or so before the First World War. The estimates for 1890 and 1900 have been

Table 7.1   *Acceptances at landmark dates: assembled estimates 1836–1913*

1836	USA	Germany	Total
Kirkman Finlay[1]	£20m.		
Morning Chronicle[2]	£20m.		
Dr M. Collins[3]	£10m.–15m.		
J. B. Smith[4]			£30m.–40m.
c. 1860–80			
Dr J. J. Madden[5]	£15m.–20m.		
1875–6			
E. Seyd[6]			£50m.–60m.
1890[10]			£90m.
1900[10]			£72m.
1913			
Accepting Houses Committee[7]		£28m.	
R. Kindersley[8]			£140m.
US Sources[9]	£30m.–35m.		

1. [Colm Brogan], *James Finlay & Co. Ltd., 1750–1850* (Glasgow, 1951), p. 195.
2. Cited by L. H. Jenks, *Migration of British Capital*, p. 87.
3. M. Collins, *The Bank of England and the Liverpool Money Market 1825–1850*, Ph.D. thesis, London, 1972, citing:
   (a)   Bank of England Liverpool Agent's letters, 29 Oct. 1836.
   (b)   A. Williams, *Historical Notes on the Bank of Liverpool* (typescript, 1929), pp. 52–3, at the Bank.
4. J. B. Smith, *Report … on the Effects of the Administration of the Bank of England* (Manchester, 1839), p.15.
5. J. J. Madden, *British Investment in the US 1860–1880*, Ph.D. thesis Cambridge, 1957, pp. 155–7.
6. E. Seyd, 'Our wealth in relation to imports and exports', *Journal Society of Arts*, XXVI (1878), p. 409n.
7. PRO T172/134, Accepting Houses Conference, 12 Aug. 1914.
8. Sir Robert Kindersley in evidence to *Committee on Finance and Industry*, Parl. Papers, 1931, I, p. 76.
9. This figure is calculated from the following:
   (a)   aggregate US short-term foreign liabilities of $450m. (£90m.) in 1914, C. Lewis, *America's Stake in International Investments* (Washington, 1938), pp. 442, 445.
   (b)   the reasonable assumption that US short-term indebtedness centred on London: National Monetary Commission [USA] *Bank Acceptances* (Washington, 1910).
   (c)   Kindersley's statement (note 8) that 60% of prewar acceptances were finance bills, i.e. 40% were trade bills. 40% of £90m. = £36m.
   (d)   It is realistic to recognise that some acceptances were taken outside Britain.
10. Calculations in Appendix 4.

calculated on the basis of the series for these firms (see Appendix 5).

The components of this prewar figure are even more difficult to estimate. Actually, prewar prime acceptances totalled £350m., but 60 per cent of these were finance bills and consequently only 40 per cent, or £140m., were trade bills. After a careful study of the data, Nishimura concludes that 'the vigorous increase in bills after 1894 was principally due to the growth in the amount of finance bills.'[6] Of these £140m. acceptances, some £24m. or so (40 per cent of £60m.) were attributable to the joint-stock banks that had recently moved into the acceptance business.[7] Home acceptances did not exceed 10–15 per cent of the total acceptances current prior to 1931 – no more than £21m.[8] These two deductions mean that the acceptance houses themselves were financing foreign trade to the tune of about £100m. in 1913, 45 per cent of them by the seven leading houses listed in the last paragraph.

In 1914 it was estimated that London acceptance credits to Germany alone amounted to £60m.–£70m., but again this figure must be reduced by 60 per cent to take account of the major component of finance bills. The gross figure also included some £15m. of acceptances taken by the three great German banks operating in London, the Deutsche, Discontogesellschaft and Dresdner banks. London acceptances for German trade were therefore more like £28m., with perhaps £6m.–£8m. (21–28 per cent) accounted for by German enterprises – a quarter in round figures. Calculation of figures for other countries can be little more than guesswork. There are no official or unofficial figures for the USA, but a calculation based on the country's aggregate short-term foreign liabilities (see notes to Table 7.1) would suggest £30m.–£35m. Similarly, figures are available for foreign short-term credits to Russian commercial banks, which amounted to 500m. roubles or £50m. in 1913. It has been assumed that this arose largely from borrowings from French and German banks, but the records of individual London merchant banks (notably Rothschilds, Kleinworts, Lazards and Brandts) show considerable credits to these concerns, so it is quite clear that they had not surrendered London's mid-century dominance of trade credit in Russia. At the outbreak of the First World War, outstanding short-term loans of French banking establishments to Russian banks and business concerns were estimated to have amounted to 500m. francs (£20m.).[9] It must be supposed that German credits were significantly smaller, which left a large gap to be filled by London, probably between £10m. and £20m. Familiarity with the structure of British international trade at this period would suggest that India and the Far East took a large share of commercial credit but in fact, as will be shown later in this chapter, the system of telegraphic transfers had largely superseded acceptances by the early 1890s.

Bringing these rather unsatisfactory figures together, we may suppose that the USA retained its position as London's premier debtor of acceptance account with about a third of the total of £100m., closely followed by Germany with between a quarter and third and then by Russia with perhaps a sixth. The remaining 20–25 per cent was shared by the other sectors of British trade with the rest of the world, the rest of Europe, the Empire, Latin America and the Orient. These orders of magnitude appear plausible in the final pages of this chapter, when the policies of the leading merchant banks in the twenty years or so before 1914 is examined.

Data from individual firms add little to this picture. Only two firms, Barings and Rothschilds, have records of their acceptances for the whole of the nineteenth century, and the former will not permit publication of their whole series. (The occasional Baring figures already cited in the text, and the post-1890 series, are derived from other contemporary sources.) Rothschilds' year-end figures show slow growth until the late 1880s, when they begin to move up sharply, probably reflecting the increase in finance bills as much as anything. Barings were of course much more energetic in this area but information presently available suggests that the acceptances did not commence their steep ascent until after mid-century (Table 3.2). Data for other firms (Brandts, Kleinworts, Schröders, Gibbs) show there was nothing like a 'take-off' before the last two decades of the century. This is of course entirely consistent with earlier recognition of the need of merchant bankers to remain diversified until information became faster and more exact. Before the establishment of the telegraph, acceptance credits were generally limited to a small circle known personally to one (or more) of the partners, and the few attempts that were made to go beyond this (notably in the mid-1830s) ended in disaster.

The earliest reference in surviving records to the use of the telegraph by merchant banks occurs in 1843, when Rothschilds and Behrens of Hamburg opened a telegraphic correspondence to swap information on prices on the international stock and currency exchanges. Behrens wrote: 'As far as we know, no Hamburg bankers have yet taken advantage of this means of communication. It is, so far, used only by the grain trade and other merchants.' But Behrens proposed to use it only once a week and, twenty years later, the weekly routine at Barings still revolved round the 'foreign post days', Tuesdays and Fridays. However, in the early 1870s, the telegraph had considerably accelerated the tempo of business. Isaac Seligman, who was sent to represent his brother's New York house in London in 1872, and was involved in the arbitrage of stocks and exchanges between the two centres, recalled the nervous strain of 'sending and receiving telegrams every few minutes.' Arbitrage evidently led the way, but showed the method for better information flows on clients.[10]

US Credits

The earliest and strongest development of 'commission merchants' or 'commission bankers' was evidently in the transatlantic trade. The system was well established in 1836 when Bates described it in some detail. To facilitate understanding of the chain of connections the role of the six main parties is illustrated in Figure 7.1. British agents or partners of New York or Philadelphia merchant houses gave orders to British manufacturers or warehouses, characteristically on regular tours of the City warehouse region and northern centres. The means of payment for

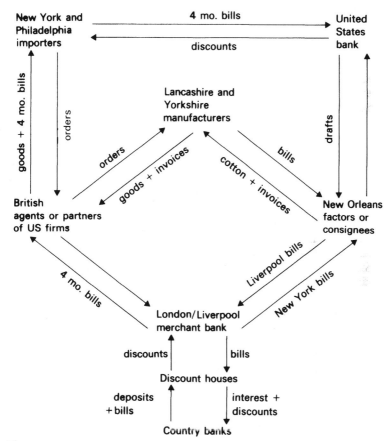

Figure 7.1 *The credit system in the transatlantic trade in 1836*

Sources: Based on Bank of England Committee of Treasury Minute Books, XXII, pp. 114–15; *Circular to Bankers* 1832, p. 205, 1837, p. 290.

Note: 'bills' always mean bills of exchange in this figure these orders was raised by these agents drawing four-monthly bills on their merchant bankers, their credit having been recommended by the bank's partner or agent in North America. At this period, US importers were in the habit of sending these bills to the United States Bank which, for a commission, exchanged them for US exporters' bills from New Orleans, the centre of the cotton and tobacco exporting business. The merchants of the plantation states made their purchases of British goods in New York and Philadelphia and for this purpose purchased drafts of the US Bank's agents. Meanwhile those sending cotton and tobacco to New Orleans for sale anticipated the proceeds by drafts on the factors or consignees there, and these drafts were exchanged by the Bank agents for the money received for drafts on Philadelphia or New York. With the money thus placed at New Orleans the bills of the Liverpool import merchants were taken and remitted to London, meeting the drafts drawn to the order of the importers of British goods. The London and Liverpool functions are not shown separately in the diagram partly to simplify, but also because by this date most of the Anglo-American merchant banks had offices in Liverpool.

Around this date the accepting houses earned their commissions in four distinct ways. As soon as a particular deal had been agreed, 1 per cent was charged for accepting the bills of the manufacturers and for effecting insurance. Interest was charged at 5 per cent according to the period of credit, which was three or four months for sales in Europe and North America, and up to twelve months for oriental markets. Two per cent was charged for remittances in produce and one per cent for remittances in bills. The accepting houses were conventionally prepared to advance up to two-thirds of the invoice to recognised clients, but in the boom conditions of the mid-1830s, some pushing houses offered up to 100 per cent for six months in the transatlantic trade.[11] In such periods discount houses might try to encroach on the business, for demarcation lines between specialists were as yet ill-formulated. 'I learn that one of the partners in Overend's house [that is Overend, Gurney & Co.] is now in Birmingham offering round at the houses of foreign merchants money at $3\frac{1}{2}$ per cent on first rate acceptances', the Bank of England agent there reported to his directors.[12] When Morrison, Cryder & Co. thought of opening an office in Glasgow and sent an agent north to assess the situation he reported that

under existing circumstances I think it would be useless to fix an agency here, we cannot come into competition with the liberal system which our neighbours have adopted, that is, to advance the invoice regulating their commissions according to the profits, if there is no profit, they charge no commission.[13]

It is an eloquent comment on the intensity of the competition that such a pushing cut-price house should think that it was not worth entering this particular market. In subsequent years even Barings contracted their transatlantic interests, no doubt foreseeing more opportunities in Europe, Latin America and elsewhere.[14] As will be explained in the next chapter, the system lasted until the far-reaching changes in the cotton trade, and merchanting generally, in the 1880s, when a succession of merchant banks pulled out of Liverpool. It might easily be supposed that this was the signal for the merchant banks to invade the imperial markets (and especially those of India and the Far East) in strength, but in fact this area had already been occupied by the joint-stock banks.

Credits for Indian and Oriental Trade

It is a strange fact that although there are competent house histories of half-a-dozen leading firms engaged in the trade to India and the Far East, scarcely any of them mentions whether the firms ever became involved in acceptance credits. Consequently it is necessary to piece together some of the story from scattered fragments. It has generally been supposed that at least down to 1813, when Indian commerce was opened to 'the more active competition of private adventurers', almost all the advances were made by the Company. The correspondence between Barings and John Palmer & Co., until 1833 the leading agency house, lends support to this view, and a letter of 1809 from Calcutta refers to the problems of 'employing a vast capital now inert, or growing so' due to some disruption in the opium trade. The agency houses employed their growing capital making advances to native merchants, or dealing in loans to the Company.[15]

The early group of agency houses (those that became insolvent in the 1830s) differed from the accepting houses at home because a large proportion of their capital from the first came from deposits. The partners had many friends and connections in the Company's service from whom they received deposits as well as business, because ex-patriots had few opportunities of obtaining safe investments, or remittances for the funds they wished to send home. In the early 1820s, when the Company drastically reduced the interest paid on its debts (from 8 to 4 or 5 per cent), large sums were deposited with the agency houses on which they paid similar rates to the Company, but lent to natives at 10 or 12 per cent. In addition, they charged high commissions on every kind of service undertaken for their clients, for instance 1 per cent when they received deposits. They also directed that some, at least, of their deposits, should not be withdrawn without notice but lodged for fixed periods. It was the overflowing deposits of these years that induced the houses to invest in indigo factories, sugar plantations, ships and estate developments, as well as loans to mercantile firms in Singapore, Java, Manila and other rising centres of trade.[16]

Obviously this local capital and expertise left little scope for the accepting houses in London, and in general the only way in which they could participate in this trade was by lending to French, German and US merchants trading to the Far East. It seems that at first there were few London houses prepared to sponsor such trade because the commissions charged were exceptionally high compared with those charged on transatlantic bills. After the French Wars 2.5 per cent was a usual commission, but this slipped down by degrees until, led by Rothschild, it bottomed at 1 per cent in 1836. By this date it was said that 'the number of London houses able and willing to grant India credits are daily increasing', while Parisian finance houses threatened competition by their attempts to get their names recognised in Calcutta. Barings, as we saw in Chapter 2, thought the prospects in India and China so enticing that they financed Boston merchants Russell, Sturgis & Co., and fitted out their own ships for the Far Eastern trade. A £2m. project of 1836 to launch a Bank of India was said to have had their support but like so many other joint-stock ventures of the period, it foundered.[17]

When the old agency houses disappeared the remaining houses were smaller and more dependent on Liverpool or London credit. Expectations of the China market were far too high, with manufacturers consigning too much to the Far East. A system of raising money by drawing bills in India at nine or ten months on firms in London, and sending them home to be discounted with the endorsement of produce-broking houses in London, came into fairly general use. Commissions remained at 1 per cent, while credit was offered to entrepreneurs entering the trade with little capital (£10,000–£15,000). In 1847 twenty-two Calcutta firms suspended payment and one of the most reputable London merchant banks, Reid Irving & Co., collapsed. Even the most reputable houses came under a cloud during this period.[18]

This background explains why the surviving East India merchants, taken as a group, repudiated banking as a legitimate branch of their activities. The Indian trade had always been unusually speculative, and merchants came to believe that banks provided more facilities for speculation to people who had insufficient capital, so making trade even less stable. Moreover, a merchant in India and China in those days who had capital stood in no need of banking accommodation. He bought his neighbour's first-class credits for his remittances, and his neighbour purchased his in turn. Again, the India and China trades were then more like barter and a merchant who had money on hand would keep it for months until the exports fell to what he considered to be safe prices. Foreign merchants trading in the Far East did not borrow from the 'local' banks for they could always raise money by using the facilities which their London correspondents were ready to provide. The prejudice against the banks in the East continued at least until the change of business habits that began in the late 1860s.[19]

The vacuum left by the old agency houses of the Palmer era and the hostility of their successors was eventually occupied by the joint-stock banks, but not without some initial difficulties, for there was at first little remittance business for them to do. The East India Company naturally wanted to maintain its traditional interest in remittance, and at first opposed the chartering of new joint-stock concerns, but the Oriental Bank was founded in 1845, to be followed by the Chartered Bank of India and the Chartered Bank of Asia in 1853, the Chartered Mercantile Bank of India, London & China and the Agra & United Services Bank in 1857, and a flush of further concerns during the 'cotton famine' of the early 1860s.[20] Most of this group foundered, but one with strong local mercantile support, the Hong Kong & Shanghai Banking Corporation (HSBC), chartered in 1865, went from strength to strength.

The ultimate reason for the success of these concerns was the abundance of their capital, or rather deposits, and more particular those of the HSBC. In 1876 the five principal Eastern banks operating in India (the Agra, Chartered Bank, Chartered Mercantile, National of India, and Oriental) had deposits of £21.25m., while the HSBC had £2.65m. In 1891 the five had £27.84m. and the HSBC £25.66m. (There are no means of ascertaining how much of these deposits were British, but that does not matter for our purposes.) When the commercial atmosphere began to clear after the storm of 1866, the British Eastern banks that survived came to an agreement among themselves neither to buy nor to sell bills of exchange drawn for periods of more than four months. The dramatic improvements in transport and communications to the East had made the old six month bill system unnecessary some years earlier; at mid-century it took only thirty days for news from London to reach Calcutta. But unfortunately for the London and Liverpool houses, the India and China firms generally would not agree to it and what was worse for them in the end, the HSBC refused to join in the agreement. The consequence was that that bank rapidly improved its position in China and Japan (it had then no branches in Malaya or India) and gained the favour of the mercantile communities there. While the agreement among the other banks lasted, a lucrative part of the business of the HSBC was to purchase six months bills, and to sell its own four months drafts on London to its competitors at a good profit, which was sometimes the only way in which they could obtain remittances. After a while the agreement fell apart, and four months bills became more common, but not before numbers of other merchant houses had collapsed from overstrained credit. So late as 1910, it was still being reported that Far Eastern bills, 'which used to be six months, are getting shorter.'[21]

The most far-reaching change in Far Eastern commercial finance came with the extension of the telegraph to India, Malaya, China and Japan. The banks began to sell telegraphic transfers on London and India and from the first they largely took the place of drafts on firms in Bombay and Calcutta. By degrees, British and other merchants purchased telegraphic transfers in preference to the bank drafts and bills which they had traditionally used. In 1892 an authority on Eastern banking wrote that

> By far the larger part of the mercantile remittances from the East have for some years been made in transfers. One effect of this has been to diminish to a very great extent the acceptances of Eastern banks and those of their London bankers for their account. These are not now a tenth of what they were before transfers came so much into use.

Consequently the merchant houses were in a much easier financial position, for the money paid in the East for a transfer was handed over to the payee on the same or on the next day. Their assets were now much more liquid, a matter of paramount importance in a trade in which so many bankruptcies had been caused by 'lock-ups', and in which profit margins were now very thin. Telegraphic transfers also had important consequences for the trade in inland bills, for the acceptances which London firms offered for Lancashire and Yorkshire exports to the East fell away to nothing in the 1870s and 1880s.[22]

At the end of the century the chartered banks claimed that they had 'practically financed the whole export and import trade' of India for the last forty years, a claim that was disputed by the Indian Presidency banks but not (so far as is known) by the London accepting houses. The agency houses had long since sunk their banking interests in those of the joint-stock banks. The HSBC was supported by leading Far Eastern merchant houses like Sassoons and Dents from the first, but the most eminent British firm in China, Jardine Matheson & Co., held aloof for a dozen years, until 1877. Other agency houses were already represented on the boards of other banks; James Blyth of Blyth, Greene & Jourdain became chairman of the Oriental Banking Corporation, while partners in Ogilvy, Gillanders & Co. were directors of the Bank of Bengal for seventy years.[23] The 1850s and early 1860s were a period of great prosperity for such firms, with commissions flowing in from the prospering tea and silk trades, which may have been another reason for neglecting opportunities in banking. At any rate, by the time that growing competition compelled them to diversify, the joint-stock banks were well entrenched in acceptance business. This was no doubt one reason for the agency houses turning to investment banking rather than accepting house activities (Chapter 5). But the main reason was that the agency houses were for the most part organised as commission houses concerned with purchases or sales in the Far East on behalf of principals in Europe and the USA, and until well after mid-century traded on very modest capitals. Wallace Bros, one of the most successful firms operating in the Far East, conducted their acceptance credits through the National Bank of Scotland; their own capital in 1914 reached £0.8m. Jardine, Matheson & Co., the most successful firm in China, had a nominal £200,000 on incorporation in 1909.[24]

The Clients of Accepting Houses

A leading accepting house would of course have scores, if not hundreds, of client firms whose international trade it supported. It is not possible within the compass of a modest volume to range over all the possible variations in credit arrangements, and in any case it would make for very dull reading. A more interesting approach is to take some representative cases, chosen from different sectors of trade and types of exporters. The first case has also been chosen because, like so much else in the Rothschild business archive, it is unusually rich in detail. It concerns a German client, one of a large class on whom relatively little has been written.

Meyer & Schönfeld were only a small firm but in several respects they represent the way in which a business – especially a foreign export firm – might be set up and financed in the textile trade of the English industrial regions in the first half of the nineteenth century. Their business combined familiarity and close personal connections in the continental markets with immediate access to the local producers in the Bradford, Leeds and Manchester areas. The partners appear to have been newcomers to this region, but had gained some mercantile experience as clerks to another firm – most probably Michaelson & Benedicks, Rothschild's principal correspondents in Stockholm. Herr Benedicks was an uncle of Schönfeld's.[25]

At the close of 1838, after Meyer & Schönfeld had established a firm in Hamburg, Herr G. S. Meyer called at N. M. Rothschild & Sons in London and, having proved his firm's sound financial standing by presenting a letter of credit by the firm of Michaelson & Benedicks and having been granted their wish to do business with Rothschild & Sons, he summarised the outcome of their talks in a memorandum written the same day in the London Coffee House and addressed it to Rothschilds:

> Thanking you for the very friendly reception you gave to our Herr
> Meyer, we take the liberty, with your kind permission, of asking you

most politely to allow us to dispose of the credit of £5,000 provided by Messrs. Michaelson & Benedicks by drawing upon you in small bills. Furthermore, we would esteem it a great favour if you would be kind enough to provide us with references to bankers and other houses we might approach in the markets of Leeds, Bradford, and Manchester where we intend to purchase goods from the small manufacturers. Finally, we wish to express our warmest gratitude for your permission to mention your most highly esteemed house in our circulars.

This credit, the guarantee of which was renewed on two subsequent occasions at the slightly lower amounts of £2,000 and £3,000 respectively, provided the financial basis for the establishment in Bradford. Michaelson & Benedicks had in fact been assisting the new firm even earlier, at the stage when Meyer & Schönfeld were launching their first house in Hamburg. Obviously, they played a part similar to those 'mother-firms' where sons of the family were sent abroad in order to found new branches in other relevant centres of trade or industry, but with the difference that Michaelson & Benedicks did not – or not directly – invest their surplus money that way, nor did they mean to expand their own business: the capital support they gave to Meyer & Schönfeld for their start was a loan, and for the branch in England they functioned merely as guarantors.

Michaelson & Benedicks had been known to Rothschilds for at least fifteen years as a respectable firm and good customers, so their guarantee was acceptable beyond any doubt. Some years later, in November 1841, the relationship was resumed in a letter:

Yesterday our Herr Meyer had the pleasure to see you [Lionel Rothschild] in person and to deliver a letter of Mr. Benedick's asking for your approval to a standing credit [the new guarantee of £3,000 replacing the initial one]. We were very pleased to hear that you are inclined to accept that suggestion and take the liberty, accordingly to your request, to apply for the said credit again in writing. We also feel that it would be appropriate to add some further information about the conditions and commodities of our business. Three years ago we established a firm in Hamburg specialising in manufactured goods in support of which we received – in addition to our own capital – a considerable amount, at 10 years terms, from Messrs. Michaelson & Benedicks. Fortunately we have been enjoying a period of success which has enabled us to gain a fair amount of capital and we wish to acknowledge gratefully that this is to a large degree owing, apart from the friendship of Messrs. Michaelson & Benedicks, to your recommendations and those we received from Mr. Salomon Heine.

The importance of such third-party backing is also confirmed by an event in July 1844, when Meyer & Schönfeld pointed out that they must have proved their reliability in almost six years of business with Rothschilds, and that Uncle Benedicks was now 76 years old and could not expect to live for ever, so they would like to be granted the same £3,000 credit on their own merits. Rothschild and Sons preferred to keep the old arrangement so the Stockholm firm renewed their existing guarantee.

There is one further condition for a policy of this kind to work, an easy flow of cash. Thus, the letter of November 1841 continues:

> for keeping this type of business running we need more cash than those who are depending on the credit granted by the stuff [worsted] merchants, as we have to give ready cash to the manufacturers. Our transactions are not of a kind which would make us face any considerable risk as we observe the principle of never handing too large an account to any one merchant, but tend to spread the risk by splitting it into more but smaller sums. From the very favourable recommendation you received from Mr. Benedicks you will learn that you would not take any risk with us, and we do not doubt you would agree to grant us a credit of £2,000 [in addition to Benedick's £3,000 – Rothschild granted £1,000]. At present, there is much advantage in buying and therefore we should highly appreciate an early answer which would enable us to plan our purchases accordingly.

The emphasis here is on 'ready cash'. Financing purchases at credit terms with local wholesale merchants would cost, at least, a commission and interest. Neither was what Meyer & Schönfeld had in mind for, in that case, they would not need to maintain a business branch in Bradford, but could just as easily buy their wares through the merchants. So the aim was to make purchases for cash (at cash or discount prices, probably with reductions) with no commission or wholesale merchants between the manufacturer and the exporter. This elimination of intermediate traders reduced costs considerably and allowed Meyer & Schönfeld two possible gains, higher profit rates (in a later context an expected profit rate of 10 per cent is mentioned) and higher competitiveness through lower prices. Most likely both options were pragmatically weighed against one another, using whichever was more advantageous at the time. But the basic question remained of how to retain a reasonable amount of cash in hand at all times. Meyer & Schönfeld had arranged funds by third party credit (Benedicks) and its acceptance by Rothschild & Sons. They also provided money of their own by remitting bills of exchange to Rothschilds. In exchange, Rothschilds would protect their bills of exchange which were generally to be paid into their account with a local bank, in this instance the Bradford Banking Company. From this

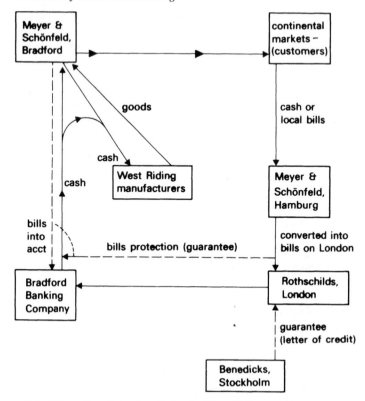

Figure 7.2   *Flow of goods and credit in the West Riding export trade*

Note: The crucial role of a locally established bank providing cash can readily be appreciated. This is particularly important when most big business was done in bills and shortages of ready money were not infrequent.

account Meyer & Schönfeld could then withdraw cash to pay their suppliers, the local manufacturers. In this way, a scheme of these transactions would resemble an almost closed circuit (the producers might as well be included in this circuit but, in this case, they form some kind of extension, and this also applies to the guarantors, Messrs Michaelson & Benedicks).

However, most of the clients of the well-known accepting houses were evidently in a much larger and diversified way of business than this small German house. As US and European merchants or their agents came to Britain to buy textiles, so British mercantile enterprise was forced to venture into the more distant European, Eastern and Latin American markets, and the changing orientation of British exports is inevitably reflected in the acceptance market. Henry & James Barton may be taken to represent the old kind of Manchester merchants of the age of Arkwright and the Peels. The family had started as fustian manufacturers towards the middle of the eighteenth century, working the familiar domestic system of the region, and exporting through Finlays, the leading Glasgow merchants of the late eighteenth century. Joining a characteristic development of the 1790s, the second generation had moved into cotton spinning and calico printing. By 1830 the third generation had some £120,000 invested in a large calico printing works (payroll 600–700) and a total capital of some £470,000, making them one of the richest manufacturing families in Lancashire. They nevertheless still occasionally drew on three London houses – Finlay, Hodgson & Co., Brown Janson & Co., and McLachlan, MacIntyre & Co. – because of the nature of textile marketing. The patterns sent out each year in September or October did not begin to find orders until the following spring and summer, while the expensive engraving and printing was in progress through the winter months. Remittances sent in the summer from distant markets might not reach Manchester until the end of the year, and then might not be easy to discount; in particular Bartons received a lot of 'foreign and promiscuous paper'.[26]

The younger, more pushing kind of successful house may be represented by Butterworth, Brooks & Co., another Manchester firm of calico weavers and printers. The firm started in 1808 and twenty years later were reckoned to be the second largest printers in the country, and the largest printers of their own calicoes, employing a capital of £200,000. A self-confessed plagiarist of other manufacturers' designs, in the 1830s Brooks was producing some 300,000 pieces (of 28 yards each) a year at a clear profit of £20,000, evidently mass sales at a low average profit margin of 1s 4d (£0.066) each. His prints were sold 'to all quarters of the globe', including (at the time) such remote places as Brazil, Chile, Peru, Siam and China. To support this extensive operation, he drew on a dozen firms, mostly in Manchester and Liverpool, and discounted over half-a-million pounds' worth of bills a year. Strong financial support was obtained from Antony Gibbs & Co. and John McVicar, who was the Liverpool agent of Jardine, Matheson & Co. of Canton, but most of the support came from mercantile houses whose names have now been forgotten. In other words, the credit system was by no means dominated by London; a good deal of 'local power' was retained in the North of England. But what is perhaps most interesting about this particular case is that John Brooks' brother was Samuel Brooks, a partner in Cunliffe, Brooks & Co., the well-known Manchester bankers of the period. The capital of the bank (£350,000 in 1838 and £500,000 in 1854) was not much greater than that of the manufacturers (£300,000+ in 1834) and so the latter drew entirely on 'outside' credit except during the crisis of 1839. Cunliffe Brooks & Co.

provided credit for numbers of Greek merchants in Manchester and it is easy to suppose that the details of their credit-worthiness came from John Brooks' assessments.[27]

Moving forward in the nineteenth century, the more representative exporter may have been James Greaves & Co., a firm established around the middle of the century to send milling and other machinery to Bombay, where they had an agency known as Greaves, Cotton & Co. In 1887 they became main agents for the textile machine builders Howard & Bullough of Accrington, who were able to equip whole factories and stood second only to Platt Bros of Oldham in their worldwide connections and prestige. At this time the firm's capital was said to be £120,000. At the turn of the century they were considered an 'old established firm' with capital 'ample for their requirements'. A decade later they were identified as a 'good all round merchant business' that had acquired substantial interests in mills around Bombay 'one of which is entirely their own and making good profits'; their capital now stood at £310,000. This solid position enabled them to draw on as many as six merchant banks and three other banks. The prescribed credit limits were listed as follows:

J. H. Schröder & Co.	£45,000	1.5% commission
König Bros	£30,000	1.5% commission
Chaplin, Milne & Co	£30,000	1.5% commission
C. J. Hambro & Son	£20,000	1.5% commission
Kleinwort, Sons & Co.	£20,000	1.5% commission
Blydenstein & Co.	£10,000	1.5% commission
National Bank of India	£15,000	1.5% commission
Manchester & County Bank	£45,000	} 0.5% over bank rate,
Lancs. & Yorks Bank	£20,000	} minimum 3.5%
	£235,000	

It looks as if Greaves enjoyed a total revolving credit of almost a quarter of a million pounds. From the angle of the merchant banks, two points are worth underlining. One is the extent to which large credits were shared on an *ad hoc* basis between a group of autonomous houses, much in the way that public issues were shared. The other is the energetic role taken by the Anglo-German group, notwithstanding that Greaves were specialists in exporting to a region completely outside their traditional area of activity in Europe and North America. We shall recur to this development in the concluding pages of this chapter.[28] Meanwhile the more general development needs to be recapitulated. The accepting houses faced growing competition in all sectors of world trade, but they did not lead the search for diversification so much as follow their clients into it. The most preferred clients preferred to maintain support from a group of accepting houses, and this also compelled the latter to spread their interests in search of business.

Competition for Acceptances

The evidence of this book serves to emphasise that, with very few exceptions, the merchant banks were much more continuously interested in acceptances than issues; in Baron Schröder's words they were the 'bread and butter' of their income. Unfortunately there is no means of estimating the varying roles of the numerous accepting houses within the overall picture of growth, but information for some of the leading houses and their foreign rivals (Table 7.2) gives a much more favourable

Table 7.2   *Acceptances of some leading London merchant banks and their rivals 1890–1914 (£m.)*

London merchant banks	c. 1890	1900	1913
Kleinwort, Sons & Co. (1796)	4.9	8.2	13.6
J. Henry Schröder & Co. (1815)	n.d.	5.9	11.6
W. Brandt's Sons & Co. (1805)	0.7	1.2	3.3
Baring Bros & Co. Ltd. (1763)	15.0	3.9	6.6
C. J. Hambro & Son (c.1800)	1.9	1.9	3.0
N. M. Rothschild & Sons (1798)	1.4	1.5	3.2
Brown, Shipley & Co. (1805)	10.6 (1888)	n.d.	5.1
British joint-stock banks			
Union of London & Smiths Bank (1839)		3.1	5.8
Parr's Bank (1865)		2.4	5.4
London Joint-Stock Bank (1836)		1.4	3.2
Manchester & Liverpool District (1829)		1.7	2.7
London Country & Westminster (1834)		0.2	7.8
Glyn, Mills & Co. (1753)		1.2	1.4
Continental banks			
Dresdner Bank (1872)		6.1	14.4
Discontogesellschaft (1851)		3.0	12.5
Crédit Lyonnais (1863)		0.04	5.7
Russian Bank for Foreign Trade (1871)		2.2	3.7
Credito Italiano (1870)		n.d.	1.9

Sources: T. Skinner, *The London Banks*, 1890, 1900, 1914–15. Kleinwort Benson MSS, Schröder Wagg MSS, Brown Shipley MSS, B. Bramsen and K. Wain, *The Hambros* (1980) pp. 330, 370. Brandt records at the London School of Economics Library, WC2.

impression of response to the opportunities of commercial credits, than that offered by issues at the period. Barings lost a great deal of business after the 1890 crisis, but other firms more than made up for these losses, maintaining a respectable place among the world leaders. They did so in conditions of intensive competition; as a leading merchant banker said of the Dresdner Bank: 'They, like the Deutsche Bank and Crédit Lyonnais, are fearful poachers and will stick at nothing in order to get business.'[29]

The available data suggests that the most enterprising accepting houses of the period were the Anglo-German houses, particularly Kleinworts, Brandts, Schröders, Rothschilds and Hambros. The importance of De Jerseys (Knoops) has already been explained (Chapter 5) and the leading role of Huths has been alluded to from time to time; in 1914 their acceptances were around £3.3m.[30] Other firms with a German background were evidently pacemakers even though there are no data to define their importance; König Bros and A. Rüffer & Sons are most prominent in the records.[31] Meanwhile, Barings' never recovered their pre-1890 leadership while such houses as Brown Shipley, Gibbs and Sassoons lost their earlier pre-eminence. It would be easy to suppose that this position reflected the rise of the German trade in the world, which continued to be financed from London to a remarkable degree, and the falling-off of opportunities in other sectors, notably the USA and (so far as London accepting houses were concerned) the Far East. But this can be only part of the story, for on closer examination the Anglo-German houses did not restrict themselves to European trade or sponsoring rising German firms. Indeed, it was only the most conservative of them, Rothschilds, that retained their preponderant interests in Europe.[32] The other houses in fact showed a remarkable degree of diversification. The most striking instance is that of W. Brandt's Sons & Co., a house established in 1805 for trade with Russia, and until 1875 solely concerned with that country. In that year one of the family went out to Buenos Aires to build a connection and in 1886 Brandts took over a Calcutta house called Scholvin & Co. Meanwhile the tenuous family connection with St Petersburg broke up. In August 1914 the £8.9m. acceptance liabilities of the firm was divided as follows:

Russia	£ 860,000	9.65%
Germany	£1,850,000	20.77%
Rest of Europe	£1,250,000	14.03%
USA	£3,085,000	34.63%
S. America	£1,318,000	14.80%
Far East	£ 545,000	6.12%
	£8,908,000	100.00

Russia was now less than 10 per cent, and only 45 per cent was committed to Europe. Kleinworts' acceptances and commodity trade also bear eloquent testimony to the developments of the period. By the Edwardian years (1900–8), only 12.3 per cent went to the firm's stamping ground in Germany, while 39.1 per cent went to the USA, 6.3 to Latin America, 4.9 to Russia and 3.2 to India and the Far East.[33]

It would be easy to assume that the last was a safe haven for British trade and finance, but under the prevailing free trade connections this was far from the case. Indeed, it is possible to cite cases where German firms, through their long-established connections in the North of England textile centres, maintained a strong competitive position in British imperial markets. Thus L. Behrens & Sons of Hamburg, for long Rothschilds' leading correspondents in Germany, retained the closest connections with S. L. Behrens & Co. in Manchester and Sir Jacob Behrens & Sons of Bradford, Manchester, London, Calcutta and Bombay. In 1885 the parent house began to grant acceptance credits for German imports and in the best years reached 30m. marks (£3m.), a facility no doubt used by the English branches and their friends in all their international connections.[34]

This intense competition with German banks deserves rather closer attention. Until the 1870s bills in the many German currencies were unfamiliar and therefore disliked in international commerce, and being disliked were subject to higher rates of discount than bills on London. The founding of the German Empire in 1871 of course created opportunities for the Reichsmark. In the same year the Deutsche Bank acquired an interest in the German Bank of London Ltd and opened a branch in Bremen. The next year a share was taken in Knoblauch & Lichtenstein of New York and a Hamburg branch opened. These investments in British and US financial expertise evidently proved to be the best way forward, for independent initiatives in the Far East, branches at Shanghai and Yokohama opened expressly for the purpose of freeing German commerce from the tutelage of British and French bankers, failed after a short period. The endeavour was renewed some fifteen years later, with greater success, when the Deutsche Bank participated in the founding of the Deutsche-Asiatische Bank at Shanghai (1889), then numerous other foreign banks along the same lines, sometimes in partnership with old private banks, for instance with Lazard-Speyer-Ellisen of Frankfurt in Central America (1905), and with Speyer Bros of New York in Mexico (1906). Meanwhile, the vigorous Berlin enterprise bought out the old Anglo-American accepting house of Dennistoun, Cross & Co.

According to Dr J. Riesser, writing in 1908, the Deutsche Bank's enterprise eventually enjoyed 'brilliant success', and its example was shortly followed by the Discontogesellschaft. 'The time may be said to have passed', Riesser proclaimed, 'at least in the majority of cases, when

German exporters ... and foreign exporters when selling goods to Germans, had to draw on London, or when German importers had to settle the credits of their sellers via London.' However he had to acknowledge that this success, pretty inevitable in the context of the rise of German industrialism and nationalism, was less impressive in the international setting. For one thing, the reality of the figures assembled in Table 7.2 was less impressive than the appearance. A large percentage of the total acceptance credit granted by German bankers in this period was composed of credit in the form of industrial acceptances of the 'doubtful sort' – that is of the kind that was constantly renewed to maintain a flow of working capital to a firm, rather than finance a specific transaction in international trade. Another part of the so-called acceptances was in fact 'speculative' – that is provincial bankers financing their stock exchange speculations or those of their clients.[35]

It is of course impossible to estimate the proportion of German bank acceptances that represented genuine trade bills, but it was certainly not a preponderant part. One of the few ways in which it is possible to get a feel of the real situation is to examine the evidence of Sir Felix Schuster, the Governor of the Union of London & Smiths Bank, to the United States National Monetary Commission in 1910. He declared, 'We do an accepting business, but when we think the bill is drawn purely for finance reasons, such as stock exchange speculation, we do not care for the business; we decline. Our acceptances are only £4,000,000 [per annum]. If we chose to go in for accepting finance bills, that might be five times the amount very easily.' There was a steady rise in German bank acceptances for overseas trade, especially from Hamburg, Bremen and London branches, but the totals for trade finance were much smaller than those given in the banks' published figures. In other words, the German banks were not conducting business on a comparable scale to that of the leading British accepting houses of the period.

Other evidence cited by Riesser leaves no doubt that in 1914 British accepting houses still dominated the finance of world trade. The number of bills drawn in London on foreign countries was very small compared to the number of bills drawn by foreign countries on London; the ratio of the first to the second in 1908 was reckoned to be about one to nine. In 1914 – and indeed until the crisis of 1931 – international trade was still largely conducted in sterling bills on London, but the traditional standing of sterling as a world currency is not the only reason for the continuing leadership of the London merchant banks. Nor was it simply a question of British firms being more experienced or efficient than new foreign rivals. It was very much more to do with the fact that German, US, French and other international houses based in London continued to maintain their ascendancy of their own compatriots, and maintained an efficient working relationship with each other and with their British connections. A closer study would no doubt demonstrate that London-based credits provided a significant proportion of the working capital for German trade expansion in the last quarter of the nineteenth century just as, half a century earlier, migrant German capital and mercantile experience vitally contributed to the growth of British overseas trade. This interesting theme evidently takes us beyond the confines of the present study and must be left for elaboration in some other research.

The German context also helps to explain the varying performance of the leading accepting houses and in particular the top-of-the-league position of Kleinworts and Schröders in 1914. In earlier chapters we have identified the merchant banks' need to maintain their 'indubitable credit' and the consequent emphasis on 'safe' business. During the course of the century, competition between the various houses increased rather than slackened, and on the eve of the First World War the accepting commission for conventional business could be as low as 0.25 per cent, plus the prevailing rate of interest for the bill period.[36] Ambitious firms looking for larger profit margins could earn them only by taking more risky or at any rate less conventional business. Oral testimony recalls that Kleinworts had a reputation for their independent approach to acceptances, and were known for their willingness to take risks. Their ample records, and those of Schröders, show that a lot of these risks were taken in connection with the rising German industrial firms, and with Anglo-German houses in Liverpool, Manchester and other North of England towns. Obviously these firms benefited from their former German backgrounds, but that was only part of it, for Rothschilds, Hambros and Montagus with similar backgrounds were regarded by bill brokers as 'stodgy'. The enterprise of the ambitious firms serves to refute any notions of overall second- or third-generation entrepreneurial failure; and shows that London-based firms not only kept abreast of German banks but continued to take a share of German accepting house business.[37]

8 The Decline of Merchanting

It is possible to assemble a list of books covering some thirty firms that functioned at one time or another as merchant banks but, incredibly, very few of these attempt to offer any reasoned account of how, why and when particular firms effected the transition from merchanting to finance. In fact the only house histories that make a point of defining and explaining the change are those of the US firms, Seligman and Morton, and that is because, in the exceptionally favourable conditions of post-Civil War finance, the founders of both concerns formally renounced the 'dry goods' trade in favour of finance. Books on British firms, by contrast, sometimes do not even mention the interest of the partners in accepting house business, exchange, railroad investments and other financial activities, while others simply allude to them in a casual or passing kind of way. This taciturnity may sometimes be explained simply by the limitations of the firms' amateur historians, but its very ubiquity provokes the suspicion that modesty and ignorance cannot be the only causes. The transition from merchanting to pure finance is so central to the story of merchant banking that it is necessary to probe evidence of the published work and to comb the available archives more thoroughly than most of the house historians have done.

In earlier chapters two 'models' of development were noticed: that of the London Rothschilds, in which a decision to abandon trade for finance can be traced to a particular date, and that of Barings and Browns in which a number of landmarks can be discerned but the transition was spread over a generation or more. In this matter the Rothschilds are evidently different from most of their English rivals because NM came of a Jewish background in which for centuries mercantile (as distinct from financial) enterprise had been suppressed or allowed only restricted opportunity to develop, and it is clear that some of the other families that made an early and clean cut away from commodity trade came from similar backgrounds; in this respect not only Seligman, but also Lazards, Sterns, Speyers and Montagus are adequately documented.[1] It is possible to find a small number of English firms that explicitly renounced trade for finance, but their very obscurity adds substance to the point that such public manifestations of the change in direction were untypical. The clearest examples are Timothy Wiggin and James Morrison who in the early 1830s abandoned the textile trade in favour of an all-out drive to secure the ascendancy in transatlantic finance. Their collapse in 1837 is all too well known, and cannot have recommended their policies to contemporaries.[2] Similarly in 1845 George Peabody publicly severed his connection with 'dry goods' after thirty years in the trade, but his position at the period appears unique. He was an American whose business had suffered from the decline of Baltimore and the US tariff of 1842, and in no way representative of general experience.

Turning then to the large majority of emergent merchant banks that were based in Britain, there can be no doubt that in general they maintained their roles as general merchants as long as possible. They had won their position as 'first-class' houses by their skill and expertise in general trade and diversified trade and financial business was in itself an insurance against adversity. It was well understood that the business of the general merchant comprehended acceptances, exchange, insurance and, perhaps on an occasion, issues as well; their financial services were a traditional mercantile activity.

The way in which a small group of merchant houses in a particular sector of trade might evolve into the source of financial services for the remainder of the group can be illustrated by the experience of the Greek merchants. The names of the leading houses – Ralli, Rodocanachi, Spartali, Argenti, and so on – are known to historians, but there are no house histories beyond a small booklet on Rallis. As mentioned in an earlier chapter, from the late eighteenth century the Greeks emerged as the leading international specialists in the Levant Trade, settling in Amsterdam from the 1760s onwards. After the French Wars they turned their attention to Britain and a few of the earliest arrivals appear to have made their fortunes in the grain trade from Odessa to London and Liverpool. The Rallis are said to have perfected a technique for accelerating the turnover of capital which essentially consisted of dispatching the bill of lading and sample of grain to the London partner ahead of the cargo, who sold it in what was currently the most profitable corn market. The sum realised could then be laid out on a return cargo of cotton piece goods, yarns or coal – and it will not escape notice that by mid-century the Levant was one of the most imporant destinations of the former.[3]

Very little is known about the capital accumulated by the leading houses, but according to a report sent to Baring Bros in 1860, Argenti had accumulated £500,000 and two Rodocanachi houses together £500,000 – £600,000. The Bank of England's assessment of the largest firm, Ralli Bros, suggests that they were two to three times as big, but that Spartali & Lascardi, the only other large firm, were worth about £100,000. The great number of Greek houses at the period (over eighty in Barings' records alone) were listed as 'small' or 'very small'; one of the more prominent of this group, Alexander Ionides, who was Greek Consul

General in London from 1854 to 1866, had a capital of about £30,000 in 1860, but the typical capital seems to have been no more than £10,000.[4] The connection between the three or four major firms and the remainder was described in the anonymous *Bubbles of Finance* in 1865:

> There are in London a vast number of small Greek firms, commission agents and other individuals. ... The great difficulty with these men is to know where to discount the paper that is remitted them from abroad, and if it were not for the wealthier firms of their own countrymen they would find it an utter impossibility to do so in London. They manage to melt their paper by taking it to one of the better known Greek firms who – '*for a consideration*' – endorse it, and pass it into their bankers with their own bills, making over the proceeds to those who give them the paper to discount. The commission charged is generally very high, often as much as nine or ten per cent for three months... of course the risk incurred by the larger house is proportionately great. If all goes well, one set of bills is provided for by fresh bills being drawn, and the wheel is thus kept rolling on. But should there be a hitch anywhere, and one bill not be met, or should a commercial crisis come on, and bills of all kinds be difficult – sometimes impossible – to discount, not only does the party who is discounting fall, but in all probability he drags down with him half a dozen firms even weaker than himself, and injures most materially the larger firm that have discounted for him, often ruining it irretrievably.[5]

By the 1830s profit margins in textiles were already modest and set on a long downward trend, so it looks rather as if Rallis and their Chian connections accumulated their fortunes serving their less fortunate compatriots than in the import–export trade. This interpretation is lent additional substance by reports that the earlier Greek migrants were men of modest substance and some integrity, entrepreneurs who were evidently able to sustain their patrons. Moreover, when Greeks of inferior means and character began to flood into London in the late 1840s and 1850s, Rallis turned to the trade to Persia and India, while Rodocanachi, Spartali and other families moved their investment into steamships, which in the innovating period were said to pay as much as 40 per cent.

The story of the Greek merchant houses has been taken far enough to make the point that acceptances and exchange were simply one option available to A1 firms in any given sector of international trade, and that such firms might move in or out of finance according to the times and opportunities. Indeed, the firm that committed itself to finance alone might easily be frowned upon for that very reason. In the case of the Greek houses, Zarifi Bros & Co. were scarcely approved of; their report read: 'Very clever and have large means, but are altogether in finance.'[6] Consequently merchants shifted all their resources into finance only if (or when) changes in the structure or conditions of trade made their traditional expertise obsolete or quite unprofitable. Though none of the house histories is prepared to concede this position, it is possible to examine it at fairly close range in one or two telling instances from other sectors of international trade.

The first Robert Benson began his mercantile career in Liverpool in 1789 in partnership with the Rathbones, and later with another well-known Quaker family, the Croppers. Benson and his various partners were a typical Liverpool merchant house, exporting piece goods to co-religionist agents in New York and importing raw cotton. In the 1820s Cropper Benson & Co. were in the premier league of cotton importers, and consequently became a respectable accepting house. Meanwhile they had turned to India and conducted a large trade through Calcutta for two generations. When the Manchester-Liverpool railway was projected the Quaker cousinhood became heavily involved and the Benson family maintained their interest in railway investment for almost a century. Seeking more capital and connections, Robert Benson II moved to London in 1853, maintaining his mercantile business with the aid of various partners, but also making some ventures in diversification, moving into the tea and tobacco trade, issuing and dealing in US railroad stocks, and joining his strength with several other small-to-medium firms in the International Financial Society in 1864. In 1870 Benson's capital stood at £110,000, but the next year he lost something between £30,000 and £50,000, and then in 1875 went bankrupt as a result of financing the exports of the Aberdare & Plymouth Iron Companies. Robert Benson III, scarcely out of college, returned hastily from New York to face the seemingly impossible task of rebuilding the old family firm without capital. He eventually succeeded in doing so by converting the old mercantile business into a highly specialised investment house. Young Benson invested the capital of connections in Liverpool, and others acquired during his Eton and Balliol education, in the Middle West. Later he advanced his position by marrying into the aristocracy and becoming one of the more successful promoters of investment trusts. However, he never built up a large capital, and down to 1960, when it united with Kleinworts, his firm remained a specialised Anglo-American investment house.[7]

Bensons may be taken as broadly representative of the smaller houses that were forced to specialise for want of adequate capital to do more. However, their experience was similar to some larger and more prestigious firms in so far as they did not begin to specialise in pure finance until forced to do so. In this respect, Antony Gibbs & Sons, the leading firm of Latin American specialists, makes a revealing case study.

In 1902 the senior partner of Gibbs reviewed his firm's long-term policy and financial position and circulated an important document among the other five partners. In it he divided the history of his firm into three periods: (1) the foundation years, 1808–c.1845, when it was basically a commission house consigning British textiles to Spain and South America; (2) the halcyon years of the famous guano monopoly, when profits were running at £80,000–£100,000 a year; and (3) the last quarter-century or so when the wealthy third-generation partners had achieved some eminence in public life but had, in their own estimation, failed to re-establish the identity of the house. Vicary Gibbs's comment on this last period is particularly pertinent to the problems of transition from merchanting to banking, not least because his firm was reckoned to be among the most successful of the nineteenth century. He disclosed that since about 1870 'Consignment business had practically ceased and the firm was forced into all sorts of enterprises of which it had no experience,' and often inadequate capital, which slipped from £1.9m. in 1866 to less than £400,000 at the end of the century. Moreover, he added, 'The business became extraordinarily various and widespread' and except 'for the one business left which the firm understood, viz. Nitrate, the business as a whole was extraordinarily speculative and unprofitable.' Part of the problem was that (as Vicary Gibbs put it) 'There was no active working head and latterly our junior members [partners] went into Parliament,' but the case serves to emphasise the point that the shift towards pure finance was no easy pre-ordained course. Like other commission houses, Gibbs acted as private bankers to many of their clients in Spain and South America, and advanced credit to both textile manufacturers in Britain and to local merchants and miners in Chile, Bolivia and Peru, but when the commission business fell away it was not obvious how the firm's experience and capital could be adapted to new opportunities. The old trade to the West Indies was shrinking in the 1870s and in 1887 the Bristol house that had conducted it was closed down. Some of the capital generated in the guano trade was diverted to establishing agencies in Melbourne and other Australian cities and opening a shipping line there, but by 1883 it was clear that this was soaking up too much capital with little return, and the antipodean enterprises were placed under increasing restraints. Gibbs opened a branch in Liverpool at a time when other acceptance houses there were closing down or moving to London, and this had to be closed in 1909. These experiences evidently raised the possibility of more activity in pure finance, but the firm's investments were not very encouraging and caused a liquidity crisis in 1876, 1884 and 1890; in 1890 the partners lost nearly £390,000 and warnings of their imperilled position were telegraphed abroad. Acceptances followed a sluggish path, topping £1m. in the late 1880s and briefly reaching £2m. just before the First World War, but showing none of the vitality of the Anglo-German houses. In this muddled situation it is not possible to identify any particular time or circumstances that set Gibbs on a secure course as a merchant bank. The most that can be safely recorded is that the partners' eminence in public life insulated the firm from some of the searching scrutiny to which less prestigious names were regularly subjected, and that Vicary Gibbs's appointment as 'working head of the business' at the turn of the century led to a steady improvement in its financial position, at any rate until the heavy losses that followed the First World War.[8]

Another striking instance of belated and feeble response can be seen in the history of the Sassoon dynasty. The founder David Sassoon, a Persian Jew who died in 1864, made a fortune of at least £2m. by taking the lead in the trade between Bombay and the so-called Treaty Ports of China. The First Opium War (1839–42) effectively opened China to British merchants, and Sassoon became the largest dealer in Indian opium and also re-exported large quantities of Lancashire cottons. The enterprising founder rather foolishly left control of his business empire in the hands of the eldest of his eight sons Abdullah (Sir Albert), who shortly settled in London. But the most energetic son was undoubtedly Elias David, who had pioneered his father's trade to Canton, Hong Kong and Shanghai. Shortly after father's death he quarrelled with his elder brother and broke away to form his own business, beginning in Bombay in 1867, and quickly extending his trade to China, Japan, Europe, America and Africa; his London office was opened in 1887. Elias's eldest son Jacob evidently inherited his father's business acumen, while Albert's son was conscientious but unadventurous. The result was that by the later Edwardian years the capital of E. D. Sassoon & Co. was two or three times that of the parent firm (£1.25m. to £1.5m. compared with a nominal £0.5m.), and the reputation of the older concern was steadily sinking. The contrast is very clear in confidential bank reports of the period. Of E. D. Sassoon it was written:

All the Eastern Banks look upon this firm as quite A1. They are very keen energetic people ... spending very little money. ... They possess very considerable property in Hong Kong and other eastern centres and do a very large trade in opium.

But David Sassoon & Co. Ltd was no longer in the same league:

The general opinion among the Eastern Banks is that this firm is perfectly good but at the same time they regard them as a more or less declining firm. In the old days the firm at one time possessed some millions of money but made very heavy losses [by risky undertakings] from time to time. ... They do a very large business in the export of opium from India to China.

From its earliest years, David Sassoon & Co. had involved itself in banking activities in India and China, and the migration of its centre of operations to London and marriage links with the Rothschilds provided ample opportunity to build on this experience. Meanwhile the opium trade came under increasing restraints as the Victorian social conscience gradually identified its habit-forming and hallucinatory effects. Both branches of the Sassoons, but more particularly the older one, were slow to respond to the openings in pure finance. They preferred their mercantile past and left much of the initiative in banking and Chinese loans to the Hong Kong & Shanghai Bank, of which they had been co-founders in 1864. Sir Albert and the brothers who stayed with him were major shareholders in the Imperial Bank of Persia but were distressed by poor returns in the early years. They made regular losses in opium and silver, while their piece goods trade suffered from over-production of Indian mills, but still failed to adapt. Though David Sassoon & Co. appeared in Skinner's *London Banks* for many years, it seems doubtful whether they ever made the full transition to a merchant bank.[9] In other words, in the nineteenth century the expression 'merchant bank', though coming into use at the end of the period, was in general less accurate than the traditional description of 'merchant'. For most of the century even the vanguard firms were at some stage in a long transitional period between merchanting and commission banking.

Joint-Stock Banking Connections

At the time that the Crédit Mobilier idea was launched in France, almost all the firms that were evolving into what later became known as merchant banks were still primarily merchants. If these merchants were going to be 'flexible' enough to match the French or German type of investment banks, they would clearly have to multiply their capital and acquire new expertise very quickly indeed, and knowledge of business history suggests that such dramatic developments happen only when existing policies are seriously challenged by the imminent collapse of traditional trade. In fact there was no serious challenge to the traditional business lines. Nishimura's *Decline of Inland Bills of Exchange in the London Money Market* (Cambridge, 1971) calculates that the volume of *foreign* bills issued in Britain doubled between 1855 and 1870 and then, after a lull, doubled again between 1890 and 1913. This rate of growth, along with the multiplication of issues, arbitrage, bullion broking and international trade in general, left ample room for development of traditional expertise. Moreover, the decline of agricultural rentals and of the 'moral' standing of landownership in the last quarter of the nineteenth century shifted landowners' interest towards investment portfolios.[10]

There can be little doubt that the very notion of the Crédit Mobilier was anathema to conventional British bankers. William Newmarch was doing little more than summarising a widespread view when he told the British Association Meeting of 1858 that it was 'an institution declaring itself to be almost entirely at variance with all that has been established by reasoning and experiment to be sound and right in institutions of this kind ... the entire concern is simply a large stock-jobbing association'.[11] The Rothschilds, as is well known, deeply resented the upstart rival; 'The House must keep up the same attitude as taken in 1848, remaining strong, wise, and cautious, while leaving to others chimerical planning of paper money, finance reform and a revival of St. Simonianism', Baron Alphonse advised his London cousins.[12] But Barings were not so hostile, and indeed Rothschilds' fury was created more by jealousy of the Pereires than invasion of principle. In fact both firms had been connected with the abortive Société commanditaire de l'Industrie, launched by Jacques Lafitte in 1825 with a proposed capital of 100m. francs (£4m.) and aims which anticipated those of the Crédit Mobilier. Barings' closest friends in London, the Glyns, were enthusiasts for joint-stock development of all kinds, while Hottinguer, their principal connection in Paris, was delighted to contemplate the vast potential of industrial investment. Bates calmly recorded, 'It appears to me that these sorts of Banks will get all the public loans and that BB & Co. must content themselves with the commission and banking business for a time.' He could afford to be complacent because for Barings loans had been little more than the gilt on the gingerbread. For all the publicity given to issues, most British merchant banks' business lay elsewhere, and from the first there was a diversity of views.[13]

There was a rash of joint-stock bank promotions in the early 1860s, a handful promoted by firms that might be classified as merchant banks. Easily the best-documented is the International Financial Society (IFS, 1863), in effect a consortium of seven respectable but second-rank concerns, Robert Benson & Co., Samuel Dobrée & Sons, Frühling & Goschen, Frederick Huth & Co., Heath & Co., George Peabody, and Stern Brothers. But the prospectus emphasised foreign loans rather than transport and industry, and as the various firms continued their family concerns, the IFS might be more accurately described as an incorporated syndicate than a Crédit Mobilier type of issue house. There were several contemporary rivals, but the London sponsors were mostly fringe concerns at the time, notably Bischoffsheim (a Paris-based house), Sassoons (at this time still based in Bombay) and Rallis who, though at the head of the Greek trading community, were still relative outsiders in the City. So far as is known, none of them were ever involved in industrial investments as such, and their liaisons seem to have been made for similar reasons to the IFS group.[14] Edward Blount and Samuel Laing are clearly important as railway financiers on the continent, but Landes's description of the latter as 'the English counterpart of the Pereires' is misleading, for their backers were French bankers. Blount devoted a chapter of his short *Memoirs* to 'Business Friendships' but does not include any London merchant bankers among them, unless Bertram Currie of Glyn Mills is included.[15] In a word, some British bankers could see the value of incorporation, but the Crédit Mobilier *ideal* of development of the industrial economy was seen as irrelevant to British needs.

The enthusiasm for incorporation, as already noticed in Chapter 4, was limited to a handful of firms. Glyns is the one firm that refused to conform to convention; the early incorporation of the firm was in fact only a sequel to a long involvement in a wide variety of joint-stock enterprises. George Carr Glyn appears as an original subscriber to the Union Bank of Australia in 1837, and in the burst of promotions in the early 1860s, he pursued its earlier interest by reconstituting the Ottoman Bank (1863) and playing a leading role in the foundation of both the London & South American Bank (1862) and the Anglo-Austrian Bank (1864). A scheme to merge Glyns with four of the principal Scots banks was aborted only at the Overend Gurney crisis when, as B. W. Currie wrote, the 'perils of unlimited liability alarmed our Scotch friends' and they withdrew. The interest receded for a time but by no means died. At the boom in promotion of banks in Russia, Currie was appointed to the board of management of the Russian Bank for Foreign Trade (1871), while Pascoe Glyn was closely connected with the incorporation of the great Australian merchant and banking house of Dalgety in 1884.[16]

The record of Glyns, as we have emphasised before, was unique, but a number of other merchant banks who absorbed some of their policies and outlook from their foreign background rather than English residence were strong contributors to the development of joint-stock banking enterprises abroad. The ramifications of some of these firms was obviously complex, and it is possible to provide only a few illustrations here. Possibly the most energetic promoter was Bischoffshem & Goldschmidt, who were connected with the foundation of the Bank of Constantinople (1856), the London & Brazilian Bank (1862), the Crédit Anglais (1862), and the Banque Franco-Egyptienne (*c.* 1870), but the centre of their operations remained in Paris so it is scarcely permissible to define them as a British concern. However, the Ralli family are known to have been connected with at least as many joint-stock banks: the Bank of Alexandria (1872), the Anglo-Foreign Banking Co. (also 1872), the

Ottoman Bank at some date after its reconstitution, and the Odessa Discount Bank (1879). Their family connection, the Rodocanachis, were associated with them in some of these ventures and were among the founders of the St Petersburg International Trade Bank (1872). The latter was also supported by Erglangers and Brandts. The most successful of the international joint-stock banks was of course ultimately the Hong Kong & Shanghai Banking Corporation, which was promoted by a consortium of British merchants trading in the area. They included the Sassoons, who were also instrumental in the foundation of the Anglo-Californian Bank (1873) and the Imperial Bank of Persia (1889). The Californian concern also involved Seligmans and Lazards, the Persian Bank Reuters and Chaplin Milne, an American house domiciled in London. The only purely English firm that can be discovered amongst these subscribers was Thomson, Bonar & Co., the Russia merchants, who appear among the founders of the Russian Bank for Foreign Trade in 1871.[17] But it must be added that by this time Thomson Bonar were not very successful and their policies were frowned on by more orthodox firms. It was reported to Barings in 1876 that while the partners were 'most respectable as to character' and were thought to possess 'considerable means', while their engagements were 'not supposed to be extended', yet 'the manner in which the business of the house has been of late years conducted has not been such as to inspire confidence in the connections they form, and their bills are not taken with the same readiness as formerly': in a word they were no longer regarded as a first-class house.[18]

However, there were a couple of British merchant banks that, defying the conventional wisdom of the age, became involved in joint-stock enterprises at an early date and presently merged their identity with them. Neither is very well documented, but the basic facts seem clear enough. J. & A. Dennistoun & Co. were a Glasgow firm involved in the transatlantic cotton trade with branch houses at London, Liverpool, New York and New Orleans and a capital of £770,000 at their bankruptcy in 1857 (Chapter 5). A. Dennistoun was a director of the Union Bank of Scotland and major shareholder in the Liverpool Borough Bank; the former connection certainly gave them access to a good deal of easy credit when they needed it. The bankruptcy of the Borough Bank, in which they had some £200,000 invested, had been the prime cause of Dennistoun's temporary insolvency, but their long-term decline was more closely connected with the ending of the old mercantile system. In 1913 they sold the remaining business to the German Bank of London Ltd, which had been established in 1879 to finance Anglo-German trade. John Dennistoun had been a director of the Bank for some years, and the name was changed to the London and Liverpool Bank of Commerce Ltd, which it was said would 'correspond more closely with the nature of the Bank's operations'.[19]

The other old banking family whose name was prominent on the board of directors was that of Schuster, and the limited evidence suggests that they, rather than the Dennistouns, were the dynamic element. The Schusters were an old Jewish banking family at Frankfurt who, like the Rothschilds, sent one of their more able sons to Manchester to extend their connections in 'Cottonopolis'. Leo Schuster became one of the town's most successful merchants and manufacturers, a Christian evangelical, one of the 'highly respectable' directors of the Manchester & Salford Bank, and presently of the Union Bank of London, with which his firm had close relations almost from its foundation. One of his brothers opened a warehouse in Bradford, and when Prussia annexed Frankfurt in 1866 his nephew, Francis Joseph, moved to London to take charge of Schuster, Son & Co. in the City. The firm's capital at this time was about £800,000. By the end of the 1860s the Union Bank was already one of the top dozen firms engaged in transatlantic finance, and the only member of this élite that had started life as a joint-stock venture; it is easy to suppose that it owed its unique position to the close connection with Schusters. At any rate, in 1887 the family firm merged with the Union Bank and Francis's son Felix, who had just been elected to the board, was its governor from 1896 to 1918. As Sir Felix Schuster he became one of the foremost advocates of bank amalgamation. At the close of the nineteenth century, according to *The Times,*

> many of the private banks were ill-fitted to withstand any violent and widespread strain. It seemed to Schuster that concentration of resources was necessary in the national interest. With this aim he negotiated with the proprietors of Smith, Payne and Smith and of their allied firms, which in 1902, largely through the help of Mr. Martin Ridley Smith, resulted in the amalgamation of those old and well-established businesses with the Union Bank. It greatly increased Schuster's reputation. It was followed by similar operations with the London and Yorkshire Bank ... and with Messrs. Prescott, Dimsdale and Co. Some smaller private banks were also absorbed. The coping stone was put on this policy when in 1919 Lord Inchcape and Schuster matured a scheme for welding together in one institution the National Provincial Bank of England and the Union of London and Smiths Bank.

As we noticed at various points through this book, Smith, Payne & Smith also retained a quantity of the kind of business usually associated with merchant banks. Consequently the amalgamation created a colossus that had traditional strength in this area as well as the kind of High Street banking usually asssociated with its name, a worrying precedent for the future of merchant banking.[20]

The Disintegration of the Old Cotton Trade

We noticed in previous chapters that although most of the transatlantic trade passed through Liverpool and (to a much lesser extent) Glasgow, as much as nine-tenths of the bills were discounted in the City of London. From the end of the eighteenth century there were banks in Liverpool, Manchester and the satellite towns conducting a large business in bills through their London agents, and no doubt most merchants were content to delegate their financial business to them. But there were at least two reasons why they might like to open direct connections with London: the early provincial banks (as we have seen) often proved unstable, and the bank rate in Liverpool was always 1 per cent above that in London, so that if his volume of bills was constantly large, it might pay a merchant to open his own 'bill office' in the City. It seems to have been a common practice for merchants to discount their bills with 'monied persons in London and other parts of the country' and the opening of a 'bill office' simply set this on a more formal and regular basis. It is impossible to say when the practice began, or how extensive it was at any particular time.[21]

The railway, steamship and telegraph, with their regular and reliable dispatches, inaugurated the modern system of easy communications, but in the long period the consequences were by no means to the advantage of the merchant. 'In the old times it was so uncertain when goods would be received that it was absolutely essential to keep large stocks always on hand; therefore great merchants with very immense capitals grew up, owning vast warehouses in which valuables of all kinds were stored for gradual use', it was explained in 1903. But when easy direct relations could be established between the producer and consumer, the merchant became redundant and by the turn of the century was 'rapidly ceasing to exist'.[22]

In the first half of the nineteenth century, cotton textiles were the most important commodity in British trade and so most affected by these changes. We have already noticed that several Liverpool and Manchester cotton merchants became merchant bankers at one time or another through the period, so it will occasion little surprise that there was a direct connection between the decline of mercantile stockholding and the migration of merchants to London, but the effects were not immediate or dramatic. Figure 8.1 shows the trend in cotton stocks between the close of the Napoleonic War and 1884. Total stocks are divided between those at the mills and those at the ports (mostly Liverpool) to show that the latter was the fluctuating element. At the beginning of the period illustrated, stocks were at a high level not merely because of the generally poor communications just described, but also because war conditions (particularly the Napoleonic blockade) had produced some dramatic shifts of supply and prices which had encouraged speculation, and much

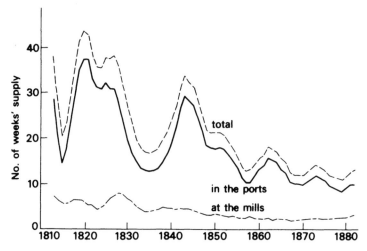

Fig. 8.1   *Stock of cotton in Great Britain 1813–82 (five-year moving average)*

money was borrowed to finance such speculative holdings.[23] The deep trough of the 1830s appears to be a reaction against the 'expensive habits' acquired during the war and early postwar years; such shifts of commercial view were equally characteristic of the period of poor communications. The steep rise in stockholding from the middle 1830s to the early 1840s was evidently connected with the dramatic rise of joint-stock banking in Liverpool and Manchester (see Chapter 2), the extension of credit giving power to 'persons of small capital' to hold stocks for more favourable markets, but as credit tightened stockholding embarked on a long downward course, interrupted only by the burst of speculative stockholding during the American Civil War (1861–5).[24] The conclusion of the war was followed by the inauguration of the transatlantic cable service (1866), which proved to be the most potent factor in restructuring the industry. Manufacturers in Britain and on the continent now bought their cotton by cable on samples previously sent to them from New Orleans, Mobile, Charleston and the other exporting ports. The system by which Liverpool merchant houses received cotton on consignment and then distributed it to brokers for sale became redundant and the old mercantile families were compelled to change their character radically or retire from business. From the old-style merchant the prospects in the cotton trade were particularly discouraging at this period as he had watched the commission slip from 3 per cent (2.5 per cent to the merchant and 0.5 per cent to the broker) down to 2 per cent (divided 1.5 to 0.5) then 1 per cent, and most of this decline took place in the twelve or fifteen years after 1870. Moreover, the trade in the early postwar years lurched from one problem to another, a distressing experience to those who were accustomed to more comfortable conditions of business.[25]

Faced with the collapse of the traditional type of mercantile activity, a few of the wealthier cotton importers discerned that they might remain in business by moving into pure finance. They had a long experience of acceptance business, for the difficulty of obtaining commissions from the late 1840s onwards had led merchants to import on their own account and to offer credit to their American suppliers. And they were accustomed to the practice of investing their surplus capital in loans and securities and dealing with seasonal liquidity problems, which was also invaluable experience for entering merchant banking on a continuous basis. A small but interesting group of cotton merchants in Liverpool, Manchester and Glasgow now made the transition from trade to finance and from the provinces to the City.[26]

Scarcely any of this group have left any records so the easiest way of chronicling this transition is to identify when they moved to London. The earliest migrant appears to have been Robert Benson, formerly a partner in the Quaker firm of Cropper, Benson & Co. of Liverpool, whose career was surveyed in the first part of this chapter. The subscribers to his railway investments included numbers of Liverpool mercantile families, the Croppers, Ewarts, Corries and others. He was followed by the old Glasgow firm of Dennistoun, Cross & Co. also noted above. In the early 1860s four of the best-known Liverpool firms opened London offices: Ogilvy Gillanders & Co. (run by members of the Gladstone family) in 1860, Brown Shipley & Co. in 1863, and Rathbone Bros & Co, in 1864, and Fraser, Trenholme & Co, in 1866. James Finlay & Co. of Glasgow followed in 1871 and two well-known Manchester firms of Frankfurt origin, Benecke Souchay & Co. and Schuster, Son & Co. around the same time. For varying periods of time, these firms ran their North of England or Scottish operations in parallel with their London business, but they were declined as international finance became increasingly centred on London.[27]

The decision to concentrate business in London can be studied at close range in the important case of Brown, Shipley & Co. Though the City office was not opened until the end of 1863 and the firm's business continued to be based overwhelmingly on transatlantic commerce, for most of the 1870s and 1880s London acceptances were 80–90 per cent of the firm's total, and the Liverpool office was losing money steadily. It was only family ties and sentiment that kept the Liverpool office open as long as it was. The 1870s and 1880s also saw the London merchant banks closing their Liverpool offices; Huths in 1877, Gibbs in 1881, Schröders in 1884 and Barings in 1891; only Kleinworts struggled on in Liverpool, trying with little success to move from cotton into cocoa, rubber and other 'new' commodities. Diversification became more difficult when the opening of the Manchester Ship Canal (1894) gave the newly created port the initiative in the new commodities of international trade.[28]

Before finally leaving the northern merchants to focus on developments in London, it is useful to record that a few of them were still conducting some banking operations alongside their trade in the traditional way down to the end of the period covered by this book. An interesting survival is Schunk & Co., a firm whose forebears, the various Souchay partnerships, were mentioned in an earlier chapter, and one of the earliest and most prosperous German houses in Manchester. In the Edwardian period they still flourished, with offices in London, Leeds and Manchester, 'doing a large merchant business and a little banking'. They never appeared in Skinner's lists but their capital (£150,000 – £200,000) was quite as large as the smaller merchant bankers, and their reputation quite as sound. Evidently they preferred to maintain their main interest in textile exports and general importing, though the greater part of their trade shifted from Europe to the Far East.[29]

Far Eastern Houses become Investment Groups

Cotton is easily the best-documented British trade but versions of the restructuring just identified can be discerned in other branches of world commerce. The main difference appears to be that merchants that had built up an intimate knowledge of underdeveloped economies had more opportunities of investing their capital in estate development, transport and perhaps factories in those countries. A review of the range of directorships held by merchant bankers in 1914 (Appendix 2) indicates that this was a widespread response. It had of course, been a common if ill-advised practice for some decades to make occasional local investments to secure clients or other openings (see Chapters 2 and 3), but in the earlier period such commitments were undertaken reluctantly as exceptions to a general policy of not 'locking up' the firm's limited capital. Records are sparse, but in several instances it is possible to trace a few details illustrating the revision of this traditional policy.

The best-documented case study must be that of James Finlay & Co., a firm of Glasgow merchants that began its long history at the middle of the eighteenth century. In the age of Arkwright the firm became importers of raw cotton and exporters of piece goods. Kirkman Finlay bought the well-known cotton mills at Ballindalloch (1798), Catrine (1801) and Deanston (1806) and built up a major trading connection with Ritchie, Steuart & Co. of Bombay, and with Dent & Co. in China. Tea, silk and other oriental goods were taken for return cargoes from the Far East. In

1837 Finlay wrote to his son in Bombay warning him against any interest in banking:

> Banking business when carried on *safely* is a very unprofitable business, and when done *wildly* – that is, a mass of business with little capital – is a most hazardous one. I therefore always refused every proposal made to me to be a Banker ... it is a business easily got into, but most exceedingly difficult to get out of. ... It is much to be feared that many of the Bills to come from the East will be quite valueless, and probably be returned, for I cannot suppose that Geo. Wildes & Co. or T. Wilson & Co. can ultimately weather the storm. I hope the others may, and I am led to believe that Barings will stand firm under every shock, but they are very wide and wild and must lose very largely.

His caution was characteristic of the better-conducted merchant houses of the period and, of course, was well justified in the stormy period of commercial credit through which he was passing.

Profit margins in cotton spinning were already under pressure in the 1830s, and in the next two or three decades the relentless competition of Lancashire squeezed the remaining Scottish industry into a corner. Under these circumstances it is not surprising that a new generation of Finlays looked for more profitable outlets for their enterprise, and eventually found it in expanding the Indian trade, and particularly the tea trade in which they had a traditional interest. But the suddenness of their conversion to financing the trade needs further explanation. Until the early 1870s the Glasgow office was opposed in principle to making advances to tea growers, or to locking up capital in estates; evidently Kirkman Finlay's policy was loyally adhered to. But by the end of the decade his firm were acting as agents for some sixteen tea estates, 'and capital investment soon transformed James Finlay & Co. from being merely agents to being principals.'

In the 1860s the last of the Finlay family retired from the business and control passed to Sir John Muir. According to the firm's official historian.

> It was John Muir who was responsible for initiating and carrying through the policy of large scale tea estate ownership. He had decided that the normal trading of the Company gave insufficient employment to the capital available and a too restricted prospect of securing profits. He considered that tea was a good investment for the surplus and it became his policy to make advances to estates in order to secure agency appointments.

By 1898 the Finlay group had £4.36m. invested in tea estates where they employed some 70,000 workers. They also invested heavily in Calcutta jute mills from 1873, in shipping from 1882 and Bombay cotton mills from 1902, and held Indian agencies for various London insurance groups. The merchant banking side of their activities, which is barely mentioned in the firm's history, appears to have been confined to making advances in the tea trade, and was evidently only one wing of their manifold interests. The Finlay group might be of only passing interest if their pattern of development was not paralleled in several other firms, though often on a later and more modest scale. The broad outline of the history of several of these firms is known.[30]

In the context of the Far Eastern trade, the 1860s is of particular significance for two reasons. One is that the period from 1850 to 1866 was one of great prosperity in the tea and silk trades, but after that competition intensified with the advent of the ocean steamer, the opening of the Suez Canal, the telegraph, and easy credits from Western banks in China. The other factor was that changes in the law governing joint-stock companies now made it easy for private trading partnerships to sponsor limited liability companies that were in fact dependent, but in law financially autonomous, so containing the risks involved in estate and factory developments. Muir was probably the earliest to realise the possibilities of this radical change in the law, quite likely because of his Scottish background, where the legal structure had traditionally been more favourable to this kind of development. But it was left to other Far Eastern houses to extract the maximum advantage from the opportunity.

The most enterprising exponents of what we may term the 'joint-stock subsidiary' were undoubtedly Jardine, Matheson & Co., originally a merchant house in the China trade. Short of capital for the transition from sail to steam, they incorporated the China Coast Steam Navigation Co. in Hong Kong in 1873 with a capital of some £120,000. Encouraged by their success, they formed the Yangtze Steam Navigation in 1879 and then turned to the London capital market for the £450,000 needed for the Indo-China Steam Navigation Co. in 1881. But in the meantime Jardine Matheson & Co. had begun to explore possibilities in banking, insurance, silk reeling, sugar refining, mining, railways and cotton mills. In thirty years or so of apparently boundless enterprise, they produced such varied joint-stock subsidiaries as the Hong Kong Fire Insurance Co. (1868), the China Sugar Refining Co. (1878), the EWO Spinning Co., Shanghai (1895), the Jardine Spinning & Weaving Co., Hong Kong (1897) and, most important of all, the British and Chinese Corporation (1898), a joint venture with the Hong Kong and Shanghai Bank to build railways in China. On present evidence,. the total capital committed to all these varied ventures cannot even be guessed at; the parent firm's capital of £1.72m. in 1891 was obviously only a fraction of its total interests. The rift between Jardine Matheson and the bank had been bridged in 1877, when one of Matheson's energetic partners (William Keswick) was appointed a bank director, and after that there was no shortage of loan funds. In this way Jardine Matheson maintained its mercantile interests in the Far East, but developed rapidly into an investment house or (in present-day terms) an investment group. By the end of the century the capital it controlled through its satellite companies must have been many times that of the parent house. As we saw in the last chapter, acceptances were a negligible part of their business; the evolution from merchanting had followed a very different path from the London-based merchant banks. However, it must not be supposed that all other firms operating in India and the Far East all followed more or less the same line of development.[31]

The clearest case study of a firm that made the transition from trade to finance more conventionally than Finlays and Jardine Matheson is that of Wallace Brothers, a Scots house that started in the usual way shipping textile piece goods and importing jute and raw cotton, but made its mark as the pioneer of the Burma teak trade. Towards the end of the 1880s the business had so increased in size that the two remaining brothers decided they would cease to be involved in the day-to-day running to concentrate on directing overall policy and controlling their credit to rice growers, textile manufactures and chartering ships. Their fixed capital investment in Burmese forests was limited by the flotation of the Bombay Burma Trading Company in 1863, and it was not until the Edwardian era that they became heavily involved in rubber estates in Johore, in railways and docks in India, and in two cotton mills near Bombay, finally turning to tea estates just before the First World War. At incorporation in 1911 the firm 'had long since derived the bulk of their income and profits not from dealings in merchandise but from commission, from financing a variety of adventures, and from banking operations on behalf of their clients and constituents'. Like Jardine Matheson, Wallaces had powerful financial backing. From their origins they had close links with the National Bank of Scotland and the Commercial Bank of India, with one or more of the brothers sitting on the respective boards. The National Bank provided acceptance credits, the ceiling on which was raised from £0.5m. in 1911 to £1m. in 1914, leaving Wallaces to concentrate their capital on managing their investments.[32]

Ogilvy, Gillanders & Co., a less well-documented case study, fits in the chronology half way between Finlays and Wallaces. When Henry Neville Gladstone (a son of W. E. G.) became a Calcutta partner of Ogilvy, Gillanders & Co. in 1881 he recognised that the old shipping agency and consigment business could no longer be relied on as a mainstay of the firm's business in India and as a result of his policy the firm devoted more attention to the development of local industries. Gladstone successfully launched the Hooghly Jute Mills Co. (1883) and the French Mill at

Chandenagor (1895), while his initiative brought the firm its first sterling loan, £475,000 for the Bettiah Raj. One of his successors in Calcutta, W. B. Gladstone, developed the firm's export trade from the Indian port, no doubt with the aid of acceptances provided by the Liverpool and London partners.[33] In 1908 it was reported that the firm's capital, now all owned by the Gladstone family, was £0.75m., 'a good deal of which is locked up in mills in India'. Other leading companies in Far Eastern trade and finance were also making heavy fixed capital investments during this period. Some of these firms appear in Skinner's lists of private bankers while others, engaged in much the same activities, do not. Thus R. & J. Henderson, 'East India merchants' established in 1818, and also listed as bankers, were by the Edwardian period principally engaged as financial and selling agents of the Borneo Co., in which they were the largest shareholders.[34] Guthrie & Co., the oldest firm in Singapore, were *not* listed as bankers but made money by several successful flotations of rubber plantation companies. Harrisons & Crosfield, also unlisted, promoted new issues for tea estates and tobacco firms in India and Java, Borneo timber and Japanese silk.[35]

Russian Investments

British trade to Russia through the Baltic was dominated by a small number of old-established mercantile families until the middle of the century, and a handful of these eventually became involved in acceptances and a few issues according to the now-familiar pattern. The best known names are E. H. Brandt & Co., Egerton Hubbard & Co. and Thomson Bonar & Co. of London, and De Jersey of Manchester. They not only conducted a general mercantile business but also at one time or another owned ships and factories – sugar mills in the case of Brandts and cotton mills in the case of the other three.[36] It has already been stressed that mercantile and banking experience emphasised the importance of liquidity, and in this instance the conventional wisdom proved all too right. De Jerseys had to stop payment in 1847, pulling down their London correspondents Thomas, Son & Lefevre with them, while W. Brandt & Sons of London, St Petersburg, Riga and Archangel became insolvent in 1861, and both Hubbards and Thomson Bonar were sporadically in difficulties and rather slipped into the second rank of merchant houses.

Nevertheless, out of this battering there emerged one of the strongest and most enterprising financial and industrial enterprises of the period, that of De Jersey and Baron Ludwig Knoop of Bremen. The details of this concern are worth reconstructing to show how an exceptional entrepreneur, starting with little capital, could defy some of the most respected canons of merchant banking to establish one of the most remarkable businesses of the age. The concern effectively began in Manchester in 1825 with C. B. De Jersey (a native of Guernsey with a little capital) and J. A. Frericks of Hamburg uniting to export cotton twist to Russia on a 'very considerable' scale. They needed capital to contract with numerous small spinners of Oldham and Rochdale with whom they dealt and so drew on John Thomas & Son (later Thomas, Son & Lefevre) a London merchant house in the Russian trade. The bankruptcy of this house was fairly anticipated in a critical bank report in 1846:

> A1 in the eyes of the world, but a degree of caution should be exercised, there is too much pig upon bacon as they generally pay by 3 mo. dfts. of their own house in Russia on their own House here.

By this time the London and Manchester houses were working together as exporters of textile machinery to Russia, and were supposed to be the largest firm in this new line at their bankruptcy in 1847. Despite the liabilities of over £600,000, the bankruptcy seems to have been little more than a setback.[37] One of their young clerks, Ludwig Knoop of Bremen, had managed to circumvent the ban on machinery exports and by 1842, when the restrictions were lifted, already had a reputation in Moscow and London. He was able to extract an agreement from Platt Bros for an exclusive agency in Russia, and no doubt on this basis was able to re-establish his firm's credit. The De Jersey name was retained, but this was in fact a front for Knoop's operations in the North of England, while more capital was brought in by William Berkfeld & Co. In 1875 it was reported that H. S. Lefevre & Co., the London merchant bankers, were now so closely allied with De Jersey (that is Knoop) and Berkfeld that 'it is impossible to say which is the most responsible of the three.' By 1870 it was guessed that De Jersey's capital was about half a million and a dozen years later not less than £1m., 'which is not too large for their enormous business.' (In 1914 the firm was incorporated with a capital of £1.25m.) They were regularly reported as 'speculative', a sure indication of a pushing firm.[38]

The main part of this capital was employed in building and equipping over 120 cotton mills in Russia between 1840 and Knoop's death in 1894. At the same time Knoop secured his sources of supply by opening a house at Bombay (1864–87) and in New York (1858), with branches in New Orleans, Charleston, Savannah and Mobile; the overall structure of his business empire is depicted in Figure 8.2. He developed an enviable capacity to fraternise with and judge the trustworthiness of his Russian customers and grant safe credits on behalf of his principals in Manchester and London. His New York house had some of its trade with Europe underwritten by Rothschilds. Knoop's Russian connections suggested

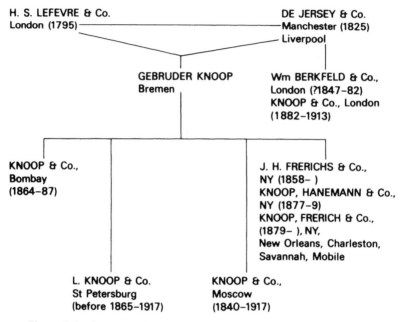

Figure 8.2   *Structure of Baron Ludwig Knoop's enterprises c. 1847–94*
Sources: Brandt Circulars 1858 p. 61, 1863 p. 109, 1864 p. 263, 1865 p. 466

another profitable line: his firm bought up cotton mills which were in themselves sound but had fallen on difficult times and ceased to be profitable. It secured representation on the board of directors of these mills and provided the necessary credit and skilled managers and foremen from England to re-establish their profitability. In later years this enterprise was supported by W. Brandt's Son & Co., the old-established firm of Russia merchants and merchant bank already referred to, and in a few instances led to joint ownership.[39]

In this instance, as in several others noticed in this chapter, merchant banks with less able leadership often followed the pacemakers without fully recognising the problems of new business. Egerton, Hubbard & Co., the Russian house of John Hubbard & Co., founded the Anglo-Russian Cotton Company to acquire the share capital of three mills in 1897. But the £470,000 investment was soon losing money and had to appeal to London for support.[40] Ludwig Knoop's financial sponsors prospered on his intimate association with the Russian manufacturing classes, his direct connections with machinery manufacturers and the principal cotton markets in New York, Bombay, Manchester and Liverpool, and his good sense in declining to lock up his capital in a few concerns. This was evidently a rare combination.

South Africa

Until the last two decades of the nineteenth century, the entrepreneurs who migrated to the City from abroad were largely Europeans (Dutch, French, Germans and Greeks) plus a sprinkling of Americans. The discovery of diamonds at Kimberley and gold on the Rand generated great wealth for a handful of settlers with the business connections and acumen to exploit the pioneer situation, and presently some part of their fortunes made its way to London. In the context of the rise of merchant banking, the story of these men is particularly interesting on two accounts, partly because their extraordinary careers telescoped the usual long transition from trade to pure finance into a very short period of years, and also because of the vast fortunes they made, which overshadowed those of most other firms described in this book.

The principal Rand houses that opened in London were Wernher Beit & Co. in 1889 and Barnato Bros soon afterwards. Julius Wernher went out to Kimberley in 1871 sponsored by Jules Porges, a Parisian diamond merchant, and quickly made himself master of the difficult art of buying diamonds. In 1876 he persuaded his principal to visit Kimberley, and as a result they started to acquire claims from the numerous small prospectors. As their holdings continued to grow, Wernher needed help and so in 1882 took Alfred Beit as partner. Beit had come out in 1875 as representative of a Hamburg merchant but set up on his own three years later. In 1884 Porges and Wernher opened a branch in London, but this was only an outlet for South African diamonds until Cecil Rhodes and the Rothschilds forged the various Kimberley groups into a monopoly. The success of De Beers Consolidated Mines immediately hoisted the price of shares, laying the foundation of the fortunes of the principal shareholders, and more particularly the 'Life Governors' of the company. When Jules Porges retired in 1889, his company was reconstituted as Wernher, Beit & Co., and the London office advertised its initial capital as £2m.[41]

The other well-known name in the De Beers amalgamation was Barney Barnato, the younger son of an East End Jewish dealer who went out to the Cape in 1873 at the age of 20 and steadily accumulated capital by buying and selling diamonds. It is said that his first break came when he bought an old nag from a seasoned dealer and allowed the horse to make its own way round the dealer's select clientele. By degrees he came to know every claim on the Diamond Fields and every turn of the reef, and used his knowledge to buy up more and more plots, which came cheaply when digging through the soft yellow earth reached the dense blue substratum, which was so much more difficult for small prospectors to work. Barnato consolidated his holdings into the Kimberley Central Company while his friend Cecil Rhodes pursued a parallel path at De

Beers mine. The South African diamond monopoly formed in 1888 had a market value of £23m., and from this apparently impregnable base both men were able to move on to make heavy investments in the then 'new frontier' gold-mining town of Johannesburg.

In 1880 Barnato made the first of a sequence of return visits to London, establishing the firm of Barnato Bros as diamond merchants and later merchant bankers. Buoyed up by the investment boom of the 1880s, the price of diamond mine shares rose quickly: De Beers shares shot up from £3 10s in 1883 to £42 in 1888, and Barnato was in his element. He had 'a genius for stock exchange manipulations which made him the most important operator in "Kaffirs" until no-one could hope to bring out a new venture, no matter how good it might be, without his help to make the market. ... The result was, as he himself frankly admitted, that he made more money by aiding or frustrating the plans of others ... than by the long years of unremitting attention to his own [mining] projects', his earliest biographer conceded. His most recent biographers adds that Barnato harboured an early but ill-formed ambition to enter banking; 'What he seemed to have in mind was a grandiose hybrid of pawn shop and company promotion rather than normal banking service.'[42]

The fortunes of the Rand houses were multiplied in the 'Kaffir boom' of 1894–5, an inflation of share values that *The Economist* believed was partly engineered by these firms, and which this sober journal thought was unprecedented in the history of Stock Exchange speculative movements. As the boom peaked, Lewis Michell, the Cape Town head of the Standard Bank, estimated the capital of the ten leading Rand operators at £33m., of which Beit was supposed to be worth £13m. and Barnato Bros £8m., but these figures could well be underestimated for Barnato himself calculated he was worth £20m. at this time. However, even on a conservative estimate, the capital of the Rand's 'top ten' was half that of the City merchant banking establishment (Table 4.2) and they simply could not be ignored. Seen from the Rand side, there were two motives for shifting from diamond and bullion dealing and mining investments towards finance in the more specialised sense. For one thing, Kimberley and the Rand evidently had more capital than it could digest locally; for instance the Standard Bank's Transvaal deposits rose rapidly to £5m. in the autumn of 1895, but its local advances were less than £0.75m., including advances against gold. Wernher Beit invested heavily in the Rand Mines Co. and Barnato in his Johannesburg Consolidated Investment Co., while the other major Rand capitalist, J. B. Robinson (who in 1895 was said to be worth £8m.) launched his South African Banking Corporation, but the course of share values was so erratic that they all looked for more stable incomes. Wernher Beit diversified into British and US government bonds, US railroad stocks, and shares in industrial companies (particularly German ones), but it should be emphasised that they by no means gave up the bullion trade; as we saw in Chapter 2, at the turn of the century they emerged as the leading exporters of South African gold, forwarding to Rothschilds who refined the metal and placed it on the London market.[43] Barnato Bros was largely interested in the diamond trade until after the First World War, when Soloman Barnato Joel (the 'Ace of Diamonds') diversified his firm's interests by investing heavily in a chain of restaurants, a brewery, a leading cotton manufacturer, the London underground transport system, and real estate in the capital. His initiative in home trade and industry was not popular with the contemporary press but was soon followed by other City investment banks.

Kimberley and the Rand threw up other less well-known financiers who at one time or another launched new merchant banks in London. Sigismund Neumann migrated from his native Bavaria to South Africa in the early 1870s to become a diamond buyer, and participated in the enterprises of other capitalists. In 1895 he was already the fourth largest Rand operator with a capital of £2.5m, and he was still busy buying up blocks of property and shares to create or increase his interest in diverse mining companies. In 1907 he went into partnership with Martin Luebeck, who had been manager of the London branch of the Dresdner Bank, as Neumann, Luebeck & Co., merchant bankers, withdrawing part of his capital from the Rand to launch out as an issuing and accepting house. Ernst Friedlander came of an old family of Berlin bankers but spent the early part of his career in South Africa where he claimed to have established the first merchant bank and later became Chairman of the Johannesburg Stock Exchange. He moved to London in 1912 to join Jules Singer's firm of stockbrokers. Singer & Friedlander commenced as bankers during the early years of the First World War when the partners, like all Stock Exchange members of German origin, were asked to resign.[44]

Only the last of these four firms lasted more than a few years in the City. What is interesting about them, in the broad context of the history of merchant banking, is that from very modest origins they and their connections were able to dominate the diamond and goldfields, preventing or discouraging Europe's existing financial houses from taking a firm grip on the mines' capital structure. London merchant banks were not 'all powerful' and the City was not an exclusive society, and it was still perfectly possible for entrepreneurs with specific expertise to find and maintain a niche there.

9 Consortiums and Syndicates

The thirty years or so before the First World War is associated with some fairly dramatic increases in the scale and organisation of industry which might be expected to have had far-reaching implications for the techniques of international trade and finance. Though the pace of industrial change was now set in the USA and Germany rather than in Britain, the London merchant banks had worldwide interests and could not isolate themselves from these changes even if they had wished to do so. It is important to inquire how these family-based mercantile organisations coped with the new challenges of growth of scale.

The data assembled in Tables 9.1 and 9.2 enable us to make some initial assessment of the merchant banks' capability by comparing their capital with that of rival concerns. Though information is incomplete, it seems that the median capital of a merchant bank in 1900 was of the order of £0.5m. – £0.6m. and in 1914 £1m.[1] Table 9.1 shows that this was not strikingly different from the merchant banks' most immediate British rivals, the group of international banks and of imperial banks. Some of the leading deposit banks already had substantially larger capitals (Table 9.2) but of course these concerns had no significant interest in the specialisms traditionally conducted by the merchant banks.[2] Measured by capital size, the latter only look inferior to the giant investment banks built up in Germany in this period (Table 9.3).

It might easily be supposed that the merchant banks attempted to meet the challenge of size by a sequence of mergers and take-overs paralleling

Table 9.1 *Capital of British imperial and international banks 1895 – 1900 and 1910–15*

| | *1895–1900* | | | *1910–15* | | |
	no.	capital	av.	no.	capital	av.
Imperial banks	19	£12.94m.	£0.68m.	18	£15.38m.	£0.85m.
International banks	25	£16.50m.	£0.66m.	24	£19.78m.	£0.82m.

Sources: A. S. J. Baster, *The Imperial Banks* (1929) p. 269, and *The International Banks* (1935) p. 245. Data for the imperial banks refer to 1895 and 1915, that for the international banks to 1900 and 1910. Both series change very gradually down to the First World War.

Table 9.2 *The growth of joint-stock banks in London, 1865-1915*

	no. of banks	total capital (where disclosed)	average capital per bank
1865	51	£26.2m. (51)	£0.513m.
1875	57	£38.2m. (55)	£0.694m.
1885	100	£236.2m. (92)	£2.568m.
1895	116	£316.7m. (108)	£2.933m.
1904–5	118	£401.0m. (109)	£3.679m.
1914–15	157	£490.1m. (137)	£3.577m.

Sources: 1865-75: *The Joint Stock Companies' Directory* (1865); *The London Banks and Kindred Companies* (from 1866). 1885-1915: Thomas Skinner, *The London Banks and Kindred Companies and Firms* (1885, 1895, 1904-5, 1914-15).

Notes:
(a) Figures cited here are intended to be paid-up capital; the published data do not always however make this explicit.
(b) A few joint-stock banks failed to record their capital. The total number recorded is represented in parentheses in column 3.
(c) Column 4 has been calculated by dividing total capital by the no. of banks disclosing this information (col. 3).

the amalgamation movement in the joint-stock banks. It is possible to discover a few instances of take-overs – for instance when Barings took control of Finlay Hodgson & Co., in 1867 and Morris Prevost in 1914, or Blyth, Greene & Jourdain acquired Benecke, Souchay & Co. (the old Manchester Huguenot house) in 1894 or Huths took over Melville Fickus in 1902 – but they are few and far between and appear to have been caused by the failure of the male line in small family partnerships rather than by the pressures of economic change.[3] We have already noticed two or three instances of London merchant banks merging with younger joint-stock concerns, notably when Schuster & Son (Manchester and London) joined with the Union Bank of London in 1887, or when the German Bank took over Dennistoun, Cross & Co. 1913, but again these developments were quite unusual and were more connected with personal and family needs than the necessities of economic change. Indeed down to the First World War, *dis*integration of firms included in Skinner's lists was evidently much more characteristic than integration, several well-known firms dividing as a result of differences between the partners – Arbuthnots, Rallis, Brandts, Sassoons, Rodoconachis, to name only those most obvious in the directories.[4] So far as concentration of capital is concerned, the only significant development in this group was the migration of several Liverpool, Manchester and Glasgow firms to

London, examined in the last chapter. As we have seen, the northern business dwindled with the decline of the merchant in the cotton trade. This development, that is to say, was prompted by underemployed capital (in its northern home) rather than by any restructuring of this sector of the money market. The actual numbers of merchant banks were increasing down to 1914 (Table 4.1), and there is no evidence of any movement to reshape the growing industry or its component firms.

The merchant banks appear to have had little difficulty in recruiting the capital they needed, simply because they made more use of two familiar sources and opened up a third, that is they made good use of monied connections (mostly relatives), they made increasing use of syndicates, and in later years they borrowed heavily from joint-stock banks and insurance companies. In this chapter each of these will in turn be examined more closely.

Family and Personal Connections

Students of the industrial revolution period of British economic history are familiar with the idea of family and personal connections constituting the principal source of capital, and it comes as no surprise that this traditional practice was maintained in family-dominated businesses in the City, and indeed wherever British interests were operating. Thus the six great agency houses in Calcutta – the group that collapsed in the early 1830s – were the usual depositories of a great portion of the savings of British residents in India. At the height of their prosperity in the early 1820s it is said that they could almost make their own terms with their depositors, and that they had large sums in their hands on which they paid 4 – 5 per cent, and which they lent at 12. In much the same way, Gibbs seem to have easily attracted deposits in Chile, while Edward Blount (the railway banker) was offered large sums on deposit by English gentlemen resident in Paris. Rothschilds and Huths achieved the same end by holding large sums for European royalty, and Barings were in the habit of holding large deposits on behalf of their 'friends' and foreign governments, and continental clients. These large deposits, a partner in Brown Shipley enviously observed in 1880, 'enables them to take up a large amount of their acceptances when they see it to be convenient.'[5]

It must be emphasised that the importance of such personal connections by no means disappeared as the century advanced, particularly in the case of the smaller firms. Thus in 1879 we read that David Sassoon & Co. have 'large sums on deposit in their hands and employ them in the East', presumably by this date in building cotton mills as well as extending their trade. Barings believed that although Sassoons 'would not obtain credit for any considerable sum in London', the partners were 'considered to have the opportunities of employing money at high rates in India.' Some further examples serve to illustrate the point that a merchant bank with good family and personal connections did not need to have a large capital.[6]

In an earlier chapter Robert Benson & Sons was mentioned as a striking instance of a merchant house that was forced to contract to the small proportions of an investment house in 1875 when the founder lost his capital. His son R. H. Benson resurrected the business by joining John Walter Cross (lately of Dennistoun, Cross & Co.) to augment his small capital and improve his US connections. His major real asset was his Eton and Balliol education, and an impetus to his business came when he married a sister of Sir George Holford of Westonbirt Arboretum fame, and of Dorchester House, W1, while his sister married Earl Grey. These connections brought him into that small cosy upper-class élite that possessed sufficient wealth to make frequent and substantial investments, and whom he now served as a kind of financial consultant.[7] As also mentioned above, John Hubbard & Co. were Russia merchants responsible for a £0.5m. investments in three cotton mills in that country. In 1903-5 Egerton Hubbard (second Lord Addington) was writing to his son-in-law, the Welsh industrialist Lord Rendel, seeking further capital for his Russian enterprises.[8] In the present state of evidence, further family sources of capital can only be inferred rather than demonstrated. Thus, Edward Boustead & Co. were a lesser-known East India house with offices in Singapore, Penang, Kuala Lumpur and other Malaysian centres. The four partners held some fifteen directorships in Malaya rubber estates between them, but this interest was only a part of that held by the family, for Boustead Bros (general merchants) held eight and Boustead Anderson & Co. a further nine directorships in Ceylon tea and rubber plantations. Similarly, Samuel Dobrée & Sons was a small old-established firm whose three partners had only one outside directorship between them, but one of the partner's brothers was Lord Kinnaird, who was chairman of the County Fire Office and a director of Barclays Bank, the Merchants' Trust, and other financial concerns that were capable of lending large sums to trusted connections. A further case is that of H. S. Lefevre & Co., another small concern established in the eighteenth century. The four partners recorded only two outside directorships but a brother was a director of six investment trusts, again granting access to large quantities of investment capital.[9]

The main problem of such personal deposits was that they were concentrated in a few hands and so vulnerable to sudden shifts; a few of the dramatic losses following partners' retirements were mentioned above in Chapter 4. The kind of crisis that might erupt can be illustrated from the experience of Brown, Shipley & Co. of London and Brown Bros of New York, Boston and Philadelphia. The smallness of the family's outside liability makes their problem all the more interesting and instructive. In the summer of 1914 they calculated what their capital would be following the imminent retirement of Sir Alexander Hargreaves Brown, the senior partner in London, and Waldron Post Brown, the New York senior, and were evidently shaken. The actual figures were

	capital	'responsibility'	totals
London and USA	£2.32m.	£2.77m.	£5.09m.
threatened withdrawals	£0.48m.	£2.06m.	£2.54m.
reduced capital	£1.84m.	£0.71m.	£2.55m.
divided between			
London	£0.78m.	£0.15m.	£0.93m.
USA	£1.06m.	£0.56m.	£1.62m.

About $10m. (£2.06m.) of this, the New York partners sadly observed, 'goes out of the London firm where by far the greater part of our direct and indirect obligations are payable'. The partners were forced to plan their withdrawal from two of their strongest interests, discounting bills and dealing in securities, and the internal crisis came to a head just at the time when there was an 'enormous increase in commercial transactions between England and the United States due to the war', offering 'just the class of business that our two companies should share in and should be fully equipped to do'. The situation was saved only when the London and US partners prevailed on a reluctant Sir Alexander to remain in harness for the duration of the war. The crisis compelled the New York partners to recommend incorporation, acknowledging that their financial interest was now reinforced by American prejudice against private banks. In London, as we noticed in an earlier chapter, the prejudice ran the other way and at Browns, as at Barings, only an internal crisis of this dimension was powerful enough to force the partners to rethink their entrenched attitudes.[10] Not all firms were fortunate enough to save the situation in this way; for instance the capital of Guinness Mahon & Co. was reduced from £730,000 (1914) to £167,000 (1920) by the death of a retired partner and the retirement of three others at the same time.[11]

It is only at the close of the period covered by this book that there is the least sign that there was any inclination to look beyond these traditional kinds of connections for more capital, and then the example has to be drawn from the history of what was probably the most ambitious and fastest-growing house. Lazard Bros of London was originally very much satellite to the firm's operations in New York and Paris, simply a 'bill office' opened during the Franco-Prussian War to enable the firm to maintain regular payment of its maturing bills. When Kindersley and Brand took over the management in 1905 a large additional capital became desirable, but it was not found until the latter part of the First

World War, when Kindersley was brought into close contact with the contractors S. Pearson & Son as a result of arranging an acceptance credit for them. In 1919 Lazards was reformed with a capital of £2.25m., of which nearly half was owned by Pearsons, and Clive Pearson joined the board. Though there was a number of merchant bank mergers in the postwar years, this connection was in a class by itself at the time, and indeed it is difficult to find precedents since.[12] The city was still dominated by family business and connections until long after the period covered by this book.

It would be valuable to compare the size of the partners' capital with that of their deposits, but unfortunately evidence is not available to support any generalisations. Quite clearly the various merchant banks varied enormously in their policies, connections and their ability to command deposits, and it is impossible to hazard any general conclusions from the few firms for which information has survived, or can be made available to researchers. The variety in 1914 is illustrated by the fact that Blydenstein's deposits and loans from bankers were sixteen times the partners' capital, Barings were nearly eight times and Chaplin Milne's four times, while Browns' outside 'responsibility' (as they termed their deposits) was only just over a quarter of the partners' capital.[13] The only other point that can safely be made is that it was not unusual for deposits to be connected with particular partners and their special interests, so that the retirement or withdrawal of a partner not only diminished the firm's capital but also might lead to a sudden contraction of money deposited with it.

Syndicates

It has been shown in an earlier chapter that the business of raising large public issues by means of syndicates became a familiar practice in London during the Napoleonic War. The British Treasury admitted all loans to competitive tender but in these years various contractors formed the habit of acting together, sharing loans between them. The liaisons formed during these years, particularly those between Baring, Hope and Hottinguer, continued until after mid-century, while Rothschilds retained their satellite concerns in London, Paris and Vienna.[14] Nevertheless, for the leading London merchant banks, syndicating was generally a last resort when all other arrangements failed. Rothschilds' attitude is exemplified in a letter from Baron Nathaniel to his brothers in London in 1865:

Our Vienna friends and the great Baron [James of Paris] will be delighted that you entertain hopes of succeeding with an Austrian loan

– till now we have not been very lucky with Baring and I think you will not only require your friend Baring, but likewise some of the joint-stock banks to unite with you, and however disagreeable it may be to have such partners, if it is the means of making the affair go down, you ought not to mind it.[15]

In the event, neither of the two London houses secured the loan, and it went to Agra & Masterman's to be issued as low as 66, a figure that suggests want of interest in London.

Table 9.3   *Leading German banks and their syndicates 1908 (£m.)*

	Capital + reserves	nos.	Syndicates sums involved
Schaffhausen'scher Bankverein (1848)	8.957	(4)	4.969
Darmstadter Bank (1853)	9.213	(5)	5.659
Berliner Handelsgesellschaft (1856)	7.225		n.d.
Commerz u. Disconto-Bank, Hamburg (1870)	4.890		0.968
Deutsche Bank (1870)	15.091	(18)	24.251
Disconto-Gesellschaft Bank (1851)	11.380	(6)	16.858
Dresdner Bank (1872)	11.575	(8)	2.622
National Bank für Deutschland, Berlin	4.661	(6+)	4.450

Sources: R. H. I. Palgrave, 'The great commercial banks of Germany', *Banker's Magazine*, Oct. 1916. J. Reisser, 'The great commercial banks of Germany', *Banker's Magazine*, July 1914.

There is no very clear evidence, but it appears that these attitudes began to change after the American Civil War, when a number of American financiers opened in London and challenged the position of the established leadership (see Chapter 3). The landmark was Jay Cooke's success in organising an English syndicate for the 1871 United States Federal loan. In London the great finance houses had held aloof from this initiative, but it so enhanced Cooke's reputation that the following year both Rothschilds and Barings joined the Morgan and Morton Rose party that were syndicated with Jay Cooke & Co. The 1872 loan was not a success (partly because Raphaels and other members of the first syndicate were antagonised), but from this time the rise of strong US and continental houses put the London leaders under increasing pressure to share major issues, so that Rothschilds were compelled to partner Morgans, Seligmans and Morton Rose & Co. for US issues (1876, 1877), while Barings were associated at different times with Hambros (Italian loans, 1881–2, 1887, 1889), with Mathesons (Chinese loan, 1855), and with Morgans (Argentine loans of 1887, 1907, 1909, 1910).[16]

However, it must added that the leading English houses were much more reluctant to be involved in syndicates than their foreign rivals were, and even when they were in partnership with others tried to conceal the fact from everyone, including their City rivals. Some instructive details appear in the Brown Shipley letter books of the period. 'We know that when Rothschilds were at the head of the previous syndicate', reported Brown Shipley, 'they managed the finances wholly themselves, declining any contribution from any of the parties interested; and on the last occasion [of a US loan in 1877] we believe that Mr Morgan took the same line – at least vis-a-vis the parties interested with him on this side, but this involved a cash advance here of £1.25m.' Actually, the other two leading US houses, Seligmans and Morton Rose, took part of this issue, while the earlier (1871–3) issues were shared with Barings, Jay Cooke, Morgans and Morton Rose & Co. Again in 1880, Rothschilds tried to insist on a position at the head of the consortium. A huge demand for the loan, as much as three-quarters of it from within the United States, was anticipated, and Rothschilds were not surprisingly unable to secure the exclusive management of the loan in Europe. A new syndicate was formed of eight firms, five American and three Anglo-American, the latter J. S. Morgan & Co., Brown Bros, and August Belmont & Co., Rothschilds' New York agents. Despite these capitulations, Rothschilds continued to try to take exclusive control. Thus in 1888 they declined to share £2.3m. Egyptian loan with London competitors who were consequently 'furious', according to their senior clerk Carl Meyer.[17] Attitudes did not really change until after the humiliation of the Baring crisis of 1890.

It is difficult to know precisely when the use of syndicates became widespread because most of the public issues continued to be made in the name of the house that took the lead, while such private records as have survived offer little information on the point. One of the few contemporary references to change in the financial press was made in a complaint in *The Statist*, which was normally a very matter-of-fact journal, in 1888:

We have commented more than once upon the change that has come over the character of the great English financial houses. They are no longer distinguished by the old prudence and caution, nor by the old regard for the public interest. These are superseded by Continental methods. Upon the Continent syndicates, groups and combinations of bankers have long been common, and in London now the same mode of doing business is in fashion. The result is that men have ceased to feel individual responsibility, each is but one of a set, and is only to a comparatively small extent, liable either in purse or in reputation for what is done.[18]

The passage obviously reflects a confusion of two distinct issues. On the one side there was the fever of issues that was shortly to lead to the Baring crisis, but this crisis occurred, according to one view, precisely because Barings were too proud to have their Argentine issues underwritten by other firms. On the other side, it must be insisted that there was nothing new in syndicating, and the technique, if it had any specific national origins, was born in Britain. The only substance in the contention is that in the 1880s it was obvious that London private bankers were no longer the only catalysts at work in the international scene, and that the shares taken in London were sometimes small. Thus, a massive Russian issue of 1880 (£20m.), was floated for the first time in Paris, but shared among fifteen banks, seven French, three German, two Russian, one Dutch, and only two British. Barings took 5 per cent and Hambros 2.5 per cent. The more modest Swedish loan of the same year was shared by six firms, only one (Hambros) London-based. The only difference between this practice and that of 1818 was that in the earlier year and down to 1870, 'the lead' was invariably allowed to London, while in the 1880s French and German houses began to seize major loans, but were forced by modest capital and inexperience to share them abroad.[19]

Of course, a large number of issues continued to emanate from London, and it is possible that the writer in *The Statist* was thinking of those made by the less prestigious houses that had to be shared among a wide group of subcontractors. Details of such issues are also difficult to trace. The kind of issue that the writer had in mind was possibly that for the Argentine North-Eastern Railway in 1888, which is analysed in Table 9.4. The issue was formally made by Gibbs, but in fact they took only 7.9 per cent of the total, and the nine London merchant banks that bought stock took only 35 per cent of the total. Considerable quantities were sold in Paris and Berlin, and to English trusts and stockbrokers, as well as nearly 200 other capitalists. This particular stock was not very successful, but the leading group of merchant banks were so busy pouring out new issues through the 1880s that it is difficult to suppose that this problem unnerved them at the time, though with advantage of hindsight we can see that it was one of the factors that was evaporating public confidence and leading to the Baring crisis.

The reference in *The Statist* to a change in the 'fashion' of doing business in the City is not, however, entirely misleading. According to the Browns' correspondence in 1879, 'there is much more intimacy between Barings and Rothschilds than in former years, and if you see an indication of such a combination we should be very glad to get in with them; or you may see your way to *faire valour* your position with Mr. J. S. Morgan so as to be invited to join.' In other words, the third generation in the City felt a stronger community of interest than their grandfathers and fathers had done, encourged by the increasing competition of foreign banks. Barings

Table 9.4 *The composition of an 'anonymous' syndicate: the Argentine North-Eastern Railway Company £1.5m. issue of 1888*

Merchant banks in London	no. of shares of £20 each	value (£)
Antony Gibbs & Sons	5,900	118,000
Baring Bros & Co.	4,215	84,300
Glyn & Co.	4,215	84,300
C. J. Hambro & Co.	4,214	84,280
N. M. Rothschild & Sons	4,214	84,280
Lewis Cohen & Sons	1,412	28,240
Mildred, Goyeneche & Co.	1,053	21,060
M. Corgialegno & Co.	500	10,000
Arbuthnot, Latham & Co.	250	5,000
British Trusts		
Army & Navy	500	10,000
Mercantile & General	250	5,000
Investment banks in Paris		
L. R. Cohen d'Anvers	2,395	47,900
Heine & Co.	1,765	35,300
A. J. Stern & Co.	1,765	35,300
Bank de Paris et de Pays-Bas	1,412	28,240
Société Générale	2,541	50,820
Comptoir d'Excompte	1,412	28,240
London stockbrokers		
Cazenove & Ackroyds	4,215	84,300
Gordon, Hill & Co.	1,054	21,080
W. O. Dodgson	150	3,000
Berlin brokers and banks		
six concerns totalling	13,908	278,160
Paris brokers and others		
seven concerns totalling	2,859	57,180
Others		
nine large shareholders	7,419	148,380
187 other shareholders	7,382	147,640
Totals	75,000	1,500,000

Source: calculated from *The Statist*, XXI (1888), p.277. Some of the bank-holdings were registered in the names of their respective partners or directors, e.g. Lord Rothschild for N. M. Rothschild & Sons.

and Rothschilds jointly sponsored the Bengal Railway (1881-2), the Manchester Ship Canal (1889) and the Pennsylvania Railroad (1908), but their anonymous participation in numerous issues like the Argentine North-Eastern Railway of 1888 was perhaps cumulatively more important than the public demonstrations of willingness to work together. Down to 1914 most London houses tried to maintain a veneer of proud independence. In City mythology syndicates were an American and German invention and, except in rare instances such as national emergencies, City houses did not like to compromise their status by being *seen* to have to share issues with their rivals.[20]

Nevertheless, apart from the Jay Cooke initiative, the most important landmark is no doubt that of the Baring crisis. The effect of the crisis was to evaporate public confidence in any single house, however august. The reputation and marketability of a loan was now more enhanced by association with a group of influential names. The crisis served to restrain overseas issues for several years, but as they picked up again, the leading French, German and US banks, which were characteristically linked in a chain of syndicates, persuaded the leading London houses to integrate with them.[21] The Rothschilds in particular were still largely concerned in Central European finance, which was now being dominated by eight German banks whose capital was much larger than that of almost all the London merchant banks (Table 9.3). N. M. Rothschild & Sons helped to establish a group known as the Consortium Rothschild consisting of a dozen firms, the three surviving Rothschild houses (London, Paris and Vienna), four German Jewish family firms (Mendelsohn, Bleichroder, Oppenheimer and Wodianer), and five company banks, the Credit-anstalt, the Bodenkreditanstalt (also of Vienna), the Budapest Kredit-bank, and two German banks, the Discontogesellschaft and the Bank für Handel und Industrie. The French scholar Bertrand Gille described Rothschilds as the 'fulcrum' of European syndicates, but this exaggerates the role of the London house.[22]

At the turn of the century a new factor suddenly appeared in the tangle of syndicating relations. Advised by Morgans' London partner, Sir Clinton Dawkins, the Chancellor of the Exchequer decided to bolster the government's flagging wartime credit by floating half of a new £10m. loan in New York. The alternative was seen to be a 7 per cent bank rate, at that time unthinkable. Morgans easily sold the £5m. stock, but the City at large were intensely jealous and (in Meyer's words) there was 'a hell of a row'. When a further issue of Consols was made in 1902 and Morgans again took £5m., Dawkins wrote that 'Friends don't exist in this kind of thing, and the very big houses *dare not* be left out.' This experience appears in the perspective of the twentieth century as a mere preface to the massive transatlantic funding which Morgans conducted for the British government during the First World War. That period lies beyond the scope of this book, but it is worth recognising here that the precedents were firmly established within our period. In the years between the Boer War and 1914, it became common for British governments to promote syndicates (or syndicating situations) to bolster allied interests in strategic areas of the world by providing loans. The aim was clearly political rather than economic, a tacit acknowledgement that the traditional (Palmerston) doctrine that the Foreign Office had no duty to promote or protect City loans to foreign states had given way to the French (Caillaux) notion of foreign credit as an instrument of state policy. Again, this is a subject that carries us far outside the realm of this book. It is enough to mention here that several of the loans to Egypt, Turkey, Persia and China in this period were the outcome of pressure from Whitehall, and in some instances the City houses are known to have been reluctant to join such syndicates. In the context of the present work, the (quite legitimate) suspicion of government motives was yet another reason for fighting shy of syndicates.[23]

In practice it was not always necessary to form a syndicate or even have a permanent working partnership with another firm to share the issue of a loan. We may take Jacob Schiff, Sir Ernest Cassel's US correspondent, as a prime example of the continuing prosperity of individualists. He was one of the principal promoters of the Japanese loans of 1904 and 1905, not because he had any specific knowledge of the Orient, but because he despised Russian anti-semitism. His partner in this successful venture was the Hong Kong & Shanghai Banking Corporation. Numerous other *ad hoc* connections of an apparently unlikely kind can be glimpsed in the literature. Hambros made investments in US railroads and municipal loans through J. P. Morgan, despite the American's general unpopularity in the City, and later on both Barings and Rothschilds were prepared to join forces with the Americans despite earlier hostility.[24] In the last analysis, opportunity and interest can be seen to have overrun the boundaries of religion, race, prejudice and government.

Borrowed Capital

The nature of the merchant banks' connections brings us readily to a third source of their capital, joint-stock banks and insurance companies. Merchants engaged in overseas trade were traditionally involved in insurance, often as brokers for particular vessels and cargoes. As already explained, the leading houses were active in both private and company insurance from an early period (see Chapter 2), and in the 1860s several emergent merchant banks became partners in Crédit Mobilier type banks (Chapter 8). But as late as 1885 the direct involvement in 'home' banks and insurance companies was limited to a handful of pacemakers, notably

Fletcher Alexander & Co. with seventeen directorships, mostly in banks and insurance companies, Morton Rose & Co. (the New York based house) with sixteen, Antony Gibbs and Frühling & Goschen with ten each. By 1914 this involvement was much more widespread. The 111 firms extracted from Skinner's lists (see Appendix 1) held between them 117 directorships in banks and investment trusts and 79 in insurance companies. Half of the firms (56 out of 111) held one or more such directors, and a few were heavily involved, particularly Frühling & Goschen, Glyn Mills, and Brown Shipley. In several instances merchant bankers were chairmen of such companies, for instance Baron Schröder of the North British & Mercantile Insurance Co.

The opportunities for partners in merchant banks to become directors of insurance companies and joint-stock banks are explained in some of the literature of the period. In his celebrated work on *Lombard Street*, Walter Bagehot explained that most City merchants

> have a good deal of leisure; for the life of a man of business who employs only his own capital, and employs it nearly always in the same way, is by no means fully employed. Hardly any capital is enough to employ the principal partner's time, and, if such a man is very busy, it is a sign of something wrong. Either he is working at detail, which subordinates could do better, and which he had better leave alone, or he is engaged in too many speculations, is incurring more liabilities than his capital will bear, and so may be ruined. In consequence, every commercial city abounds in men who have great business ability and experience, who are not fully occupied, and who are very glad to become directors of public companies in order to be occupied. ... There is in all ordinary joint stock companies a fixed executive specially skilled, and a somewhat varying council not specially skilled. The fixed manager ensures continuity and experience in the management, and a good board of directors ensures general wisdom.[25]

An article in the *Banker's Magazine* of 1888 on Lord Revelstoke, the head of Barings, endorsed this point. 'Of course, in the main, an acceptance business like that of Baring Brothers & Co. will run alone, without much attention from the head partner', it insisted. However, it must be added that some of the merchant bankers who had made their way up from the bottom of the ladder more recently did not see the matter in such dispassionate terms. James Blyth, founder of Blyth, Greene & Jourdain, wrote from his sweating Mauritius office to his brother in London: 'I shall be glad to find that you have been able to pave the way to our getting into some of the snug things in London ... say a director's seat for each in a Fire Office, a life insurance company etc.' Some of his ambitions were eventually fulfilled, for he became a director of the London Assurance

Company and chairman of both the Oriental Bank Corporation and the East & West India Dock Company.[26]

Of course, it is one thing to identify this growth of connections and quite another to assess precisely what use was made of them. It must be conceded at once that, despite the extensive listing of bank and insurance records in recent years, there remains such a shortage of specific evidence that it is possible only to indicate where general practice probably lay. According to the authoritative *Circular to Bankers* in a passage written in 1832, the most characteristic passage of credit occurred when country bankers in farming areas like Norfolk and Suffolk lent their surpluses to their agents in London, who lent them to Barings, who in turn lent them to the Bank of the United States, who then lent them to construct roads, canals, railroads and other public works, and to finance private industry. Gurneys were particularly favoured by the farmers because (unlike the Bank of England branches) they would redeem their notes issued at one office at any other branch, and it seems that the prosperity of this country bank promoted the leading discount house of Overend, Gurney & Co. They in turn appointed the fastest-rising US house, J. S. Morgan & Co., as their confidential agents, and through them started buying US railroad stock.[27]

This outline needs a little refinement from the side of the merchant banks, and specifically from the policy of Barings. Joshua Bates, the senior partner from about 1830 to 1864, was a New England puritan who took a particular pride in *not* borrowing money, or at any rate, in the absolute independence of his firm. Thus in 1834 we find him writing to Nicholas Biddle in the United States that

> the House [of Baring] has never discounted a bill since the writer belonged to it. On two occasions only have they borrowed money on stocks. One of these was a fore cautionary measure where the loan of a million was made for the bank but the money was never wanted, on the other occasion we borrowed for a very short time being under heavy advances on American stocks.

At the time of the crisis of 1837 this policy seemed amply justified and Bates confided to his journal that

> It is a source of pride and satisfaction to me that by foresight on the part of myself and partners our House has never discounted a bill and never had aid from the Bank in any way, so that our skill and judgement has excited the admiration and astonishment of everybody.[28]

Of course, this ultra-conservative policy was by no means dictated by lack of access to credit; on the contrary, at this period Barings could borrow money more easily than anyone else in the City. The thinking of the partners is again carefully recorded by Bates

> Lord A [shburton] remarked that we should always have £100[000] in hand free to embrace any profitable business that might offer. I remarked that in a business like ours that reserve should be at least £500,000, that £100,000 one way or the other was of very little use and it would be impossible that anyone could calculate so nearly in a business so large.

But having stressed the paramount importance of liquidity – that £0.5m. out of £0.75m. partners' capital should be available on short call – he wrote to Ashburton to concede that '*There is nothing in our wanting £100,000 since we have abundant securities to raise a million.*' The financial stability of a firm like Barings was much greater than indicated by the partners' capital; when Ashburton died in 1848 he left nearly £3m. ('all accumulated by himself', according to Bates) while at this time Barings' partners' capital was still under half-a-million. The firm borrowed £200,000 from Overend, Gurney & Co. for a short period in 1854 and again in 1858, but even such modest debts as these seem to have been quite exceptional.[29]

Barings' policy in the middle decades of the century might be of little consequence but that it set a standard for other prudent houses, who were compelled to notice the way in which it came through successive crises (1837, 1848, 1857) stronger than ever. Firms that had to have recourse to the Bank of England at such times, however strong their overall financial positions, received a very black mark in Barings' and other firms' 'character books'. Nevertheless, it was perfectly possible for respectable houses to borrow large sums on security, and a few did so. Thus when George Peabody, the American who pioneered the sale of US state and public utility bonds in London, ran into liquidity problems in 1841 and 1842, he borrowed from Morrison, Sons & Co. (the former Morrison, Cryder & Co.), the London Joint-Stock Bank, Overend, Gurney & Co. and the Alliance Bank of Manchester, among others. Within a decade he recovered his position and was subsequently able to finance his growing business without difficulty.[30] However, it seems that, by 1830, the largest loans were being made by the Bank of England to four bill-broking firms (discount houses), the only ones of any significance at this time, and it is fair to assume that these houses were in turn discounting the bills of the emergent merchant banks. At any rate, such discounting was standard procedure later in the century, and there is no reason to suppose that Bates' refusal to discount a bill reflected any general practice.[31]

N. M. Rothschild took a very different view of credit from the Barings and from 1823 to his death in 1836 regularly borrowed large sums from the Bank of England. Again according to the respected *Circular to Bankers,* Rothschild's prestige was such that he could borrow any sum that the market could raise. 'The influence of Mr Rothschild is so great that if much money should be wanted for any operations in which he is deeply engaged, there will be but little chance for other speculators to obtain the requisite accommodation.' His accounts show that he periodically had large dealings with Overend, Gurney & Co., the leading discount house.[32] The Barings evidently did not approve of this practice. In a memo on the approaching crisis of 1836, Ashburton wrote

> In my days of Bank direction we never let the new money jobbers discount there. The Goldsmids who were the Rothschilds of their day and conducted an immense circulation during the week never had an account of discount. I apprehend this is all changed and that Rothschilds, Gurney, and the other great money dealers are admitted to occasionally very large sums. I hold this to be a great mistake and to form no inconsiderable portion of the danger apprehended.[33]

However, Rothschild's account at the Bank was closed in 1843, a fact that J. H. Clapham, its official historian, found difficult to explain because it was evidently nothing to do with Bank policy. Specific evidence is elusive but the context shows that NM's sons and grandsons abandoned his bolder projects, or indeed anything that might be interpreted as at all risky. Only three years after his death they declined to join a consortium of a dozen English and French houses formed to negotiate a credit of £2m. for the Bank of England with the Bank of France. Baron Anselm Soloman Rothschild instructed his young London cousins:

> Do not take any rash step in a large operation. Your mother tells me that *Herries* told your good father in her presence to mind and not trust the Bank without any guarantee ... as the Bank being involved in difficulties may *stop* suddenly. ... Mind, my good cousins, that you are not your good father and do not have his influence, and he was capable of acting in other ways than prudence would direct you.[34]

In other words, even the Bank of England was not to be trusted, and it was finally left to Bates of Barings to lead the consortium. Pursuing an ultra-cautious policy with a vast capital, the second- and third-generation London Rothschilds scarcely ever needed recourse to borrowing, at any rate until the turn of the century. And then, as we saw in the pages of Chapter 6 devoted to underwriting, Lord Rothschild found it easy to borrow for short periods from the clearing banks, a practice that by that time was commonplace.

The Greek houses as we noticed above were conspiciously involved in promoting new joint-stock banks, and their experience is instructive. In the company promotion boom of the early 1860s, Rodoconachis helped to launch the London Financial Association and Rallis and Zarifis promoted the rival Mercantile Credit Association. Rallis and other Levantine merchants formed the Bank of Alexandria and the Bank of Constantinople in 1872 and were later active in the Ottoman Bank. Rodoconachis were among the founders of the St Petersburg International Trade Bank, also in 1872, and Rallis in the Odessa Discount Bank (1879). This string of promotions may be interpreted as part of the Greeks' attempt to retain the grain trade against the challenge of Dreyfus and the Jewish houses, but at the time they were thought to be a manoeuvre to secure an unlimited quantity of easy credit.[35] According to the shrewd author of *The Bubbles of Finance* (1865), a fictional account in which the 'characters are types not personalities' and the real names of companies suitably disguised, on the accession of 'Mr Velardi' to the board of the joint-stock 'Onyx Bank'

> it was believed that establishment would in future be very largely supported by the Greek interest in London. This disinterested surmise proved much more correct than similar prophecies generally do, for as Greek commercial men generally follow and often help each other, no sooner was the name of one of their community seen on the board of a joint-stock bank, than a perfect flood of current accounts poured into the concern. ... Mr Velardi continued a director of the Onyx Bank, and took a very active part in the management of that establishment, which gave us almost unlimited facilities in the way of discount.[36]

The records of all these concerns appear to have perished, but Bank of England sources confirm that most bills were discounted within the Greek community. Meanwhile, high profits were made, the new Middle East banks borrowing at 3–6 per cent in London and Paris and lending at well over 10 per cent in Alexandria and elsewhere.[37] The sources used here are by no means unbiased, but they serve as a reminder that the foreign banking clans that settled in London often continued to maintain the system of mutual support that had carried them through the difficult periods of their early settlement.

When the whole truth of business history can be uncovered, the behaviour of the less competent or responsible firms can be far graver than the wilder insinuations of fiction writers. We noticed in the last chapter that Antony Gibbs & Co. raised a capital of nearly £2m. out of the profits of the guano trade, but that their attempts to reinvest it in other branches of international trade (notably Australia) did not turn out very profitably. Meanwhile the various members of the family moved into politics and country life, and became accustomed to living beyond their

Table 9.5 *Antony Gibbs & Sons: partners' capital and borrowed capital 1866–1900*

	partners	borrowed	capital in accounts	acceptances
1866	£1.90m.	£1.10m.	n.d.	n.d.
1870	£1.10m.	£1.40m.	n.d.	n.d.
1876	£0.09m.	£1.80m.	n.d.	n.d.
1884	£0.06m.	£1.75m.	0.41	0.51
1888	£0.11m.	£2.10m.	0.91	1.16
1900	£0.41m.	£1.75m.	0.42	0.56

Source: Guildhall Library MSS 11,042/1 pp. 277–85, 11, 064/1

means, leaving the management of the business to their clerks. Their drawings, along with capital taken out by retiring partners, became so heavy that the partners' united capital fell to under £100,000 in the 1890s (Table 9.5). This drain was made good by increasingly heavy external borrowing until, according to a confidential memo prepared by Vicary Gibbs in 1902, the partners' capital was scarcely more than one-twentieth of the borrowed capital. The situation was evidenty a dangerous one, and in 1876, 1884 and 1890 the losses threatened to submerge the partners' capital. Despite heavy reining in of liabilities in the latter two years, especially in Australia, the financial situation was hardly under control when Vicary Gibbs took control at the turn of the century. Gibbs' position steadily improved over the next twenty years but the lessons were hard to learn; in 1906 Vicary Gibbs was writing that 'In my opinion it is essential for the good of the House that Partners should have some inducement to economise.'[38] Unfortunately, Gibbs' surviving records do not disclose which banks or other institutions were lending them such large sums for long periods, so further evidence must be sought in the better-documented experience of other merchant banks.

In the provinces at least, the early joint-stock banks were founded and functioned as a kind of self-help institution for merchants and manufacturers of the town and locality, and some of the provincial acceptance houses took advantage of the system. A useful case study is again offered by J. & A. Dennistoun, the Glasgow-based Anglo-American acceptance house. In the 1850s, when the partners' capital was already over £0.5m., they were regularly granted credits for short periods by the Union Bank of Scotland, up to £100,000 for four months at a time, as well as £10,000 open credit for a new enterprise in Australia. It seems that advances were made on the security of the £100,000 of Union bank shares held by Dennistoun's senior partners.[39] However, such practices were viewed with considerable distaste in the City – or at any rate, among the more orthodox elements in it – not least as the early joint-stock banks were notoriously inexperienced and unstable. Consequently the most instructive case, and the final example of this chapter, comes from the City itself and relates largely to the early years of this century.

Saemy Japhet, whose firm continues as a component of Charterhouse Japhet, started his independent career in Frankfurt in 1880, and came to London via Berlin in 1896 with a capital of only £15,000. He retained good connections in his native city and in Berlin but his capital was quite inadequate for his ambitions, and his stockbroking business was largely maintained by acting as an agent for the Deutsche Bank. The limitations of this arrangement soon became clear: 'they gave us moral support, spoke well of us, helped us even in London, introduced us at Schröders, Hambros ... but otherwise they wanted us to make money and to work for them. Instead of becoming more independent, we felt that we had, even more than before, to rely on our brokers, because we had not sufficient loan accounts to finance all our open positions.' Then at the turn of the century Japhet managed to persuade R. Warschauer & Co. of Berlin to put £50,000 into his little firm, and in 1902 this was increased to £150,000, giving the new house a total capital of £200,000, which was comparable with the smaller merchant banks of the period. One of Warschauer's most talented young men, 'a first class arbitragist', joined Japhet in London and so far raised the credit of the house that the firm was able to draw three month bills on the Crédit Lyonnais, on the Société Générale, and on Sulzbach. After a short period (1907–9) during which the Darmstaedter Bank invested capital in Japhet's rapidly growing concern, he turned to Sir Ernest Cassel, who added £200,000 to the capital making a new total of £400,000. Cassel generously gave advice down to his death in 1921, when the newly incorporated S. Japhet & Co. Ltd registered a capital of £0.75m. It was a meteoric rise, and in no way to be counted as typical, but it clearly illustrates the way in which talent and dedication could draw funds from the big banks.[40]

10 Performance

Merchant bankers have been peculiarly reluctant to commit their views and stories of their careers to publishers, and the handful that have written autobiographies are probably not typical. The only really literary one is Sir Lawrence Jones's trilogy of reminiscences, the final volume of which includes the following striking passage about the author's life in a City merchant bank:

> No doubt there are one-man businesses where decisions are made swiftly. But in houses where there are many partners, and at board meetings, the tempo is for the most part leisurely indeed. There is gossip and chaff and the latest good story before a conference or a board meeting gets under way; it is all friendliness and informality; the debate saunters off into by-ways; the real point is sometimes not reached until we are washing our hands for lunch. The comfort of our partners' rooms, the deep leather sofas, the open fires, the pictures on the walls, all encourage a rather cosy, lounging method of discussion. Accuracy, punctuality, and dispatch belonged to the counting-house downstairs, not to the partners' room. ... Again, friendship, subject always to unwritten hierarchical laws, played a part in all our relations with other firms ... it was agreeable to work in an atmosphere where mutual liking played as large a part as the cash nexus. There was competition, but it was amicable, even generous.[1]

Jones was writing about Helbert, Wagg & Co. in the 1920s and 1930s, but he no doubt believed that the atmosphere he described was inherited from earlier generations.

The letters of Sir Clinton Dawkins of Morgans confirms that a similar unhurried atmosphere, redolent of the gentleman's club and country house weekend, was equally a feature of City life at the turn of the century. Moving into banking from the upper echelons of the Colonial civil service, he found the City 'does not involve long hours or much fatigue. ... I am happy enough in the City, but there is *not* enough to do there, and I feel the want of handling big questions again.' However, he saw the strongest contrast when his firm, Morgans, invited him to their New York office. He wrote:

> But it is extremely interesting to find oneself in the very heart of the Wall Street excitement and combinations and to note the prodigious amount of nervous excitement and energy the Americans throw into

their work. Part of the buoyancy and excitement is also due, I suppose, to the comparative youth of the vast majority of them. Few of them live through it to advanced years except physical and intellectual giants like Morgan who has something Titanic about him when he really gets to work. Most of them drop out suddenly. Total collapse very often.[2]

But of course this dedication to money-making was not something peculiar to New York, and among the ranks of fast-rising entrepreneurs in London there is adequate evidence of comparative single-mindedness. The clearest published account comes from the autobiography of H. O. O'Hagan, the foremost company promoter of the 1880s and 1890s. He insisted that

> Success rarely comes to those who take to their offices, their sports, their theatricals, or other amusements. To really succeed, a man must make his work his first love. It has been said to me, 'if you are thinking of your business day and night, how can you get any pleasure out of life?' To which I replied that I loved pleasure as much as anyone, and the busy man, no matter how hard he may at times be put to it, will find time to taste of the pleasures; but when I was hard put to it, then I found my business my greatest pleasure, for it was like playing a lot of games of chess at the same time. I believe I was one of the first to make it a practice not to go to the City on Saturdays, except when exceptionally busy; but I took my Saturdays off not for enjoyment and sport, but because I found that my Saturdays and Sundays could best be employed at my country home in studying papers and in getting out important schemes, which would not come to me in the hurry and confusion of a day's City life.[3]

These quotations serve as a reminder that the City financiers of last century were by no means a homogeneous group, and theories that interpret them as a single class interest are likely to conceal more than they illuminate. In particular, Marxist theories of the concentration of the aristocracy, commercial, financial and industrial élites into one class fail to comprehend the diversity of the City of London, let alone other economic groups. Recent refinements of the theory claiming that the 'model of leadership' in the nineteenth-century middle class was aristocratic, and consequently amateur and leisure-oriented, still fail to grasp the full complexity of traditions and relationships, though social connection was evidently important.[4] Dr Y. Cassis of Geneva has tried to measure this phenomenon in a fascinating thesis on *Les Banquiers Anglais 1890–1914*. He is able to demonstrate that most of the leading City merchant banks united themselves into a tight community based on education at a few expensive public schools and the ancient English universities, and on intermarriage and an aristocratic life-style. But the really significant finding is the contrast with firms like Kleinworts and Schröders who forged ahead so fast in this period. Thus while all the partners in Rothschilds, Hambros and Gibbs and most of them in Barings and Morgan Grenfell had public school and/or Oxbridge educations, none of those at Kleinworts or Schröders was educated in this way. And while the partners in the firms mentioned married the sisters or daughters of partners in other merchant banks, or those of other old private banking families, or aristocratic ladies, Kleinworts and Schröders kept to continental brides. Forty-five per cent of all City bank directors and partners in the period had an address in London *and* the country, and 20 per cent in the country alone, but this did not include Kleinworts, Schröders or Brandts, while Cassel was obviously ill-at-ease there and probably used his country mansions much as O'Hagan used his retreat. The explanation – not pursued by Dr Cassis – cannot simply be cultural isolation in the Lutheran Church or in work-a-day Camberwell rather than the Church of England, Wimbledon or Richmond; it is probably much more to do with imbibed habits of work. Records of City office hours are sparse but, by any external standard, not even the clerks worked long hours; except when there was a large delivery of overseas mail, 10 a.m. to 5 p.m. was quite usual. By contrast, we are told that German clerks worked sixty, seventy and even more hours a week and the only holidays formally allowed were Sunday afternoons and a few Christian festivals. Moreover, the mercantile tradition of sending sons and apprentices abroad for experience was falling into disuse by 1890 in England, but not in Germany. Documentation is sparse, but the preponderance of Anglo-German families with diverse interests among the accepting houses (Table 3.4) suggests that the conclusion reached for a few firms has wider validity.[5]

The other predominant influence in the City according to popular belief was that of Jewish money-making. In the course of this book it has been shown that several Jewish families played a prominent role in the development of the City in the ninteenth century, but that their traditions and ideology constituted only one strand among several. However, W. D. Rubinstein in *Men of Property* (1981) has suggested from his identification of the British millionaires and half-millionaires of last century that the 'merchant banking community in the City of London was overwhelmingly foreign and disproportionately Jewish, especially at the very top levels', and Cassis adds substance to this by showing that merchant bankers as a group were significantly more wealthy than other bankers. There is no reason to infer from this that the Jewish merchant bankers were necessarily acting together either as syndicates or on some informal basis. The Rothschilds, as we have seen, regarded themselves as a separate order from all other bankers, Jewish and non-Jewish, and resisted connections with Seligmans, Raphaels, and all other houses. Evidently a few Jewish families accumulated immense wealth but it was in the characteristic Victorian manner of dedication to their own businesses. Single-minded entrepreneurship may have been relatively more common among Jews but of course was by no means confined to them.[6]

A recommended textbook for entrants to merchant banking bluntly describes the characteristic histories of accepting houses as 'historical novels', an opinion not to be wondered at in view of the numbers of novelists, journalists and retired executives commissioned by bank directors for this task.[7] When the heroic sagas are scrutinised rather more closely the achievements of earlier generations do not always look as impressive as they might considering the qualifications of the founders and boundless opportunities of the age. Perhaps the one most outstanding feature of the emergent merchant banks in the nineteenth century was their conservatism. Led by the survivors of the financial turmoil of the French Wars, a heterodox group of British, German, Greek and American merchants built up an unrivalled and generally unsullied business in acceptances, and a few of them went with varying degrees of success into state loans in their respective geographical sectors. But when fresh opportunities came they were occupied by new specialists: railway finance by the contractors and their financial partners, arbitrage and foreign exchange by Jews and 'Greeks', industrial issues and underwriting by company promoters. When new areas of the world were opened to international finance and investment the old firms were often slow off the mark and ineffective, as for instance in the industrialisation of Russian textiles (dominated by Ludwig Knoop), the development of South African gold mines (dominated by the 'Rand lords'), and issue of Chinese loans (Panmure Gordon and the Hong Kong & Shanghai Bank). Even in areas in which the merchant banks had an early start they lost ground within a generation or so, for instances the early 'Greek' leadership of the grain trade was lost to Jewish and Dutch houses (Dreyfus, Bunge, and Fribourg), while imperial banks easily won the field in India and the Far East (Chapter 8). Merchant banks were slow to sense the possibilities of joint-stock organisation, whether for themselves or satellite enterprises, and long held aloof from it. The facts refute any suggestion that the houses dealt with in this book were ignorant of new developments. If the railways are taken as a case in point, Huth and Hodgson accompanied George Stephenson on his early forays to establish the route of the Midland Railway while James Rothschild saw the birth of the French system, but neither Huths nor the English Rothschilds made the best of their splendid opportunity.[8] The endless possibilities of railway finance are illustrated by the impressive enterprise of the Glyns. More generally, the specific expertise of the merchant banks in the economies of particular trading partners evidently gave them enviable opportunities, and their record should be judged against this backcloth.

However, in recognising the very real limitations of the merchant banks, it is important not to fall into the trap of overstating their late-Victorian decline as (for instance) Marcello de Cecco does through the pages of his useful book *Money and Empire: the International Gold Standard 1890-1914* (1974). It is a clear overstatement to say that the joint-stock banks were replacing merchant banks even in the latter's most specialised function, acceptances, and consequently 'suffocating' them. Equally, we cannot stay with Dr Cassis all the way as he draws a picture of the pre-1914 City in which the merchant banks were still dominating British finance through directorships of the Bank of England, representation on the boards of other large companies, and social cohesion of their group. A more realistic (if less dramatic) view must recognise the pace-making merchant banks holding their own against the pressure of both the British joint-stock banks and the German giants (Table 7.2), and make a more sober assessment of the performance of the houses that have left a record.

The actual achievement of the accepting houses was at once more pedestrian and more useful than the adventures described in the heroic literature. It was of fundamental importance to the development of the British economy, and hence also of the international economy last century. Economic historians are now beginning to recognise that the working capital of manufacturers that exported a large proportion of their output had to be two or three times that of their fixed capital, and that even with such a ratio, liquidity crises remained a familiar feature because payments for exports were so slow to materialise. Case studies show that even the biggest firms were vulnerable to such risks.[9] Acceptances and other credit facilities for exporters in Britain and suppliers abroad helped to obviate the considerable risks of exporting, so facilitating the great growth in international trade in the period. In the mean time, scarce domestic means were released for productive internal employment.

The other great financial problem in the growth of the international economy of the nineteenth century was that of overcoming the immobility of capital. Immobile capital appears to be characteristic of newly developing economies, with the pioneers of modern industry typically drawing on family resources, personal contacts and retained profits for their establishment and growth. But in the railway age such local resources invariably proved inadequate and means had to be sought to recruit capital from a much wider circle. The merchant banks did not possess sufficient capital or deposits to finance development loans but, more importantly, the most eminent of them enjoyed a reputation which enabled them to act as *catalysts* for the generation of capital from the particular country or locality where it was needed. That is to say that most of the foreign loans raised in London were subscribed to by foreigners who recognised the name of the London issue as a guarantee of the soundness of the bonds he was buying. The practice can easily be identified in Barings' taking the lead in the French indemnity loan in 1818; most of the loan was sold to French investors by the five French firms that joined Barings' and Hopes' syndicate and took half the paper off their hands. Similarly, in writing of the early capitalisation of French railways, Jean Bouvier refers to James Rothschild playing 'en quelque sorte un rôle de catalyseur'.[10] The other French scholar eminent in this area, Bertrand Gille, wrote that Rothschild's own subscriptions to French railways he was interested in averaged only 10 per cent, the remaining 90 per cent being subscribed by those who followed him. This theme is repeated again and again in issues through the century, but touching a wider circle of states. When Barings made their first Russian issue in 1850 Bates thought £5.5m. was too large but he was soon recording that the 'Russian loan goes wonderfully well. ... It seems to suit the Dutch and the French', who took most of it. And at the turn of the century, when the main interest focused on a series of massive loans to develop China, the British & China Corporation was formed by Jardine Matheson and the Hong Kong & Shanghai Bank as 'the catalyst for financing and developing much of China's railway system'.[11]

Defenders of the export of British capital always maintained that foreign loans brought immediate benefits to the exporter by way of orders for British manufacturers. It was an arrangement by which Britain was enabled to sell her industrial surplus abroad at a time when it was difficult for underdeveloped countries to pay for them with a comparable flow of exports. 'Seven-eighths or fifteen-sixteenths of any loan issued are employed in buying goods' from the lending country, James Rothschild maintained to a French government inquiry in 1866.[12] But in acknowledging the truth of this familiar notion, we must now take into account the scaling down of the estimates of British capital exports in the period. Professor D. C. M. Platt, the instigator of this revision, has written that

Britain was *not* a great exporter of capital before 1870. ... British investors, before the end of the 1860s, were preoccupied with opportunities for home investment. When they placed their money abroad, they seldom looked further than the British colonies or the United States.[13]

A sequence of earlier estimates had failed to recognise that the issue of a loan in London did not necessarily imply that it was taken up by British investors; indeed it is quite possible to demonstrate that, following the precedent of Barings' Indemnity Loan (1818) and Rothschilds' Prussian Loan (1819), most of the bonds were bought in the country of origin and others soon made their way there. Platt has so far dealt in less detail with the period 1870–1913, but has made a provisional reduction in the usual 1913 estimate of £3.7 billion to £2.5 billion. It is easy to guess that further downward revisions are imminent. The consequences of this for an assessment of Britain's role in international economic development can at present be discerned only in outline, but it will inevitably tone down the stridency of earlier assessments of the role of finance in imperialism and the maintenance of what Jenks called a 'rentier governing class'.[14] Equally it must diminish the role of merchant bankers in those dramas. Such a revision would harmonise with the more modest economic performances ascribed to them in this volume, suggesting trade credit to be of more far-reaching importance than foreign loans.

It is practically impossible to *measure* the relative importance of issues and acceptances through the period, but a few further points can be made by way of comparing and contrasting the relative performances of the two principal arms of merchant banking. It might easily be supposed that the 'whiter than white' notion of indubitable credit and the conventions governing the ratio of capital to acceptances held back initiatives in this sector, but the experience of Kleinworts, Schröders, Huths and several smaller firms shows that such a view could be exaggerated. Kleinworts were occasionally restrained by opinion in the City, but they and other members of the Anglo-German group set a pace that strongly contributed to maintaining the momentum of growth in the generation that preceded 1914. Without their enterprise, the Baring crisis could have been followed by a downward movement in acceptances, much as the period 1890–1914 saw a fall in the volume of issues handled by the merchant banks.[15]

It can be calculated that the private banks' share of public issues fell from 53 per cent in 1870–4 to 35 per cent in 1910–14. British investment in America continued to grow at an impressive rate – from perhaps £40m. in 1870 to £400m. at the turn of the century – but British issuing houses took a diminishing role in this business.[16] As early as 1888 it was authoritatively stated that 'very rarely have our great issuing houses taken part in placing American shares in London', preferring rather to retail issues of US houses.[17] Some may argue that it was inevitable that the rise of joint-stock banking and of Wall Street as a financial centre would make inroads into British private banking; and few would question that some *relative* loss of world market must have occurred, but in the period from 1885–9 to 1905–9 the fall was an absolute one. The actual capital of most of the merchant banks was, as we have seen in Chapters 3 and 4, quite modest, but it has been shown that their real power lay in their reputation and connections. Merchant bankers were directors of any number of joint-stock and chartered banks, investment trusts and insurance companies, and were able, even with the most slender personal means, to recruit capital with ease (Chapter 9). Alternatively, they could sponsor joint-stock enterprises (Chapter 8) or, like the continental Rothschilds, use their name to become the pivot of international syndicates.[18] Set alongside such exciting possibilities, the performance of the leading issue houses appears sluggish. The record of the accepting houses shows that enterprise was not dead, but it was not a marked characteristic of the leading houses in the later Victorian and Edwardian years. Newer wealth migrating to the City – the Sassoons, Seligmans, Barnato, Wernher Beit & Co. – seem to be all too easily absorbed into the system.

This critical assessment is not intended to suggest that by 1914 the Germans or Americans had become better at their respective equivalents of merchant banking. Both the two systems were the subject of rigorous appraisal shortly before the First World War, the German by Dr Riesser and the American by the National Monetary Commission, and both inquiries looked primarily to London for models of what their system might be.[19] Both of course had strong and weak, enterprising and conservative firms. The American system was closest to that of Britain and set the pace with Morgans, who made $1.9 billion (£380m.) of issues between 1902 and 1912, while the partners held seventy-two directorships in forty-seven major US corporations.[20] But other New York based enterprises were not nearly so competent or pushing; Chaplin Milne & Co. (formerly Morton Rose) went bankrupt in 1914 and Seligmans, according to the Company's centenary history, were very conservative:

> Historically, the firm's underwritings had been confined [until *c.* 1920] largely to bond and preferred issues of companies with which Seligmans had maintained long-term investment banking relationships and of a quality which normally appealed to conservative clients with substantial portfolios.[21]

It looks as if most London firms lived on similar safe connections.

Explanations for the uninspired British performance are not far to seek, and implicit in several of the chapters of this book. Much of it is attributable to the now-familiar story of family firms that, having accumulated a modest fortune, were anxious not to squander it by taking excessive risks or disperse it by bringing in too many clever outsiders. They secured their futures, and those of less bright members of the family, by the usual practice of investing their money in landed estate and their time in the prestige of parliamentary careers and government office. Such activities were by no means irrelevant to continued success in the

City, for the 'great houses' lived, above all, on the prestige of their names, and titles and estate gave lustre to these names. Bagehot's celebrated remarks about the deference of the English middle class was nowhere more true than in the City. 'In all countries new wealth is ready to worship old wealth, if old wealth will only let it', he observed, and as a City man he had had ample opportunity to notice how London's cosmopolitan community were allowed to fawn to its aristocracy of wealth and rank.[22]

Of course the Baring crisis called the position and practices of some of the leaders into question. As explained in Chapter 5, Barings never recovered their former prestige, but here we are concerned with the City leadership as a whole. The position is best understood by reference to an adulatory article on Revelstoke in the *Banker's Magazine* in 1888. The writer insisted that

> Without that unimpeachable virtue known as first-class credit the firm could not keep afloat the mass of acceptances which bear its name. Messrs. Baring Bros ... have never known, during the present century, anything but first class credit, into which enters *the elements of dignity – moral, personal, and commercial alike*[23]

But after Barings' fall the same discreet journal could not resist quoting a continental criticism of it. 'The firm entered upon speculations out of all reasonable proportion to its resources .. and the famous banking house of Baring Bros. & Co., *before whose signature only a little while ago every business man in the world bowed low*, has fallen.'[24] In other words, the collapse of Barings was not simply a business catastrophe; it was also an affront to the proud commercial ethics of the City, and consequently to its self-esteem and confidence.

Another approach to the question of merchant bank prestige is connected with the engagement of their partners as non-executive directors of other concerns, particularly of joint-stock banks and insurance companies; it has been estimated that in 1914 as many as half the boards of joint-stock banks were recruited from this source.[25] Directors lent their time and expertise to less experienced firms but in so doing they mortgaged the futures of their own businesses in various ways. Not only did they provide the means for the new banks to grow much faster and bigger than their own firms but, more significantly, they diverted enterprise from their own family interests. If Bagehot's comment could be relied on for the following half-century, delegation presented few problems, but the actual experience of some leading firms (notably Barings and Browns) suggests some neglect of the home base.[26] The available data on capital offer a measure of relative decline: despite the dramatic growth in world trade in the period, several leading banks failed to make good the capital taken out by retiring partners (Barings, Browns, Hambros), while others contracted sharply from this cause (Raphael, Gibbs, Guinness Mahon). There is some contemporary comment to suggest that it was often the owners of stagnant merchant banks who sought to be directors and then governors of the Bank of England – Sir August Prevost of Morris Prevost & Co. (closed 1914) and Lord Cunliffe of Cunliffe Brooks (amalgamated 1920) are clear-cut cases.[27]

A third explanation of the real decline of some merchant banks is the absorption of their partners in politics and drive for public honours. This no doubt reinforced the banker's public image but again diverted him from his family business. Among the numerous honours of the late Victorian and Edwardian age, the ranks of the 'steel barons' and 'beerage' look thin compared with the City nobility. Merchant bankers were honoured by at least a dozen peerages, nearly a score of knights and at least ten barons (foreign creations). Public figures like Lord 'Natty' Rothschild, Lord Revelstoke (E. C. Baring), Lord Swaythling (Samuel Montagu), Sir Edward Speyer and Sir Ernest Cassel were said to have been advisers to successive governments though it is difficult to assess how much value was attached to their views. The Gladstone family was represented in two City merchant banks (Ogilvy, Gillanders & Co. and Thomson Bonar & Co.) while Disraeli had an intimate connection with the Rothschilds, and later Jewish financiers (Rothschilds, Sassoons, Hirsch and Cassel) are supposed to have been close to King Edward VII. Political connections and influence are evidently a large and important subject in their own right and can be only mentioned here; but enough has been said to illustrate the fact that these activities absorbed much time that was lost to the family business, without necessarily contributing much to the political scene.[28] Some contributions were made late in the century to the furtherance of British imperialist interests, such as in Egypt, Persia and China but for the established merchant banks these were little more than time-consuming forays into high-risk areas that their banking instincts alone would have restrained them from.

Popular imagination has long invested merchant banking with a glamour and romance all of its own, and its expertise with awe-inspiring mystery. City men have contributed to this by shrouding their activities in secrecy; there has been little for writers to draw on beyond reverence for upper-class connections, anti-Semitic gossip and the kind of official 'histories' already complained of. But stripped of these trappings and irrelevancies, the Victorian merchant banking scene presents a fairly familiar picture to economic historians: a predominance of family businesses with a high turnover of firms, new entrants taking high risks to build up their capital while second- and third-generation firms stick to safe business with modest profit margins, the diversification of services offered by established firms, increasing competition from faster-growing and more capital-intensive American and German rivals, and in several prominent firms the diversion of the partners' time and enterprise to politics and country life. The 'technologies' of the industry were (and are) by no means difficult for newcomers or outsiders to understand, and to the vast majority of those daily occupied in the various branches of finance, theories and doctrines of economics or any other discipline were of no concern.[29] The only factors that distinguished this industry from others was the high entry requirement ('indubitable credit') for accepting houses, and the extraordinary international mix of the membership. However, the entry requirement was by no means required of issue houses, where connection was the thing that mattered, and it is possible to identify other service industries whose membership exhibited comparable ethnic diversity, for instance the mid-nineteenth-century export merchants of Manchester and Bradford.[30]

It is difficult to resist the conclusion that in the quarter-century before 1914 the merchant banks, or at any rate the prestige names, had lost much of their vigour and boldness. The 1890 crisis had enervated the two greatest houses and strong competition from the joint-stock banks had proved overwhelming in some sectors (India and the Far East, home and foreign 'rails'), while Schuster's Union Bank combine showed that the functions and resources of joint-stock and merchant banks could be united with striking success. Despite the strongest prejudice against them, Morgans stole the lead from London both in the USA and in British industrials. While other British and foreign banks united their strength, the merchant banks stood aloof but failed to make as much as they might of the syndicate and other alternatives. Many firms simply turned to short-term loans, as seen in the massive development of finance bills before 1914. There were of course still some lively innovators making their fortunes in the City – Sir Ernest Cassel, Sir Alexander Kleinwort, Robert Fleming, Saemy Japhet, Max Bonn and perhaps a few others – but they were a minority in the system. Much of the real enterprise lay elsewhere in the City, with men like H. O. O'Hagan, Sir Edward Holden, Panmure Gordon, Sir Charles Addis (of the Hong Kong & Shanghai Bank), Arthur Lampard (Harrisons & Crosfield), Sir Felix Schuster and others. The other pacemakers were foreign-trained – Hirsch, Cassel, Speyer, Werhner, Beit, and some of the German accepting houses listed in Chapter 3.

And what of the future? The First World War was a major setback to one of the most enterprising sectors of the City, the Anglo-German banks, and it took them several years to recover their position, by which time the crisis of 1931 was on them. In 1928, the peak year for acceptances in the interwar period, total acceptances reached £170m. or 80 per cent of the 1913 figure cited in Table 7.1.[31] The Anglo-American banks,

Morgans and to a lesser extent Seligmans, derived most benefit from the war, and other firms benefited in proportion to their ability to meet the massive expansion of transatlantic credit.[32] Similarly the postwar boom best suited those ready to catch the wind of the spate of new industrial issues – Morgans again, but also a new crop of firms such as Helbert Wagg, Cazenoves, Edward de Stein and Sir Arthur Wheeler's City operation (Charterhouse); once again fresh opportunities drew in new blood rather than reinvigorating the old. Meanwhile older concerns continued the sedate and amiable pace of the partners' room in a way that reflected past glories and the leisurely tempo of the gentleman's club rather than future challenges.[33] Relations between firms were generally easy-going and competition 'amiable'. Partners jealously guarded their old family independence and mergers were rare until after 1945. Rothschilds, Hambros, Montagus and other firms remained 'stodgy' in the view of the bill brokers who knew all the accepting houses; the former did not begin to divert their capital into domestic investments until the 1930s, and only then because they were persuaded by Philip Hill, the self-made financier and founder of what became Hill Samuel.[34] These details carry as well beyond the nineteenth-century City, but they contribute to a growing recognition that this parochial square mile did not change very much until after the Second World War. It would far too sweeping to speak of entrepreneurial failure in the third generation, for there were too many exceptions and too many newcomers to offer exceptions to such an easy generalisation, but it is difficult to resist the conclusion that the revered City establishment dawdled into the twentieth century.

This critical commentary is not intended to imply that the merchant banks, taken as a group, did not possess considerable resilience and potential for future growth; post-1945 experience clearly shows that they did. By international banking standards their capital looked increasingly modest and their family dynasties less and less relevant, but in the long term other assets proved of greater significance. The most important of these was the flexibility and specialism derived from their long mercantile background, so that in the interwar years several made the transition to industrial issues and corporate finance, and in the post-war years most of the survivors extended into insurance (if they were not already in it), financial consultancy and investment portfolios. When acceptances and public issues picked up they had the expertise to resume their earlier roles. Even the early mercantile role was not entirely discarded: several leading merchant banks continue as merchants in the sense that they are bullion brokers, represent companies at international fairs, ship out samples to test export markets for clients, and are active in compensation trade. Minnows in the international banking scene, they survive on their flexibility and capacity to innovate. Modest size has itself come to be seen as an asset, for the most successful have retained the rapid speed of response of the smaller firm. Most of the City's present-day meritocracy is only dimly aware of the value of its long mercantile inheritance, but few will fail to be recognise that diversity, flexibility and lively entrepreneurship will be as much the key to future success as past achievements.

Notes and References

The following abbreviations are used throughout the references:

Archives

BBAB	Baring Bros Archives at Barings, 8 Bishopsgate, London EC2.
BBAG	Baring Bros Archives at Guildhall Library, London EC2.
BBAC	Baring Bros Archives in the Canadian National Archives, Ottawa.
Brandt	40 vols of trade circulars collected by Wm Brandt & Sons, 1829–1934, Nottingham University Library Archives.
Gibbs	Business records of Antony Gibbs & Sons at Guildhall Library, London EC2.
Hambros	Business records of C. J. Hambro & Son deposited at Guildhall Library, EC2.
MC	Records of Morrison, Cryder & Co. at Guildhall Library.
Meyer	Letters of Sir Carl Meyer, 1884–1914, copies kindly lent by his grandson, Sir Antony Meyer Bt, MP.
Milner	Letters sent by Sir Clinton Dawkins to Sir Alfred (later Lord) Milner, Bodleian Library, Oxford.
PRO	Public Record Office, London WC1 and Kew.
RAL	Rothschild records in the Company archives of N. M. Rothschild & Sons, London EC4.
KB	Business records of Kleinwort Benson & Co. EC3, stored at the Company's records department at Newbury, but a few transferred to Guildhall Library.
B of E	Bank of England records at the Bank, London EC2. The principal series used in this book is the Agents' letters and letter books written at the branch offices at Manchester (abbreviated M), Liverpool (Lp) and Leeds (Le).
R. G. Dun	Dun & Bradstreet credit registers, Baker Library, Harvard University, Cambridge, Mass.

Journals and other published sources

BHR	*Business History Review*
BM	*Banker's Magazine*
CB	*Circular to Bankers*
EcHR	*Economic History Review*
JC	*Jewish Chronicle*
J Ec H	*Journal of Economic History*
J Eur Ec H	*Journal of European Economic History*.

Chapter 1

1   C. Wilson, *Anglo-Dutch Commerce and Finance in the Eighteenth Century* (Cambridge, 1941), *passim.*
2   C. Wilson, op. cit., p. 90. Acceptance credits are considered in detail in Chapter 7.
3   G. Yogev, *Diamonds and Coral. Anglo-Dutch Jews and Eighteenth Century Trade* (Leicester, 1978) esp. pp. 55-9. For the late survival of the system see S. Japhet, *Recollections from my Business Life* (1931) pp. 17-18.
4   C. Wilson, op. cit., esp. pp. 69, 142-3. M. G. Buist, *At Spes non Fracta: Hope & Co. 1770-1815* (The Hague, 1974) chs 2, 5. P. J. van Winter, *American Finance and Dutch Investment 1780-1805* (New York, 1977), I, ch. 3.
5   G. Yogev, op. cit., p. 58. C. Wilson, op. cit., pp. 111-14. R. W. Hidy, *The House of Baring in American Trade and Finance* (Harvard, Mass., 1949), ch. I.
6   S. D. Chapman, 'The international houses: the continental contribution to British commerce 1800-1860' *J Eur Ec H,* VI (1977). H. Luthy, *La Banque protestante en France,* II *1730-94* (Paris, 1961) p. 318. C. Wilson, loc. cit.
7   F. Redlich, *The Moulding of American Banking. Part II 1840-1910* (New York, 1951), pp. 311-15, offers the best short summary of London-based loan contractors at the period. S. R. Cope, *The History of Boyd, Benfield & Co: a Study in Merchant Banking in the Last Decade of the 18th Century,* Ph. D. thesis, London, 1947, esp. ch. 6. S. R. Cope, 'The Goldsmids and the development of the London money market', *Economica* IX (1942). P. K. O'Brien, *Government Revenue 1793-1815,* D. Phil. thesis, Oxford, 1966, ch. 2. J. J. Grellier, *The Terms of All the Loans* (3rd edn, 1812).
8   S. D. Chapman, 'The foundation of the English Rothschilds', *Textile History,* VIII (1977).
9   P. J. van Winter, op. cit., I, pp. 148-9, 166-8, 184. For the specific example see S. D. Chapman, 'British marketing enterprise: the changing roles of merchants, manufacturers and financers 1700-1860', *BHR,* LIII (1979).
10   S. D. Chapman, 'Marketing enterprise', loc. cit. The details assembled in the following paragraphs are also collected in the same article, where further examples appear.
11   S. D. Chapman, 'International houses', loc. cit.
12   S. D. Chapman, 'Marketing enterprise', loc. cit.
13   H. Thornton, *An Inquiry into Paper Credit* (1802), p. 59.
14   The generalisations of this section are again based on a wide literature assembled in S. D. Chapman, 'Marketing enterprise', loc. cit.
15   S. D. Chapman, 'Foundation of the English Rothschilds', loc. cit., and 'International houses', loc. cit.
16   MC. *passim.*
17   S. D. Chapman, 'Marketing enterprise', loc. cit., and see also Chapter 3.
18   ibid.
19   V. Nolte, *Fifty Years in Both Hemispheres; or Reminiscences of a Merchant's Life* (1854), and see also Chapter 7.
20   S. D. Chapman, 'Marketing enterprise', loc. cit., and see also Chapters 3 and 4.
21   ibid.

Chapter 2

1   cf. G. Yogev, *Diamonds and Coral. Anglo-Dutch Jews and Eighteenth Century Trade* (Leicester, 1978), pp. 55-6.
2   *Gentleman's Magazine,* Sept. 1836, p. 326. B. Gille, *Histoire de la maison Rothschild,* I (Geneva, 1965) pp. 193-4, 469-70.

3   RAL T4/61, J. Stern to NMR 8 May 1815.
4   *Sel. Comm. on Cash Payments*, Parl. Papers, 1819, III, p. 159.
5   For example *Gentleman's Magazine,* 1836, p. 328. B. Gille, op. cit., I, p. 192.
6   D. E. W. Gibb, *Lloyd's of London* (1972) pp. 146-7. Gibb treats these chairmen only as prominent politicians, missing their bank connections.
7   B. Gille, op. cit., I, pp. 414-15. RAL 109/53/1, 13, letters from James de R. and Weisweller (Madrid) to NMR & Sons, Jan.-June 1843.
8   R. Liebeschutz, 'August Belmont and the House of Rothschild', *Leo Baeck Inst. Year Book,* XIV, p. 224.
9   B. Gille, op. cit., esp. I, pp 469-70, 484-5.
10 B. Gille, op, cit., II, pp. 558-9. See also Chapter 6.
11 Cardiff RO, Dowlais Iron Works, London letter books 1837-67.
12 RAL T7/157, Nathaniel to London brothers, n.d. (1847).
13 RAL T7/158, Nathaniel to London brothers, n.d. (1847). T9/4, same to same, 22 Mar. 1862.
14 J. H. Clapham, *The Bank of England: a History* (1944), II, pp. 168-72.
15 RAL T7/16, 17, A.S. de R to London cousins, 28 and 31 July 1839.
16 Bates's Journals, 7 Jan. 1840.
17 RAL T58/57 Belmont to NMR & Sons, 27 Apr. 1870 cf. R. Liebeschutz, op. cit., p. 227.
18 RAL T54/310, Belmont to NMR & Sons, 27 Nov 1849. cf. I. Katz, *August Belmont: a Political Biography* (New York, 1968)
19 R. Liebeschutz, loc. cit, cf. RAL T10/157, Alphonse to London cousins, 30 Sept. 1869.
    RAL T10/176, Anthony R. to his brothers, n.d. (Nov. 1869).
20 RAL T54/313 Belmont to NMR & Sons 19 Feb. 1850.
    T54/344, same to same, 15 July 1851 RAL ledgers II/81/0-7.
21 RAL T10/79, Baron James to London nephews, 18 July 1868, cf. *The Economist,* 3 Mar. 1866, citing Baron James's evidence to the French government's monetary inquiry of that year.
22 H. A. Chilvers, *The Story of De Beers* (1959) pp. 56-7. Letters of (Sir) Carl Meyer (1851-1922), 4 vols 1884-1914, kindly lent by his grandson, Sir Anthony Meyer, MP. RAL Gansl letters XI/4/47, esp. 16. Nov. 1882.
    R. Turrell, 'Rhodes, De Beers, and monopoly', *Journal of Imperial and Commonwealth History,* X (1982). J. J. Van-Helton, 'Empire and high finance', *Journal of African History,* XXIII (1982).
23 F. C. Gerretson, *History of the Royal Dutch,* (1953-7), I pp. 213-16, III, pp. 115-17. R. W. Hidy and M. E. Hidy, *Pioneering in Big Business* (New York, 1955) pp. 132-252, 259. R. Henriques, *Marcus Samuel* (1960) p. 67. D. Avery, *Not on Queen Victoria's Birthday* (1974) p. 156. J. D. Henry, *Baku: an Eventful History* (1905), pp. 113-14.
24 cf. John Francis, *Chronicles and Characters of the Stock Exchange* (1849), p. 303.
25 RAL T10/389, 11 Apr. 1872.
26 *The Times,* 4 June 1879, cf. A. R. Wagg, *History of the Firm* (typescript, n.d., in archives of J. Schröder Wagg Ltd).
27 Analysis of RAL ledgers VI/10/0-113 (1815-1914). T11/62, Baron Edmond to London cousins, 18 Feb. 1874.
28 RAL T13/163, 203, Baron Alphonse to London cousins, 16 Jan. and 10 Dec. 1885.
29 John Francis, op. cit., p. 308. Obituaries in *The Times,* 1 April 1915, 30 May 1917. A. R. Wagg, loc, cit., Carl Meyer letters, III, 263, 15 Feb. 1905, and *passim.*
30 J. Ayer, *A Century of Finance, 1804-1904: the London House of Rothschild* (1905) lists all Rothschild issues in the period. H. O. O'Hagan, *Leaves from My Life,* I (1929) pp. 377-8; the author was the most successful company promoter of the period.
31 Information from Clive Trebilcock, the historian of Vickers, 10 Mar. 1982.

32 *The Times*, 1 Apr, 1915. On Chinese loans, see Chapter 8, on Panmure Gordon see H. O. O'Hagan, op. cit., p. 368, and A. R. Wagg, loc. cit.

33 R. Hidy, *The House of Baring in American Trade and Finance 1763–1861* (Harvard, 1949). Canadian Public Archives, Ottawa: Baring Bros MSS, esp. trade circulars (1833). Joshua Bates's Journals, seven vols, 1830–64 (private ownership). Until an authorised history of the firm has been published, Baring Bros' retained records are available only for specifically approved projects.

34 William Rathbone VI, *A Sketch of Family History during Four Generations* (Liverpool, privately published, 1894) pp. 129–30. BBAC 3,048, 3,082–4.

35 W. Rathbone, loc. cit. Bates's Journals, 12 Jan. 1839. R. Hidy, op. cit., p. 79. On Ward see also RAL T54/290, Belmont to NMR & Sons, 15 May 1849.

36 Bates's Journal, 30 Aug. 1831, 23 Sept. 1838, 3 Apr. 1858. BBAC 3055 Bates to Biddle 20 Dec. 1834. On the Lancashire context, see S. D. Chapman, 'Financial restraints on the growth of firms', *Ec H R*, XXXII (1979).

37 Julian Sturgis, *From Books and Papers of Russell Sturgis* (Oxford, 1893) esp. pp. 210, 237, 254. BBAC, esp. 10,935–6, Russell & Sturgis to BB, 21 Sept. 1862.

38 BBAC 80,056–7, 80,123–4 (trade circulars, 1833).

39 Bates's Journals 8 June 1837, 4 June 1842, 18 June 1848, 15 Feb. 1851, 7 Jan. 1856, and *passim*. F. Hidy, *House of Baring in American Trade*, pp. 43–4, 79–82. B. W. Currie, *Recollections, Letters and Journals 1827–96* (privately printed, 1901), I, esp. p. 43.

40 Baring Bros & Co.'s ledgers are not open to research so it is not possible at present to make a full analysis of sources of income, but occasional figures scattered through Bates's Journals suggest that commissions fluctuated from over half to two-thirds as a percentage of gross profits; see esp. Journals 15 Sept. 1832, 12 Feb. 1834, 23 Jan. 1851.

41 M. Gérard, *Messieurs Hottinguer, Banquiers à Paris*, II (1968) pp. 152–3. R. Fulford, *Glyn's 1753–1953* (1953), p. 159. Williams & Glyn's Archives: Pascoe Glyn's letterbook, 28 Sept. 1863.

42 P. L. Cottrell, *Investment Banking in England 1856–82*, Ph.D. thesis, Hull, 1974, p. 164. Bates's Journals, 6, 11 May 1863.

43 *The Times*, 15 May 1848. Bates's Journals, 20 Nov. 1853, 1 April 1858.

44 *The Times*, 20 Nov. 1873. T. G. Baring (Earl Northbrook), *Journals and Correspondence of Sir Francis Thornhill Baring* (privately published, 1905), p. 276. Y. Cassis, *Les Banquiers Anglais 1890–1914: Etude Sociale*, D-ès-L. thesis, Univ. of Geneva, 1982, esp. p. 294.

45 M. E. Hidy, *George Peabody, Merchant and Financier 1829–1854* (New York, 1978) pp. 270–1, 345–8. R. Hidy, op. cit., pp. 386, 423. D. A. Adler, *British Investment in American Railways 1834–98* (Charlottesville, 1970), p. 36.

46 E. J. Perkins, *Financing Anglo-American Trade: the House of Brown 1800–1880* (Harvard, Mass., 1975) pp. 119–21. RAL T49/53, 14 Jan. 1849.

47 D. A. Adler, op. cit., pp. 16–19, 205f. L. H. Jenks, *The Migration of British Capital to 1875* (1927) pp. 201–4. R. Fulford, op. cit., ch. 8.

48 Bates's Journals, 2 Apr. 1845, 4 Oct. 1846, 18 June 1848, 1 Jan 1858.

49 *The Times*, 22 Apr. 1857, 1 May 1857. J. N. Westwood, *A History of Russian Railways* (1964) pp. 40 ff.

50 *The Times* supplement, 8–9 Nov. 1927.

51 Bates's Journals, 26 Dec. 1853, 1 Jan. 1856, 3 Jan. 1857.

52 See Chapter 8.

53 Appendix 4.

54 *BM*, XLVIII (1888), pp. 607–8.

55 *The Statist*, XXII (1888), p. 624. H. O. O'Hagan, op. cit., pp. 376–9.

56 T. Skinner, *The London Banks* (1891 et seq.)

57 Appendix 4.

58 *Dictionary of Business Biography*, John, second Lord Revelstoke (1863–1929); for a less

flattering interpretation by a contemporary, see Chapter 3. Bodleian Library, Milner MSS 214/41, Clinton Dawkins to Milner, 22 Mar. 1901.

59 V. P. Carosso, *More than a Century of Investment Banking: The Kidder Peabody Story* (New York, 1979) esp. pp. 17–24, 33–4, 188.

60 E. T. Hooley, *Hooley's Confessions* (1925), pp. 26–31.

61 J. R. Killick, 'Risk, specialisation and profit in the mercantile sector of the 19th century cotton trade: Alex Brown & Sons 1820-80', *BHR*. XVI (1974).

62 See Chapters 3, 4 and 8.

63 RAL T31/61, Amshel to Jacob, 8 Feb. 1816.

64 RAL T31/53, Soloman to NMR and James, 2 Feb. 1816.

65 Bates's Journals, 3 Nov. 1834, 20 Nov. 1853, 3 Mar. 1858.

66 B. W. Currie, op. cit., I, p. 21. R. Girault, *Emprunts Russes et investissements Français en Russie 1887-1914* (Paris, 1973), pp. 148, 188 ff.

67 M. E. Hidy, op. cit., pp. 224, 328 ff. RAL T55/18, Belmont to NMR & Sons, 24 Nov. 1855.

68 Quoted in P. L. Cottrell, op. cit., p. 376. cf. Fritz Stern, *Gold and Iron: Bismarck, Bleichroder, and the Building of the German Empire* (New York, 1977).

69 RAL 58/35, 18 Nov. 1869.

70 F. C. Gerrestson, op. cit., II pp. 145-6, IV p. 185.

Chapter 3

1   *CB* 8 May 1835, 2 Sept. 1836, 23 June 1837. W. Rathbone VI, *A Sketch of Family History during Four Generations* (Liverpool, |1894), p.129. L. S. Pressnell, *Country Banking in the Industrial Revolution* (Oxford, 1956) p. 485.

2   Bates's Journals, 15 Sept. 1832, 12 Feb. 1834, 23 Jan. 1851, 7 Jan. 1856, 1 May 1857, MC, letters from Jones, Gibson & Orde of Manchester, 1836.

3   L. H. Jenks, *Migration of Capital*, p. 87. *CB* 7 Oct. 1836.

4   B of E 'American accounts 1836–42' ADV/B521. [C. Brogan], *James Finlay & Co. Ltd.* (Glasgow, 1951) p. 195. J. R. Freedman, *A London Merchant in Anglo-American Trade 1835-50* [Huth], Ph. D. thesis, London, 1968.

5   MC, letters from 9 June 1837, 24 Aug. 1837. BBA G HC 16/2.

6   S. D. Chapman, 'The International Houses: the continental contribution to British Commerce 1800-1860', *JEurEcH*, VI (1977) pp. 24 ff.

7   M. E. Hidy, *George Peabody Merchant and Financier 1829-54* (New York, 1978), pp. 188-9. A. J. Murray, *Home from the Hill*, p. 82. BBAG HC 16.

8   Brown Bros letter book 1825-7, New York Historical Society. E. J. Perkins, *Financing Anglo-American Trade: the House of Brown 1800-1880* (Harvard, Mass., 1975) pp. 34-7.

9   B of E Lp ltrs, 8 Sept. 1827. A. Ellis, *Heir of Adventure* (1960), p. 28.

10 A. Ellis, loc. cit. E. J. Perkins, op. cit., pp. 37, 39. Pennsylvania Historical Society, Cope MSS, Copes to Cropper Benson & Co. 21 Mar. 1822.

11 E. J. Perkins, op. cit., pp. 119–21, 141, 145–6. B. Gille *La maison Rothschild*, II, p. 582. RAL T54/316, Belmont to NMR & Sons, 1 Apr. 1850.

12 RAL Belmont letters T58/63, 10 June 1870; T58/35, 13 Dec. 1870.

13 RAL Belmont T59/67, 6 Sept. 1884.

14 RAL T49/53 Baron Alphonse to London cousins 14 Jan. 1849.

15 S. D. Chapman and S. Diaper, *Kleinwort Benson in the History of Merchant Banking* (Oxford, 1984), ch. 6. H. Clay, *Sir Montagu Norman* (1957) p. 53.

16 A. Deitz, *Stammbuch der Frankfurter Juden* (Frankfurt, 1907) pp. 297-8. L. H. Jenks, op. cit., pp. 270, 421-3. *BM* XLVII (1887) p. 1047. *JC* 26 Jan. 1877, 5 July 1895.

17 A. Dietz, op. cit., pp. 76-7, 335-6. P. H. Emden, *Money Powers of Europe* (1939) p. 397.

18 B. Supple, 'A business elite', *BHR* XXXI (1957) p. 156. A. Dietz, op. cit., pp. 290-1, 417. R. G. Dun, vol. 342, pp. 216, 300V, 300QQ.

19 A. Dietz, op. cit., pp. 275-6, 418. *BM* LXXI (1901) pp. 423-4. E. J. Perkins, op. cit., p. 209. See also Chapter 8.

20 K. Grunwald, *Studies in the History of German Jews in Global Banking* (Jerusalem, 1930) pp. 13-14. D. A. Adler, *British Investment in American Railways 1834-1898* (Charlottesville, Va, 1970) pp. 205-7.

21 Linton Wells, *The House of Seligman* (typescript, 1931, New York Hist. Soc.) esp. I pp. 56-80, 155-63, II pp. 259 ff. Isaac Seligman, *Reminiscences* (New York, 1925) esp. pp. v, xi-xii. S. Birmingham, *Our Crowd: the Great Jewish Families of New York* (New York 1977) p. 130.

22 S. Japhet, *Recollections from my Business Life* (1931), esp. pp. 13, 32, 37.

23 R. G. Dun, vol. 198, pp. 101B, 174. Brandt, 1877, p. 169, 1884, p. 547.

24 *BM* LXXXVIII (1909) pp. 667-8, XCI (1911) p. 283.

25 Records of R. Raphael & Sons at the firm (now Raphael Zorn, EC2), esp. newsclip of 30 Oct. 1893.

26 C. Bermant, *The Cousinhood* (1971) pp. 189, 282. R. J. D. Hart, *The Franklin Family of Liverpool and London* (1958).

27 RAL T 47/8, 5 Jan. 1898.

28 B. Bramsen and K. Wayne, *The Hambros 1779-1979* (1979) pp. 167-8. RAL T 6/67, Hambro & Son to Rothschilds 4 Mar. 1826. A. R. Wagg, *History of the Firm* (typescript at Schröder Wagg, n.d.)

29 cf. Constance de Rothschild (Lady Battersea), *Reminiscences* (1922) esp. p. 66, where she maintains that the family 'were on a different social plane from their co-religionists' and so could find few Jewish marriage partners of their own rank and had frequently to resort to intermarriage. See also Chapter 9 for syndicating connections.

30 RAL Belmont letters to NMR & Sons, T59/29, 28 Oct. 1879, T 59/32, 21 Jan. 1880, T 59/33, 19 Feb. 1880. D. A. Adler, op. cit., p. 207. *Fenn on the Funds* (1876 edn) p. 476.

31 A. Ellis, op. cit,. p. 108. Linton Wells, op. cit., pp. 259 ff, 298. S. Birmingham, op., cit., p. 131. D. Greenberg, *Financiers and Railroads 1869-1889: a Study of Morton, Bliss & Co.* (Newark, Del., 1981) pp. 149-51, 167.

32 The best summary of American developments is V. Carosso, *Investment Banking in America: a History* (Harvard, Mass., 1970), esp. ch. 2.

33 S. Japhet, op., cit., esp. pp. 17-18, 37-8.

34 R. J. Truptil, *British Banks and the London Money Market* (1936), p. 155. H. D. Kirchholtes, *Judische Privatbanken in Frankfurt-am-Main* (Frankfurt, 1969), p. 32. R. V. Kubicek, *Economic Imperialism: the Case of South African Gold Mining Finance 1886-1914* (Duke Univ. USA, 1979) pp. 155-6.

35 BBAB European Customer Reference Books, III, p. 39, 74. J. Mai, *Das Deutsche Kapital in Russland 1850-94* (Berlin, 1970) p 70. T. Skinner, *The London Banks,* gives a year of foundation for all these firms.

36 L. Corry, *The House of Morgan* (1930). A. Sinclair, *Corsair* (1981). These popular books neglect the English sources but Prof. V. Carosso is now researching to prepare a more scholarly work.

37 R. G. Dun, vol. 348, p. 882 (1863). M. E. Hidy, op. cit., pp. 19n., 343-4. RAL T 54/259, Belmont to NMR & Sons, 21 Aug. 1852. [Anon.], *George Peabody & Co., J. S. Morgan & Co., 1838-1958* (Oxford, 1958) pp. 9-12.

38 R. G. Dun, vol, 418 pp. 278 (1871), 300A (1875), 300Q (1876), 300NN (1877), 300 A28 (1882). RAL Belmont letters, T 59/50 6 July 1881, T 59/67, 6 Sept. 1884. R. A. Dayer, *Bankers and Diplomats in China, 1917-25: the Anglo-American Relationship* (1981), p. 18. D. A. Adler, op. cit., p. 196.
    For later enterprise of J. S. Morgan & Co. and Morgan Grenfell & Co. in industrial securities, see p. 101ff.

39   R. McElroy, *L. P. Morton: Banker, Diplomat and Statesman* (New York, 1930), ch. 3.
     D. Greenberg, op. cit., esp. pp. 24–5, 30–5, 70–2. R. G. Dun, vol. 200, pp. 343, 396,
     vol. 205, p. 809, vol. 416, pp. 80., 100 WW, 100 A39, 100 A96, 100 A153. D. A. Adler,
     op. cit., pp. 205 ff.
40   H. M. Larson, *Jay Cooke, Private Banker* (Cambridge, Mass., 1936) pp. 182–4,
     309–10. D. A. Adler, op. cit., p. 145. *The Times* 23 Aug. 1906.
41   BBAC 80, 343, Thomson Hankey & Co. sale, 19 July 1838. Bates's Journal 29 Nov.
     1857. D. A. Adler, op. cit., pp. 81–2, 94–5. *The Statist* XXXIV (1894), p. 574.
42   Milner MSS 214/42, 41, Dawkins to Milner, 8 Feb. and 22 Mar. 1901.
43   Linton Wells, op. cit., II, p. 341. S. Birmingham, op. cit., pp. 130–1, 190. T. Skinner,
     London Banks (1914).
44   K. Grunwald, 'Windsor-Cassel: the last Court Jew', *Leo Baeck Inst. Year Book*, XIV
     (1969). C. Adler, *Jacob H. Schiff: his Life and Letters* (New York, 1928), *passim*.
45   PRO T 172/134, report on a conference between the Chancellor of the Exchequer,
     members of the Cabinet and representatives of the accepting houses, 12 Aug. 1914.
     F. H. Jackson of Huths was critical of the estimate, but this is understandable as his
     firm's capital was significantly below the median figure of £1m. on which the estimate
     appears to have been based.

Chapter 4

 1   See Chapter 8.
 2   Bankruptcies included Reid, Irving & Co. in 1847, Wm Brandt & Co. in 1861,
     Dennistoun & Co. in 1857, Robert Benson & Co. in 1875, and Heath & Co. *c.* 1885: D.
     Morier Evans, *The Commercial Crisis 1847–8* and *The History of the Commercial Crisis
     1857–8;* C. Amburger, *William Brandt*, p.49; *The Times*, 17 June 1875, D. A. Adler,
     British Investment in American Railways (1970) p. 196n. Brandts was the parent house
     of the London firm of that name.
 3   Omissions include the firms of Argenti, Zarify, De Jersey and Cassel: *The Statist*
     XXXIV (1894), p. 574.
 4   See Chapter 8.
 5   For a case study, see Coxes in J. R. Winton, *Lloyds' Bank* (1982) ch. 6.
 6   See Chapter 2.
 7   R. Fulford, *Glyn's 1753–1953. Six Generations in Lombard Street* (1953). See also
     Chapter 9.
 8   Appendix 3. Accepting Houses Committee circular notice, 5 Aug. 1914 (at the
     Committee's Office, EC3).
 9   J. R. Winton, loc, cit.
10   Wallis Hunt, *Heir of Adventure* (1951), I, *passim*.
11   R. J. Truptil, *British Banks and the London Money Market* (1936), p. 149.
12   See Chapter 6.
13   Appendix 3. For Rothschild and Baring see also Chapter 2. For Ralli and Schilizzi,
     Brandt Circulars, 1873, pp. 215–6. For the Far Eastern houses see Chapter 8. For other
     firms see standard histories in Appendix 5.
14   R. Raphael & Sons records, EC2. Montagu records in Midland Bank archives. A.
     R. Wagg, *History of the Firm* (typescript, n.d.), Schröder Wagg archives. S. Japhet,
     Recollections from my Business Lift (1931).
15   Baring MSS, reports on London merchants in 1830 (unlisted). C. Amburger, *William
     Brandt*, pp. 50, 67.
16   S. Japhet, *Recollections*, p. 61. S. E. Franklin, *Samuel Montagu & Co.* (typescript, 1967,
     Midland Bank archives). *Jewish Chronicle*, 17 Sept. 1909.
17   Analysis of T. Skinner, *The London Banks*, 1914.

18 W. L. Fraser, *All to the Good* [Autobiography] (1963) pp. 34, 36. KB Information Books, USA II p.52.
19 Barings' salary ledgers, BBAB (unlisted). Hambros List of Salaries (uncatalogued). op. cit. Chapman and Diaper, op. cit. Chapter 7. V. P. Carosso, *Investment Banking, p. 87.*
20 See Chapter 8. W. D. Rubenstein, 'British millionaires, 1809–1949', *Bull. Inst. Hist. Research,* XLVIII (1974).
21 See Chapter 8.
22 See Chapter 9.
23 S. D. Chapman, 'The international houses', *JEur EcH,* VI (1977). B of E M. Ltr Bks, VIII (1852) pp. 4–6.
24 Bates's Journal, 24 June 1844.
25 Kent RO Collet MSS C79/5–6, 35 letters April 1865 to April 1866.
26 A. C. Pointon, *Wallace Bros.* (Oxford, 1974) pp. 23–4, 67. S. Japhet, *Recollections,* p. 76 Milner 207/30, 9 Aug. 1899.
27 The late Sir Cyril Kleinwort in conversation with the author, 1977.
28 Guildhall Lib. Gibbs. MSS 11,042/2, pp. 692–5. cf. J. C. Brown, *A Hundred Years of Merchant Banking* (New York, 1909) pp. 292-3 (Brown Shipley).
29 [Anon.] *History of Lazard Bros. & Co. Ltd., London* (typescript at the firm, *c.* 1966). J. A. Spender, *Weetman Pearson, First Viscount Cowdray 1856-1927* (1930).
30 See Chapter 2. B. Gille, *Les Rothschilds, passim.*
31 [M. R. L. Meason], *Bubbles of Finance* (1865) pp. 163-4.
32 See Chapter 8.
33 V. Nolte, *Fifty Years in Both Hemispheres* (1854), pp. 287–94, 309.
34 *CB,* 1837, pp. 94–5, 366.
35 Chapman and Diaper, op. cit., chs 2 and 3.
36 M. G. Buist, *At Spes non Fracta: Hope & Co. 1770-1815,* pp. 40, 53, 68.
37 See Chapter 2.
38 E. J. Perkins, *Financing Anglo-American Trade: the House of Brown 1800-1880* (Harvard, Mass., 1975), p. 25.
39 B of E Lp. Ltr Bks IV (1843) pp. 252, 271. J. S. Gladstone, *History* (1910), p. 20. L. H. Jenks, *Migration of Capital,* pp. 143, 176.
40 Heather Gilbert, *Awakening Continent: the Life of Lord Mountstephen* (Aberdeen, 1965), p. 18.
41 S. Birmingham, *Our Crowd* (New York, 1977), p. 190. cf. RAL T10/37, Baron Alphonse to London cousins, 1869; T13/31, 38, same to same, 16 Jan., 10 Dec. 1885.
42 S. D. Chapman, 'International houses', p. 38. C. Amburger, loc. cit. T. Skinner, *London Banks,* 1900. p. 40. H. Clay, *Sir Montague Norman,* p. 53.
43 S. D. Chapman 'Financial restraints', *EcHR,* XXXII (1979).
44 *The Statist,* 17 Jan. 1885.
45 The five Far Eastern houses in order of incorporation were Chalmers, Guthrie & Co. (1899), Forbes, Forbes, Campbell & Co. (1904), Matheson & Co. (1909), James Finlay & Co. (1909) and Wallace Bros. & Co. (1911). T. Skinner, *London Banks* (1914).
46 Baring Bros 'Character Book No. 8' (1870-83), at the firm. David Sassoon & Co. incorporated in 1901. Another Far Eastern house to become a private company at this period was Blyth, Greene, Jourdain & Co. (1894). T. Skinner, op. cit.

Chapter 5

1   The standards outlined here are synthesised from customer reference books of the leading merchant banks of the period. The most useful of these are:
    BBAG HC 16 Reports on busines houses, 1836-7, 1843, 1849-50.
    BBAB (unlisted) 'Europe', 3 vols, *c.* 1845-*c.* 1875.
    'Character Books', [No 1] 1835, No 7 1870-83.
    KB Kleinwort Information Books, UK, 3 vols 1875-1910; Germany, 6 vols 1875-1911.
    Gibbs 11,038c, 11,069c Liverpool house reports 1884-1908.
    RAL II/34/0,1: Information Books, 2 slim vols, 1876-1923.
    B of E Agents' letters and letter books for Manchester, Liverpool and Leeds contain a large quantity of similar information, 1827-*c.* 1850.
2   RAL T29/364, N. M. Rothschild to Carl, 22 Dec. 1814.
3   BBAC p. 3055, 20 Dec. 1834.
4   B of E Lp ltr boks V (1844) p.2, VII (1847) p. 7, IX (1848), p. 58.
5   Lancs.CRO DX 1923 Preston Bank Character Book pp. 110, 138.
6   R. Hidy, *House of Baring*, pp. 138, 234. Bates's Journal 17 Jan. 1849, 1 Jan. 1858.
7   J. Killick, 'The cotton operations of Alexander Brown & Sons in the Deep South, 1820-60', *Jnl of Southern History*, XLIII (1977), p. 172. E. J. Perkins, *Financing Anglo-American Trade (Harvard, Mass., 1975) pp. 53-8*.
8   Linton Wells, *The House of Seligman*, I, pp. 88-9, 218.
9   G. Meinertzhagen, *A Bremen Family* (1912), p. 253, A. J. Murray, *Home from the Hill: a Biography of Frederick Huth* (1970), p. 161. R. Meinertzhagen, *Diary of a Black Sheep* (1964), p. 13. BBAG HC 16/2, report of 1843.
10 Liverpool RO, Diaries of George A. Brown, 1837. D. A. Adler, *British Investment* pp. 13-14. BBAG HC 16/2, 1843 report.
11 B of E Lp ltr bks VII (1846) p. 115, X (1849) p. 159 BBAG HC 16/2, 1843 report.
12 Gibbs MS 11,038c, report on London, Paris & American Bank.
13 V. Nolte, *Fifty Years*, p. 309. B of E Lp ltrs 17 Jan, 1829, ltr bks XI (1848), p. 36. BBAG HC 16/2, report of 1849-50.
    D. M. Evans, *History of the Commercial Crisis 1857-8* (1859), Appendix pp. 137-9. RAL Belmont T55/73, 6 Nov. 1857.
14 *Sel. Comm. on Finance and Industry* (1931), I, p. 75.
15 Unclassified records of J. H. Schröder Wagg & Co., London.
16 Unclassified records of Brown Shipley & Co. retained by the firm.
17 Quoted in Chapman and Diaper, *Kleinwort Benson* (Oxford, 1984) ch. 6.
18 Guildhall Lib. Brown Shipley Private Letter Books, 1879-80, p. 14 (unlisted).
19 Brown Shipley Private Letter Books 1891-2 p. 30, 1896-7 p. 269, 1898-9, pp. 214, 226, 237, 269.
20 Chapman and Diaper, op. cit., ch. 6.
21 Brandt 1863 pp. 230, 333-4, 1891 p. 131, 1892 pp. 555, 576, [Anon.], *Manchester Faces and Places* XVI (1905). Guildhall Lib. Brown Shipley Private Letters to the American Houses, p. 108 (unlisted).
22 Brandt 1875 pp. 180-1, 1889 pp. 20, 150, 1897 p. 233. Brown Shipley Private Letters to the American Houses, p. 84. BBAB Customer Reference Books, Europe, II, no. 2732 Meyer I/35, 10 Aug. 1886, III/271, 22 Feb. 1905.
23 H. O. O'Hagan, *Leaves from my Life* (1929), I, pp. 377-9.
    B. W. Currie, *Recollections, Letters and Journals 1827-96* (1901), I, p. 89.
24 *The Statist*, XXII (1888), p. 685.
25 RAL T14/39, Baron Alphonse to London cousins, 12 Oct. 1888.
26 *The Statist*, XXIV (1889), p. 100; XXV (1890), p. 257.

27 Quoted by L. S. Pressnell 'Gold reserves, banking reserves and the Baring crisis', in C. R. Whittlesey and J. S. G. Wilson (eds), *Essays in Money and Banking* (Oxford, 1968) p. 195.
28 RAL T15/44, Baron Alphonse to London cousins, 15 Nov. 1890.
29 Records of Raphael, Zorn & Co., London EC2.
30 *The Statist*, XXIX (1892) pp. 207, 321. Brown Shipley Private Letters Books, 1891–2, pp. 28–9. *The Times*, 8–10 June 1914.
31 B. W. Currie, op. cit., I, pp. xi, 89.
32 A. C. Pointon, *Wallace Bros.* (Oxford, 1974), p. 64.

Chapter 6

1 M. Winkler, *Foreign Bonds: an Autopsy* (Philadelphia, 1933) pp. 134–6.
2 S. D. Chapman, 'The establishment of N. M. Rothschild as a banker', in N. Gross(ed.), *Essays in Jewish Economic History* (forthcoming, Jerusalem, 1984).
3 RAL VI/10/5, Prussian Loan issue, 1818.
4 D. C. M. Platt, 'British portfolio investment overseas before 1870', *EcHR*, XXXIII (1980).
5 J. Bouvier, *Les Rothschilds* (Paris, 1967) pp. 140–1.
    B. Bramsen and K. Wain, *The Hambros* (1979), p. 272.
6 RAL T8/334, Baron Alphonse to London cousins, 18 June 1852.
7 *The Economist*, 15 Aug. 1868, p. 925. J. Bouvier, *Le Crédit Lyonnais* (Paris, 1961), II, p.575.
8 (Anon.) *George Peabody & Co., J. S. Morgan & Co., Morgan Grenfell & Co. 1838–1958* (1958) pp. 8–12. D. S. Landes, 'The spoilers foiled', in C. P. Kindleberger and G. di Tella(eds), *Economics in the Long View* (1982), II, p. 87.
9 Linton Wells, *The House of Seligman* (typescript, New York Hist. Soc., 1931), II, pp. 259 ff.
10 Merseyside County Musuems, Fraser Trenholm MSS, Prioleau to Trenholm, 21 Oct. 1863. The Erlanger background is summarised in H. D. Kirchholtes, *Judische Privatbanken in Frankfurt* (Frankfurt, 1969) pp. 33–4.
11 Fraser Trenholm MSS, Prioleau to J. T. Welshman (partner), 9 May 1863.
12 ibid., Prioleau to Trenholm, 6 May 1864.
13 R. I. Lester, 'The Erlanger loan and the plan of 1864', *BHR* XVI (1974).
14 CB 6 Nov. 1835. *Fenn on the Funds* (1876 edn) pp. 262–3.
    R. Graham, *The Onset of Modernisation in Brazil* (1968), p. 102.
15 *Fenn on the Funds.* BBAB Stock ledgers.
16 L. H. Jenks, *Migration of British Capital to 1875* (1927), ch. 9.
17 BBAC, 10,398–10,403, Barings to Governor of S. Carolina, draft, 1857.
18 D. C. M. Platt, *The Origins, Function and Destination of Foreign Finance 1815–75* (forthcoming, 1984).
19 Quoted in A. Ellis, *Heir of Adventure* (1960) p. 108.
20 *Sel. Comm. on Foreign Loans*, Parl. Papers, 1875, XI, pp. 1–3.
21 D. C. M. Platt (ed.), *Business Imperialism 1840–1930* (Oxford, 1977) esp. ch. 9. This theme is further developed in Chapter 10.
22 *Sel. Comm. on Foreign Loans, pp 174 ff, 221 ff.*
23 1860–76 data compiled from L. H. Jenks, op. cit., Appendix C, with corrections and omissions from *Fenn on the Funds* (1876), Jules Ayer, *A Century of Finance 1804–1904*, and an internal list of Baring Bros, foreign, colonial and commercial loans.
    1877–90 data assembled from information published in *The Economist*, *The Statist*, J. Ayer, Fenn, and Barings' internal list. Increasing familiarity with merchant bank records shows that none of these published sources is complete.
24 H. O. O'Hagan, *Leaves from my Life* (1929), I pp. 150–2.

25 *The Times*, 1 Apr. 1915. RAL XI/111/36.
26 BBAB stock ledgers, 17/10 (1899–1905). Schröder Wagg Archives, 'Black Books' (issue prospectuses).
27 L. H. Jenks, op. cit., p. 140. Barings' internal list of issues.
28 L. H. Jenks, op. cit., ch. 5. S. J. Reid (ed.), *Memoirs of Sir Edward Blount* (1902). *Dictionary of National Biography* (Sup.), Samuel Laing.
29 B. Gille, *La maison Rothschild*, I, pp. 289, 334, 344, 353-6. RAL T7/55 (n.d., but 1846).
30 M. C. Reed, *Investment in Railways in Britain 1820-44* (Oxford, 1975).
31 B of E Manc. ltr books, VI, pp. 72,159. *BM*, LXXI (1901) pp. 423-4. M. C. Reed, op. cit., p. 206.
32 D. A. Adler, *British Investment in American Railways*, p. 25.
33 D. A. Adler, op. cit., esp. ch. 1.
34 D. A. Adler, op. cit., pp. 36-8. S. Marriner, *Rathbones of Liverpool 1845-73* (Liverpool, 1961) pp. 22, 59. R. Hidy, *House of Baring*, pp. 349, 356, 372. For investment in iron works see B. Gille, op. cit., I, pp. 388 ff., Bates's Journals 4 Oct. 1846, L. H. Jenks, op. cit., p. 390 (Huth).
35 M. E. Hidy, *George Peabody, Merchant and Financier* pp. 270-1, 282, 292-3, 343-5 R. Hidy, op. cit., pp. 408 f., 423.
36 RAL esp. T54/275, 20 Mar. 1848, T54/279, 7 Aug. 1848.
37 RAL T54/278, 29 Apr. 1853.
38 RAL T8/334, Baron Alphonse to London cousins, 18 June 1852.
39 RAL T54/259, 21 Aug. 1852.
40 J. Mai, *Das Deutsche Kapital in Russland* (Berlin, 1970), p. 65.
41 M. Gérard, *Messieurs Hottinguer, Banquiers à Paris*. I (1968) pp. 537-71.
42 Bates's Journals, 30 Nov., 28 Dec. 1856.
43 B of E, Samuel Dobrées's diary, 24 Apr. 1857. *The Times*, 10 Jan. 1857.
44 *The Times*, 1, 13 May 1857. Bates's Journals, 1 May 1857. B. W. Currie, *Recollections* (1901), II, p. 115. BBAC 75,210.
45 L. H. Jenks, op. cit., pp. 198-206. R. Fulford, *Glyn's 1753-1953*, ch. 8.
46 For example *Daily Globe*, 1-2 Apr. 1856.
47 L. H. Jenks, op. cit., pp. 300 f. D. C. M. Platt, *Origins, passim*.
48 K. Grunwald, *Turkenhirsch* (Jerusalem, 1966), esp. pp. 13-18. D. A. Adler, op. cit., pp. 205-7. *The Statist*, XXXVII (1896) p. 520. *JC* 24 Apr. 1896.
49 For stockbrokers see for example W. J. Reader, *A House in the City ... Foster & Braithwaite 1825-1975* (1979).
50 D. Greenberg, *Financiers and Railroads 1869-1889: a Study of Morton, Bliss & Co.* (Delaware, 1981). cf. S. D. Chapman and S. J. Diaper, *Kleinwort Benson*, ch. 3.
51 D. A. Adler, op. cit., pp. 24, 86-9, 167-9. Pore's *Railway Manual* (1893). *The Statist*, XXII (1888, 2) pp. 69, 719. L. H. Jenks, 'Britain and American railway development', *J Ec H*, XI (1951).
52 J. Savile, 'Some retarding factors in the British economy before 1914', *Yorks. Bulletin of Economic & Social Research*, XIII (1961).
53 S. D. Chapman, 'The international houses: the continental contribution to British Commerce 1800-1860' *JEurEcH*, VI (1977).
54 W. T. Jackson, *The Enterprising Scot* (Edinburgh, 1968), pp. 297, 302.
55 'Syndicate Books' at Robert Fleming & Co., London EC2.
56 P.L. Cottrell, *Industrial Finance 1830-1914* (1980) pp. 45ff. cf. 'A City man' [M. R. L. Meason], *The Bubbles of Finance* (1865).
57 *The Statist*, XXVI (1890, 2) p. 557.
58 For Grant see *Dictionary of National Biography*, L. H. Jenks, *Migration of British Capital*, p. 251, and H. O. O'Hagan, op. cit., pp. 32-5. For Adamson & Co. see P. L. Cottrell, op. cit., pp. 113 ff.
59 H. O. O'Hagan, op. cit., pp. 36, 79. W. J. Reader, *A House in the City* pp. 94-5, 106-9, 116-17.

60 John Kinross, *Fifty Years in the City* (1982), p. 48, and information from Mr Kinross, 27 Jan. 1983.
61 P. L. Payne, 'The emergence of the large-scale company in Britain 1870–1914', *EcHR*, XX (1967).
   At the regional level, the same point is even more clearly demonstrated from local directories of the type of *The Nottingham Red Book* (1885–1914) which contain sections on local joint-stock companies.
62 H. O. O'Hagan, op. cit., pp. 119 ff, 152, 377. *The Statist*, XX (1887), p. 514.
63 T. Balogh, *Studies in Financial Organisation* (Cambridge, 1950), p. 233. These figures may be revised by the current SSRC research programme of Prof. D. C. M. Platt.
64 T. R. Navin and M. V. Sears, 'The rise of a market for industrial securities', *BHR*, XXIX (1955).
65 D. Kynaston, 'The late-Victorian and Edwardian stockbroker as investment adviser', SSRC Business History Seminar, May 1982.
66 H. Withers, *International Finance* (1916), pp. 69–70.
67 John Kinross, op. cit., pp. 42, 47, 221, and information from Mr Kinross. L. Dennett, *The Charterhouse Group 1925–1979: a History* (1979), pp. 17 ff. Information from the late Sir Siegmund Warburg, 2 Sept. 1982. For a case study of the problems of merchant bank response, see S. D. Chapman and S. J. Diaper, op. cit., esp. ch. 4.

Chapter 7

1 Quoted in *The Economist*, 3 Mar. 1866, p. 254.
2 W. Maude, *Antony Gibbs & Sons Ltd* (1958), p. 31.Guildhall Lib., Hambros MSS 19,061, 19,129.
3 A. I. Bloomfield, *Short-Term Capital Movements under the pre-1914 Gold Standard* (Princeton, NJ 1963). S. Nishimura, *The Decline of Inland Bills of Exchange in the London Money Market 1855–1913* (Cambridge, 1971).
4 *Sel. Com. on Commerce*, Parl. Papers, 1833, VI, p. 123, ev. of T. Wiggin. C. Lewis, *America's Stake in International Investments* (Washington, DC, 1938), p. 560. D. C. North, 'The US balance of payments, 1790–1860', in National Bureau of Economic Research, *Trends in the American Economy in 19th Century* (Princeton, NJ 1960), pp. 623–4.
5 J. Potter, 'The Atlantic economy, 1815–60', in L. S. Pressnell (ed.), *Studies in the Industrial Revolution* (1960).
6 S. Nishimura, op. cit., p. 66.
7 *The Economist*, 31 Dec. 1913.
8 R. J. Truptil, *British Banks and the London Money Market* (1936), p. 160.
9 R. H. Brand, *War and National Finance* (1921) pp. 25, 60. A. I. Bloomfield, op. cit., p. 68. PRO T172/134, Accepting Houses Conference, 12 Aug. 1914. Major creditors of German firms included Kleinworts, Lazards, Rothschilds and Brandts.
10 RAL XI/61/10, S. Behrens & Söhne to NMR & Sons, 1 Sept. 1843. W. Rathbone, *A Sketch of Family History* (1894), p. 124. J. Seligman, *Reminiscences* (New York, 1925), p. xiv.
11 Guildhall Lib., Morrison, Cryder & Co. letters e.g. C. Vidal to MC 8 Apr. 1836, W. Harte to MC 11 May 1836, J. & F. Dorr to MC 15 Dec. 1835, F. J. Oliver to MC 28 Dec. 1835, 13 Apr. 1836 (hereafter MC ltrs)
12 B of E B'ham ltrs, 29 Jan. 1835.
13 MC ltrs, J. Archer to MC, 28 Apr. 1836.
14 See Chapter 2.
15 Bodleian Lib., Palmer MSS, J. Palmer to Barings 24 Aug. 1808.
16 J. W. MaClellan, 'Banking in India and China', *BM*, LV (1893), p. 51. *Sel. Comm. on Manufacturers*, Parl. Papers, 1833, ev. of John Innis, p. 197.

17   MC ltrs, C. J. Weber to MC, 15 May 1836. R. Hidy, *House of Baring*, p. 563.
18   *Sel. Comm. on Commercial Distress*, Parl. Papers, 1848, ev. of Charles Turner, pp. 51–5. See also Chapter 5.
19   J. W. MaClellan, op. cit., pp. 214–15.
20   J. S. Baster, *Imperial Banks*, pp. 106 ff.
21   J. W. MaClellan, op. cit., pp. 57, 735. *The Times*, 19 June 1875. National Monetary Commission, USA, *Interviews on the Banking System* (Washington, DC, 1910), ev. of Sir F. Schuster, p. 38.
22   J. W. MaClellan, op. cit., pp. 736–7.
23   J. W. MaClellan, op. cit., p. 173. M. Collis, *Wayfoong*, pp. 29, 58. A Muir, *Blyth, Greene & Jourdain, 1810–1960* (1961), p. 23. J. S. Gladstone, *History of Gillanders Arbuthnot & Co. ...* (1910), p. 75.
24   M. Keswick (ed.), *The Thistle and the Jade* (1982), p. 34. Kwang-Ching Lin, *Anglo-American Steamship Rivalry in China 1862–74* (Harvard, Mass., 1962) pp. 12–13, 57–60. A. C. Pointon, *Wallace Bros.* (1974) pp. 53, 56. T. Skinner, *The London Banks* (1910).
25   RAL XI 38/178 esp. letters of 24 Nov. 1841.
26   B of E M. Ltrs, 4 Apr. 1829. W. Bailey, *Western & Midland Directory, 1784. Universal British Directory*, III (1795), Manchester. C. Brogan, *James Finlay & Co. Ltd. 1750–1950* (Glasgow, 1951), pp. 11–12, 15. *Sel. Comm. on Copyright of Designs*, Parl. Papers, 1842, VI, ev. of S. Schwabe pp. 6–7.
27   B of E M. ltrs, 6 Dec. 1828, 12 Nov. 1834, 8 Sept. 1836, 17 Dec. 1836, 27 May 1837, 17 Aug. 1839, ltr. books IX (1854), p. 13, L. H. Grindon, *Manchester Banks and Bankers* (1877), p. 99.
28   Guildhall Lib., KB Information Books, UK I p. 49, III p. 91, KB 'Special Reports' (Newbury).
29   Midland Bank Archives 47/3: N. & S. Wales Bank Ltd., 12–14 May 1897.
30   R. S. Sayers, *The Bank of England 1891–1944* (1976), I, p. 269.
31   For König Bros and Rüffer see esp. RAL II/34/0, 1.
32   RAL general ledgers VI/10/0–113.
33   C. Amburger, *William Brandt*, pp. 52–4. S. D. Chapman and S. Diaper, *Kleinwort Benson*, ch. 6.
34   [Anon.], *175 Years: L. Behrens & Sohne, 1780–1955* (Hamburg, 1955).
35   J. Riesser, *The German Great Banks* (Washington, DC, 1911) esp. pp. 275–89, 298–9, 421–36.
36   National Monetary Commission, USA, *Interviews* p. 38.
37   Reminiscences of Michael Colefax, formerly of Kleinwort Benson Ltd, 27 Aug. 1981.

Chapter 8

1   Bibliography in Appendix 5.
2   *S. C. on Manufactures*, Parl. Papers 1833, p. 119, ev. of T. Wiggin.
    MC, numerous letters referring to the inauguration of banking by the firm in 1836. Morrison's earlier career as a textile warehouseman in the City is referred to in Chapter 3. M. E. Hidy, *George Peabody, Merchant & Financier* (1978) pp. 135, 138.
3   [Jack Vlasto], *Ralli Bros*, (1951). S. Fairlie, *The Anglo-Russian Grain Trade 1815–1861*, Ph.D. thesis, London, 1959, ch. 6. B of E M. ltrs, 18 Nov. 1839.
4   BBAB Customer Ref. Books (Europe), I. B of E Greek Firms' accounts 1848-52. B of E M. ltr bks VII (1850) p. 141, X (1857) p. 32. A. C. Ionides, *Ion: a Grandfather's Tale* (Dublin, 1927).
5   [M.R.L. Meason], *The Bubbles of Finance* (1865), pp. 187–8.
6   B of E M. ltr bks VIII (1852) pp. 4–6. P. Herlihy, 'Greek merchants in Russia in the 19th century', p. 16.

7 S. T. Zenos, *Depredations*, pp. 19. 76. Jack Vlastro, loc. cit. BBAB Customer Ref. Books, loc. cit.

8 Guildhall Lib., 11,042/1, pp. 277–85. J. A. Gibb, *The History of Antony and Dorothea Gibbs* (1922). W. M. Mathew, *The House of Gibbs and the Peruvian Guano Monopoly* (1981).

9 Cecil Roth, *The Sassoon Dynasty* (1941) esp. pp. 74-6, 97-9, 178-9.
S. Jackson, *The Sassoons* (1968) esp. pp. 21-4, 44, 98-9, 103-4.
KB Information Books, UK III, pp. 130-1. V. Berridge and G. Edwards, *Opium and the People* (1981), esp. p. 177.

10 S. Nishimura, *The Decline of Inland Bills of Exchange in the London Money Market 1855-1913* (Cambridge, 1971), p. 65. David Spring, 'Land owners in the late 19th century', paper read at Economic History Society Conference, Loughborough, 1981.

11 *Journ. Statistical Society*, XXI (1858), p. 450.

12 RAL T8/340, 15 Nov. 1852, Baron Alphonse to London cousins.

13 J. Bouvier, *Les Rothschilds (1967), p. 120*. Max Gérard, Messieurs Hottinguers, *Banquiers à Paris*, II (Paris, 1972), pp. 152-3. Bates's Journals, 6, 11 May 1863. Glyns are discussed below, see note 16.

14 P. L. Cottrell, *Investment Banking in England 1856-1882*, Ph.D. thesis, Hull, 1974, ch. 4.

15 RAL T9/5, undated note from the Paris House *c. 1862*, shows that Blount and Laing's backers included Schneider, Bartholomy, Paccard, Mirabeau, Piccard, Denière, Lucy Sedillot, Bischoffsheim, Talabot, Cahen d'Anvers and Heinch – not one English house. S. J. Reid (ed.), *Memoirs of Sir Edward Blount* (1902). cf. D. S. Landes, 'The old bank and the new: the financial revolution in the 19th century', in F. Crouzet, W. H. Chaloner and W. M. Stern (eds), *Essays in European Economic History* (1969).

16 B. W. Currie, *Recollections* I, pp. 52-3, 61-2. R. Fulford, *Glyn's 1753-1953*, p. 159. D. M. Joslin, *A Century of Banking in Latin America* (Cambridge, 1963), p. 65. Brandt 1871, p. 464 (Russian Bank). *City Press*, 1 July 1955 (Dalgety). A. S. J. Baster, *The Imperial Banks* (1929) p. 65.

17 These connections have been compiled from A. S. J. Baster, op. cit., *passim*, Brandt 1870 p. 122, 1872 pp. 85, 552, 574, 647.
J. Mai, *Das Deutsche Kapital* esp. pp. 68-70, and BBAB Customer Reference Books, Europe I pp. 436-54. For the Hong Kong & Shanghai Bank see this chapter, for the Imperial Bank of Persia, F. Kazemzadeh, *Russia and Britain in Persia 1864-1914* (Yale, 1968) ch. 2 and pp. 210 ff. For the Odessa Bank see A. K. Golubev, *Russkiye Banki* (St Petersburg, 1899), pp. 63-4.

18 BBAB Character Book 'No. 8' (1870-83), p. 104.

19 BBAG HC 16/2, Reports on Business Houses 1849-50. D. M. Evans, *Commercial Crisis 1857-8*, Appendix p. 137. Glasgow Univ. Archives: Union Bank of Scotland, Minute Book of Court of Directors UGD/129/1/6/1. Brandt 1913 pp. 108, 120.

20 B of E M. ltrs, 3 Aug. 1836, 18 Jan. 1837. *BM*, LXXI (1901) pp. 423-4. E. J. Perkins, *Financing Anglo-American Trade*, p. 209. BBAB Character Book 'No. 8' pp. 43, 193. K. Grunwald, *Studies in the History of the German Jews in Global Banking* (Jerusalem, 1980) pp. 95-6.

21 The clearest overview of the relation between the City of London and provincial financial centres is contained in the various Parliamentary inquiries: *Secret Comm. on Joint-Stock Banks*, 1836, IX, ev. of W. G. Cassels, p. 101, ev. of E. Burdekin. p.4. *Sel. Comm. on Joint-Stock Banks*, 1837-8, VII, ev. of S. Turner, p. 22. *Sel Comm. on Commercial Distress*, 1848, ev. of A. Hodgson, p. 16. *Sel. Comm. on Manufacturers*, 1833, VI, ev. of K. Finlay, p. 35.

22 Quoted by S. Nishimura, op. cit., p. 77.

23 *Sel. Comm. on Manufacturers*, 1833, VI, ev. of L. Lloyd, p. 23, of H. Houldsworth, p. 315.

24 *CB*, 1 May 1835.

25 A. Ellis, *Heir of Adventure* (1960), pp. 94-5. T. Ellison, *The Cotton Trade of Great Britain* (1886) pp. 275-80. S. Marriner, *Rathbones of Liverpool 1845-73* (Liverpool, 1961) pp. 128-32.
26 S. Marriner, op. cit., pp. 57-8, 207-23.
27 See Appendix 3.
28 A. Ellis, op. cit., p. 111. Appendix 3. cf. D. A. Farnie, *The Manchester Ship Canal* (Manchester, 1980) chs. 3-5.
29 KB Information Books, UK III, p. 116.
30 [C. Brogan,] *James Finlay & Co. 1750-1950* (Glasgow, 1951), *passim:* quotations from pp. 181, 105.
31 M. Keswick (ed.), *The Thistle and the Jade* (1981), *passim.* Kwang-Ching Liu, *Anglo-American Steamship Rivalry in China 1862-74* (Harvard, Mass., 1962) pp. 11-13, 138-9.
32 A. C. Pointon, *Wallace Bros.* (Oxford, 1974) esp. pp. 40-6, 53-5.
33 J. S. Gladstone, *History of Gillanders, Arbuthnot & Co. and Ogilvy, Gillanders & Co.* (1910) esp. pp. 79-80. KB Information Book, UK II, p. 165.
34 R. T. Stillson, 'The financing of Malayan rubber, 1905-23', *EcHR,* XXIV (1971). KB Information Books, UK III p. 166.
35 KB Information Books, UK II p. 47, III p. 151. Harrisons & Crosfield, *One Hundred Years as East India Merchants 1844-1943* (1943), ch. III.
36 PRO FO83/111, 115. C. Amburger, *William Brandt and the Story of his Enterprises* pp. 11, 17, 23. L. H. Jenks, *Migration of Capital,* p. 183. BBAG HC10. 28/7.
37 B of E M ltrs 29 Apr., 17 May, 28 June 1828. Lancs RO, Preston Bank 'Character Book' p. 128. BofE M ltr bks VI (1847) p. 147.
38 BBAG Character Book 'No. 8' (1870-83) pp. 47, 126, 189-90. R. G. Dun vol. 349 pp. 982, 1045. KB Information Books UK II p. 117. Brandt 1913 pp. 427-8, and Figure 8.2.
39 G. Schulze-Gaevernitz, *Volkswirtschaftliche Studien aus Russland* (Leipzig, 1899) pp. 91-106. R. G. Dun, vol. 349, pp. 920, 982, 1045, 1100A66. KB Information Books, Russia I, p. 40. C. Amburger, op. cit., pp. 61, 65-6.
40 H. P. Kennard, *The Russian Year Book* (1912), p. 678. Guildhall Lib., Anglo-Russian Cotton Co. records.
41 There is a large bibliography on the early developments on the Rand, much of it generated in recent years by the extensive Barlow Rand archives at Johannesburg. See esp. R. V. Kubicek, *Economic Imperialism in Theory and Practice* (1979) chs 4, 6; R. Turrell 'Rhodes, De Beers, and monopoly', *Journal of Imperial & Commonwealth History,* X (1982); S. D. Chapman, 'Rhodes and the City of London' (forthcoming article); A. P. Cartwright, *The Corner House* (Cape Town, 1965).
42 H. Raymond, *B. I. Barnato: a Memoir* (1897). S. Jackson, *The Great Barnato* (1970) esp. pp. 168-70. *The Statist,* XXI (1888) p. 274, XLII (1898) p. 457.
43 *The Economist* 1894, p. 299, 1895, p. 1075. Michell's estimates of capital is in Standard Bank Archives, Johannesburg, GMO 3/1/31 GM-LO No. 76/95, 18 Sept, 1895. R. V. Kubicek, 'The Randlords in 1895', *Journal of British Studies,* XI (1972) pp. 96-8. S. Jackson, op. cit., p. 120.
44 R. V. Kubicek, op. cit., pp. 155-7, 198. Peter Brackfield, 'And in Banking: Singer & Friedlander Ltd.', *Bowring Magazine* XXVII (1978).

Chapter 9

1 For capital of merchant banks c.1900 see Table 4.2; for 1914 see Table 7.2.
2 Except that the Midland Bank opened a foreign exchange department in 1905 and Lloyds Bank in 1911: A. S. J. Baster, *International Banks,* p. 55.

3 Brandt 1867 pp. 123–4, 1894 p. 559, 1913 p. 27. T. Skinner, *London Banks* (1914).
4 K. Grunwald, *Studies of the History of the German Jews in Global Banking* (Jerusalem, 1980) p. 96. T. Skinner, op. cit. C. Roth, *The Sassoon Dynasty* (1940) p. 97 ff. C. Amburger, *William Brandt*, p. 61.
5 'Banking in India and China', *BM*, LV (1893) pp. 50–1. W. Maude, *Antony Gibbs & Sons Ltd* (1958), p. 34. S. J. Reid (ed.), *Memoirs of Sir Edward Blount* (1902), p. 45. A. J. Murray, *Home from the Hill* (Huths) pp. 154, 158. R. Hidy, *House of Baring*, , p. 129. J. H. Clapham, *Bank of England*, II p. 334. For Rothschilds and Barings see also Chapter 2.
6 BBAB 'Character Book' 1870–83, pp. 133, 152. cf. Stanley Jackson, *The Sassoons* (1968), p. 98.
7 S. D. Chapman and S. Diaper, *Kleinwort Benson*, ch. 3.
8 Guildhall Lib. Hubbard MSS 10,364. H. P. Kennard, *Russian Year Book* (1912) p. 678.
9 T. Skinner, *London Banks* compared with the same author's *Directory of Directors*.
10 Guildhall Lib. Brown Shipley MSS, envelope marked 'Partners' File 1914'.
11 Records of Guinness Mahon & Co., London EC4.
12 'History of the London House of Lazard' (at Lazards).
13 Data published in T. Skinner, *London Banks* (1914).
14 J. J. Grellier, *The Terms of all the Loans* (1812). B. Gille, *La maison Rothschild*, I, p. 182.
15 RAL T9/76, n.d. but late 1865.
16 E. P. Oberholtzer, *Jay Cooke* (Philadelphia, 1907), II, pp. 278–88.
    H. Larson, *Jay Cooke* (Cambridge, Mass., 1936) pp. 322–5.
    Baring internal list of loans. L. Wells, *House of Seligman* (New York, 1931), II, pp. 259 ff. J. Ayer, *London House of Rothschild*, passim.
17 Brown Shipley 'Private and Confidential' letter books, 23 Feb. 1879–12 Feb. 1880. RAL T59/32, 33, Belmont to NMR & Sons 21 Jan., 19 Feb. 1880. Meyer I/72, 4 April 1888. J Ayer, op. cit.
18 *The Statist*, XXII (1888), p. 538.
19 R. Girault, *Emprunts Russes*, p. 165. Hambros MS 19,168.
20 Brown Shipley 'Private' letter books, 24 Dec. 1879. J. Ayer, op. cit. Barings' internal list of issues.
21 A. Crump, 'The Baring financial crisis', *Econ. Journal* I (1891).
    V. P. Carosso, *Investment Banking in America* (Harvard, Mass., 1970) ch. 3.
    R. Girault, *Emprunts Russes*, esp. chs 3, 6. K. E. Born, *International Banking in the 19th and 20th Centuries* (1983), ch. 5.
22 G. Diouritch, *L'expansion des banques allemandes a l'étranger* (Paris, 1909), p. 281. B. Gille, 'Finance internationale et trusts', *Revue historique*, CCXXVII (1962).
23 Milner MSS, 177/155–7, 213/158, 215/40, Dawkins to Milner, 26 July 1900, 16 Aug. 1900, 21 Mar. 1902. Meyer III/22, 7 Aug. 1900. K. E. Born, op. cit., pp. 119 ff. offers the only general account of this subject.
24 J. Ayer, op. cit., and Baring list. B. Bramsen and K. Wain, *The Hambros*, p. 329
25 W. Bagehot, *Lombard Street* (1875), 14th edn, pp. 204–5.
26 *BM*, XLVIII (1888), p. 607. A. Muir, *Blyth, Greene & Co.* (1961), p. 23.
27 *CB*, 1832, p. 205; 1837, p. 290. For Gurney and Morgan see Chapter 3. RAL T54/259, Belmont to NMR & Sons, 1852.
28 BBAC 3,057, Bates to Biddle, 20 Dec. 1834. Bates's Journals, 4 Mar. 1837.
29 Bates's Journals, 1, 8 Nov. 1835, 18 June 1848. BBAC 9,634–5, 10,036–7. The advances were made against the security of Pennsylvania Railroad stock.
30 M. E. Hidy, *George Peabody*, pp. 179 ff.
31 J. H. Clapham, op. cit., II, pp. 142–3.
32 J. H. Clapham, op. cit., II, pp. 80–2, 143–4. RAL VI/10/0–113. *CB*, 9 Oct. 1835.
33 BBAC 3,323.
34 J. H. Clapham, op. cit., II, pp. 144, 168–70. RAL T7/16, 17, 28 and 31 July 1839. Bates's Journals, 7 Jan. 1840.
35 D. Landes, *Bankers and Pashas*, pp. 66, 68. A. S. J. Baster, *International Banks*, pp. 70, 85. Brandt 1872, p. 654. A. K. Golubev, *Ruskiye Banki* (St Petersburg, 1899) pp. 63–4.

36 M. R. L. Meason, *The Bubbles of Finance* (1865) pp. 180, 186.
37 B of E MSS 3394, Greek firms' accounts, 1848–52. L. H. Jenks, *Migration of Capital*, p. 137.
38 Gibbs MSS 11,042/1, p. 308.
39 Glasgow Univ. Lib., Union Bank MSS UGD/9. D. M. Evans, *History of the Commercial Crisis 1857–8* (1859), p. cxxxvii.
40 S. Japhet, *Recollections from my Business Life* (1931).

Chapter 10

1 Sir Lawrence E. Jones, *Georgian Afternoon* (1958), pp. 143–4.
2 Milner 214/41, 213/161,46 Dawkins to Milner, 22 Mar. 1901, 2 Nov. 1900, 13 July 1901.
3 H. O. O'Hagan, *Leaves from my life*, I, p. 262.
4 See esp. Perry Anderson(ed.), *Towards Socialism* (1965) pp. 22–3.
5 Y. Cassis, *Les Banquiers Anglais 1890–1914*, D. -ès-L. thesis, Geneva (1982), chs, 2, 6, 7. F. Ladenburg, *Report on the Early Training of German Clerks*, Parl. Papers, 1889, LXXVII, pp. 495–7. S. D. Chapman and S. Diaper, *Kleinwort Benson*, chs 5, 6. K. Grunwald, 'Windsor-Cassel', *Leo Baeck Institute Year Book*, XIV (1969). Merchant bank office hours are mentioned in W. Rathbone, *A Sketch of Family History during Four Generations* (Liverpool, 1894), p. 124, Schröder Wagg Archives, MS 'Black Book' (end page regulations for clerks), Meyer I/*passim*, and W. L. Fraser, *All to the Good*, pp. 37–8. Rathbone's comment refers to his experience at Barings *c.* 1840, where the office hours were from 10 a.m. to 5 or 6 p.m. for four days in the week, but Tuesdays and Fridays were foreign post days and the clerks all had tea at the office and remained till they had finished their work. This pattern appears to have survived more or less down to the First World War in most houses.
6 W. D. Rubinstein, *Men of Property: the Very Wealthy in Britain since the Industrial Revolution* (1981), p. 92. Constance de Rothschild, *Reminiscences* (1922) p.66 for the family's unique position within Jewry.
7 C. J. J. Clay and B. S. Wheble (eds), *Modern Merchant Banking* (Cambridge, 1976), p. x.
8 F. S. Williams, *Rise and Progress of the Midland Railway* (1876) p. 38, for Huth and Hodgson. See Chapter 2 for Rothschilds. The Liverpool group (Gladstones, Rathbones, Bensons and so on) were promoters of the pioneer Liverpool–Manchester Railway (1830) but made little of their opportunities at the time, being immersed in the finance of cotton and Far Eastern trade.
9 S. D. Chapman, 'Financial restraints on the growth of firms . . . ,' *EcHR*, XXXII (1979), esp. pp. 62–5.
10 J. Bouvier, *Les Rothschilds*, p. 129. Marquess of Northampton's Baring records, Compton Wynyates.
11 B. Gille, *La maison Rothschild*, I, pp. 374–5. Bates's Journal, 13 Jan. 1850. M. Keswick (ed.), *The Thistle and the Jade* (1982), p. 194.
12 L. H. Jenks, *Migration of Capital*, p. 4 and ch. 5. James Rothschild quoted in *The Economist*, 3 Mar. 1866.
13 D. C. M. Platt, 'British portfolio investment overseas before 1870', *EcHR*, XXXIII (1980).
14 L. H. Jenks, op. cit., p. 334.
15 E. J. Perkin, *Financing Anglo-American Trade*, p. 136. D. S. Landes, *Bankers and Pashas: International Finance and Economic Imperialism in Egypt* (1958), pp. 41–2, notes that the 'established houses preferred to win and hold their clients by the quality of their services.'

16 Calculated from data in T. Balogh, *Studies in Financial Organisation* (Cambridge, 1947), p. 233, and estimates assembled in D. A. Adler, *British Investment in American Railways*, pp. 86, 169.

17 A. W. Currie, 'British attitudes towards investment in North American railroads', *BHR* XXXIV (1960).

18 B. Gille, 'Finance internationale et trusts', *Revue Historique*, CCXXVII (1962) p. 306, interpreting G. Diouritch, *L'Expansion des banques allemandes à l'étranger* (Paris, 1909), p. 281.

19 J. Riesser, *German Great Banks*, loc. cit. National Monetary Commission (USA) reports, ten vols, Washington, 1910, esp. *Report on the Banking and Currency Systems of England, Scotland, France, Germany, Switzerland and Italy*.

20 V. P. Carosso, *Investment Banking in America*, p. 69. D. M. Kotz, *Bank Control of Large Corporations* (Berkeley, Calif., 1978), pp. 36–7.

21 R. L. Muir and C. J. White, *Over the Long Term . . . the Story of J. & W. Seligman & Co. 1864–1964* (New York, 1964), p. 124.

22 W. Bagehot, *The English Constitution* (1872), Nelson edn, p. 29.

23 *BM* XVIII (1888), p. 609. My italics.

24 *BM* LI (1890), p. 621

25 This approach has been more fully developed by Y. Cassis, *Les Banquiers Anglais 1890–1914*, ch. 4.

26 cf. L. S. Pressnell, 'Gold reserves, banking reserves and the Baring Crisis', in C. R. Whittlesey and J. S. G. Wilson (eds), *Essays in Money and Banking* (Oxford, 1968). H. Clay, *Lord Norman* (1957), pp. 53 ff. See Chapter 5.

27 See Chapter 5. *BM* LXXI (1901), pp. 728–9. Midland Bank 67/2, Rowland Hughes' reports, 1897. Other Governors falling in this category might be Bonamy Dobrée of Samuel Dobrée & Sons and William Lidderdale of Rathbone Bros.

28 R. E. Pumphrey, 'The introduction of industrialists into the British peerage,' *Amer. Hist. Rev.* LXV (1959) for comparisons. The whole subject of political influence of financiers needs further research. For a sceptical view of the value of advice given, see for example *St. Stephen's Review*, 25 July 1885, 'Portrait of Lord Rothschild' (press cutting in Anglo-Jewish Archives, Mocatta Library, UCL). Victor (third Lord) Rothschild, *You Have It, Madam* (1980) shows Disraeli dependent on his grandfather's financial collaboration rather than political advice in the Suez Canal shares purchase in 1875. K. Grunwald, 'Windsor-Cassel – the last Court Jew', *Leo Baeck Institute Yearbook*, XIV (1969) surveys the scattered sources on Sir Ernest Cassel, friend of King Edward VII. A. Offer, 'Empire and social reform: British overseas investment and domestic politics 1908–14', *Historical Journal* XXVI (1983), traces the connection between Lloyd George and Sir Edgar Speyer.

29 cf. Sir Lawrence E. Jones, op. cit., p. 118.

30 S. D. Chapman, 'The international houses', *JEurEcHist*, VI(1977).

31 R. J. Truptil, *British Banks* (1936), p. 170.

32 For Seligmans' wartime expansion, see Isaac Seligman, *Reminiscences* (New York, 1925), pp. v–vi.

33 L. E. Jones, op. cit., pp. 143–4.

34 Michael Colefax (late Robert Benson & Sons) to the author, 27 Aug. 1981, citing Richard Jessel of Jessel Toynbee (bill brokers). R. Palin, *Rothschild Relish* (1970), p. 104.

Appendix 1 *Capital and Numbers of Partners in some Merchant Banks at the End of the Nineteenth Century (1896–1908)*

	date	partners	capital (£m.)	source
N. M. Rothschild & Sons, London	c. 1900	3	6.0	guesstimate[2]
Marcus Samuel & Co.[1]	1900	4	2.0	AG MSS
Kleinwort, Sons & Co.	1900	8	1.7	KB ledgers
Chaplin, Milne & Co. (late Morton Rose)[3]	1897	4	1.65	KB MSS UK
Glyn, Mills & Co.	1900	8	1.5	Skinner
J. H. Schröder & Co.	1901	3	1.5	JHS MSS
Baring Bros & Co. Ltd	1900	4	1.225	Skinner
Lazard Bros	1896	4	1.2	Hughes
R. Raphael & Sons	1900	4	1.11	RR MSS
J. S. Morgan & Co.	1900	4	1.0+	MG MSS
S. Montagu & Co.	1896	7	1.0+	Hughes
Balfour Williamson & Co. (L'pool)	1903		1.0+	W. Hunt
Brown Shipley & Co.	1900	6	0.925	BS MSS
Grace Bros & Co.	1899	5	0.75	Skinner
Chalmers Guthrie & Co.	1900	4	0.75	Skinner
König Bros	1900	2	0.675	KB MSS UK
Louis Dreyfus & Co.	1903		0.6+	KB MSS UK
Frederick Huth & Co.	1896	5	0.6	Hughes
E. D. Sassoon & Co.	1896	3	0.6–	Hughes
B. W. Blydenstein & Co.	1900	4	0.5+	Skinner
David Sassoon & Co. Ltd	1901	5	0.5	Skinner
Wallace Bros	1885		0.5+	Rothschild
Antony Gibbs & Co.	1900	6	0.42	AG MSS
C. J. Hambro & Son	1896	5	0.4	Bramsen
Cox & Co.	1900	5	0.4	Skinner
Guinness, Mahon & Co.	1900	4	0.4	GM MSS
Frühling & Goschen	1896	3	0.35–0.4	Hughes
E. Boustead & Co.	1908	8	0.3–0.5	KB MSS
H. S. Lefevre & Co.	1905	3	0.2–0.3	KB MSS USA I
Seligman Bros (London)	1897	5	0.28	Birmingham
Mildred, Goyeneche & Co.	1906	3	0.265	KB MSS UK
W. P. Bonbright & Co.	1906	3	0.26	KB MSS UK
W. Brandt's Sons & Co.	1899	4	0.22	Amburger

Rathbone Bros	1892		0.2	Rothschild
Robert Benson & Co.	1900	2	0.2	KB MSS UK
Melville, Fickus & Co.	1896	2	0.2	Skinner
S. Japhet & Co.	1902	3	0.2	Japhet
Blyth, Greene & Jourdain	1900	5	0.15	Skinner
Forbes, Forbes & Co.	1896	4	0.11	Skinner
Arthur H. Brandt & Co.	1899	2	0.11	Amburger
John Hubbard & Co.	1908	4	0.1	KB MSS UK
Haarbleicher & Schumann	1896	3	0.05	Hughes

Total capital, 42 firms[4]	*c.*1900	32.275
Average capital, 42 firms	*c.*1900	0.77
Estimated capital, 106 firms	*c.*1900	81.6

Sources:

T. Skinner, *The London Banks* (1900) records the capital of incorporated firms. The only other published sources of value are S. Birmingham, *Our Crowd* (New York, 1977) p. 190, for the Seligmans; and S. Japhet, *Recollections from my Business Life* (1931) p. 80.

The MSS sources are:

AG MSS	=	Antony Gibbs & Co. MSS, Balance Books 1882–1925, MS 11,064 Guildhall Library, London.
Amburger	=	C. Amburger, *William Brandt and the Story of his Enterprises*, (typescript trans., n.d.), Brandt MSS, Nottingham University.
Hughes	=	Business reports by T. Rowland Hughes of the North & South Wales Bank, Midland Bank archives M 153/44, 47.
KB MSS	=	Kleinwort Benson records, UK and USA 'Information Books', Guildhall Library, London.
MG MSS	=	Morgan Grenfell records (per Professor V. Carosso).
RR MSS	=	R. Raphael & Sons records.
GM MSS	=	Guinness Mahon & Co. records.
JHS MSS	=	Schröder Wagg records.

Notes:

(1) The figure for M. Samuel & Co. is that for the whole trading and transport company; only a small part of this capital would have been employed in the bank.

(2) N. M. Rothschild & Sons: this 'guesstimate' is based on the probate of the wills of the three partners; the true figure is likely to be higher rather than lower.

(3) Chaplin Milne & Co. (former Morton, Rose & Co. and Morton, Chaplin & Co.): the figure given is the firm's total capital in London *and* New York; the capital of the London house alone was said to be only £50,000, though entered in Skinner's Directory (1900) as £0.3m. at incorporation in 1899 (Kleinwort 'Information Books', UK II, p. 58).

(4) Where the estimate of capital is given as a range, a mean figure has been used to provide the totals.

Appendix 2 *Directorships and Spheres of Interest of Merchant Bankers, 1914–15*

Directorships held

Firm	banks and trusts	insurance	estate and mortgage cos.	public utilities	total	Spheres of interest
T. H. Allen & Co.			1		1	India
Arbuthnot Ewart	1	1	1	1	4	India, Siam
Arbuthnot Latham	4	3	2	0	9	India, S. America (coffee)
Armstrong & Co.					0	
Baring Bros & Co. Ltd	1				2	Latin America, Far East, France, Russia
Barnato Bros			15	1	18	S. Africa (mining)
F. J. Benson & Co.	1				1	
Robert Benson & Co.	9	1		5	15	US railways + estate
W. & J. Biggerstaff			8		12	Nigeria, Argentine
B. W. Blyderstein	1				1	Holland
Blyth, Greene, Jourdain	1	1	4		7	Mauritius, Peru, Bolivia
Wm P. Bonbright			1?	2	3	
Bonn & Co.	2				2	Brazil, Germany
Boulton Bros & Co.	3				3	Russia
Edw'd Boustead	1		14		15	Malaya (rubber)
Arthur H. Brandt					0	Russia
Wm Brandt's Sons & Co.		4			4	Russia, India
Brown, Shipley & Co.	7	3	1		11	USA, Mexico
Chalmers, Guthrie	2	3		2	10	
Chaplin, Milne & Co.	1	2	12+	2	22	USA, Canada, etc.
George Clare & Co.				2?	4	
Cox & Co.					0	India
Cunliffe Bros	1		1	2	4	India, Natal
Roger Cunliffe & Co.		1			1	
De Clermont & Donner					0	
Dent, Palmer & Co.			1		3	India
De Puri, Gautschi					0	
S. Dobrée & Sons					1	
L. Dreyfus & Co.					1	Russia (grain)
Dunn, Fischer & Co.					0	Canada
J. Elles & Sons					0	
Emile Erlanger & Co.					19	S. Africa
Jas. Finlay & Co.	1	1	12	1	23	India
Robt Fleming & Co.	3		2	5	12	USA, Canada (railways)

Firm					Total	Region
Forbes, Forbes & Co.	3	1	1	2	7	India, Central Africa
Früling & Goschen	8	7	—	—	15	W. Indies, Egypt
Antony Gibbs & Sons	1	5	4	4	17	Chile, Australia
Glyn, Mills & Co.	7	8	4	6	27	domestic; dispersed world
Grace & Co. Ltd			13	5	19	Chile, Peru (nitrates)
Grindlay & Co.		1			1	India
Guinness, Mahon & Co.					1	Ireland
Haes & Sons			1	3	6	
C. J. Hambro & Son	5	2		1	8	Scandinavia, USA
Harris, Winthrop & Co.					0	US firm
Hatton, Morris & Co.					0	
Heilbut, Symons & Co.			3		3	Malaya (rubber)
Helbert Wagg & Co.			7		7	S. Africa, Canada
R. & J. Henderson	1	1	6		8	Borneo, Sarawak
E. Von der Heydt & Co.					0	Germany
Higginson & Co.	3	2	—	—	5	Boston (Mass.) firm
L. Hirsch & Co.	—	—	6	—	6	S. Africa, Angola
Holt & Co.	3	1			4	New Zealand, USA
Horstmann & Co.					0	Germany
John Hubbard & Co.	3	3	1	1	9	Russia
F. Huth & Co.	4	2		1	7	S. America USA
Isaac & Samuel					0	
S. Japhet & Co.					1	Germany, Italy, USA
A. Keyser & Co.				10	11	mainly domestic?
Henry S. King & Co.	4	2	2	—	8	India, USA, Australia
Kleinwort, Sons & Co.		2			2	Cuba
Knowles & Foster			1	1	3	Brazil, Argentina
König Bros					0	Germany
W. Ladenburg & Co			1		1	Romania
Alex Lawrie & Co.	1	2	7	1	11	India (tea)
Lazard Bros	1	1	1	1	4	Paris, New York, Far East
H. S. Lefevre & Co.	2	—	—	—	2	USA, Canada
Wm Le Lacheur & Son	—	2	1	—	3	Costa Rica
Sir Chas McGrigor & Co.					0	
Duncan MacNeill & Co.	2	—	6	2	10	India (tea), Australia
Wm F. Malcolm & Co.					0	
M. Marshall & Son					0	
Matheson & Co.	2		2	2	8	China
F. Mendl & Co.	1			5	7	Argentina, Paraguay (corn)
Mildred, Goyeneche & Co.					0	Spain
Samuel Montagu & Co.					0	arbitrage
Morgan Grenfell & Co.	1	5	1	3	10	USA
G. F. Neame & Co.		1			1	
Neumann, Luebeck & Co.	3		4	1	8	S. Africa, Rhodesia
B. Newgass & Co. Ltd	2	—	3	9	15	USA, Peru, Ecuador
Ogilvy, Gillanders & Co.	1		2	3	7	India, Siam
Parry, Murray & Co.				1	2	India
Pinto, Leite & Co.		1			1	Portugal, Brazil

Firm					Total	Spheres of interest
Gerald Quin, Cope & Co.					0	
Ralli Bros					0	Black Sea, India
R. Raphael & Sons					0	arbitrage (New York)
Raymond Pynchon & Co					1	American bank
Richardson & Son					0	India
Robinson, Fleming & Co.	5			1	6	
P. P. Rodoconachi & Co.					0	
Rodoconachi Sons & Co.	4		2	3	10	shipowners
O. A. Rosenberg & Co.					0	
Geo. Ross & Co.			3		3	San Salvador
N. M. Rothschild & Sons		1	1	3	5	continental Europe, USA
A. Rüffer & Sons		3		4	8	France, Spain, c. Europe
Sale & Co.					0	
M. Samuel & Co.	1			3	8	Japan, Far East
D. Sassoon & Co.					0	India, China
E. D. Sassoon & Co.	1	1			2	India, China
J. H. Schröder & Co.	1	1	2		4	Russia (wheat), S. America (minerals), Chile (nitrates), Cuba
Seligman Bros	1	1			2	USA, Germany
Sperling & Co.					0	
Speyer Bros	1	1	1	2	5	USA, Brazil, Cuba
Stern Bros	1				1	Turkey, Argentine
Herbert Stern & Co.				2	2	
Stilwell & Sons					0	Navy agents
Thomson, Bonar & Co.					5	Russia, USA, Argentina
Wallace Bros & Co.	4	2			6	India, Far East
Geo. W. Wheatley & Co.					0	shipping agents (India etc.)
Wogau & Co.					0	Russia
Woodhead & Co.	1			6	10	Argentine, Uruguay, Russia
Zulueta & Co.				1	1	Spain
Totals, 111 firms	117	79	161	110	552	

Sources: T. Skinner, *The London Banks and Kindred Companies and Firms, 1914–15* (1915). T. Skinner, *Directory of Directors, 1914–15* (1915). Additional information on spheres of interest from R. J. Truptil, *British Banks* (1936) and the various bank histories listed in the notes to the chapters.

Appendix 3 *Migration of Bankers from the Provinces to London*

Glasgow	est'd	London branch	source (short title)
James Finlay & Co.	c. 1750	1871	C. Brogan, *James Finlay*, pp. 11–12, 15.
Dennistoun, Cross & Co.	c. 1790	1855	D. M. Evans, *History of the Commercial Crisis* (1859) p. cxxxvii.

Liverpool	est'd	London branch	source (short title)
Rathbone Bros	c. 1730	1864	S. Marriner, *Rathbones* (1961) p. 223. E. A. Rathbone, *Records*–p. 17.
Robert Benson & Co.	1789	1853	S. D. Chapman and S. Diaper, *Kleinwort Benson*, Chs 1–3.
Brown Shipley & Co.	1805	1863	A. Ellis, *Heir of Adventure*, p. 99
Ogilvy, Gillanders & Co.	1824	1860	J. S. Gladstone, *History* (1910)
Morris Prevost & Co.	1822	1838	*BM*, LXXI (1901) p. 728.
Balfour Williamson & Co.	1851	1899	W. Hunt, *Heirs of Great Adventure* (1951) I, 203.
Fraser Trenholm & Co.		1866	Fraser Trenholm MSS, Merseyside RO.

Manchester	est'd	London branch	source (short title)
Timothy Wiggin		c. 1826	*S. C. on Manufacturers*, 1833, p. 119.
Benecke Souchay & Co.	1806	1872	Brandt 1850 p. 184, 1872, p. 508
Schuster, Son & Co.	1808	by 1873	P. H. Emden, *Money Powers* (1937) p. 397. *BM*, LXXI (1901) p. 423.
Pinto Leite & Nephews		c. 1900	T. Skinner, *London Banks*.
Abraham Baver & Co.		1842	K. Grunwald *Studies*, pp. 153–4. Brandt 1842 p. 295.

Migration of Bankers from London to Liverpool

	open	closed	source (short title)
Newgass Rosenheim & Co.	1872	1875	Brandt P. 1875 180–1.
Frederick Huth & Co.	1839	1877	Brandt 1839 p. 217, 1877 p. 1.
Antony Gibbs & Co.		1881	J. A. Gibbs, *History*, pp. 456–7
J. H. Schröder & Co.	1839	1884	Brandt 1883 p. 477, 1884 p. 493.

Baring Bros	1832	1891	BBAG HC3.35
Drake, Kleinwort			S. D. Chapman and S. Diaper,
& Co.	1858	1962	op. cit. Ch. 5.
James Holdford & Co.	1837	1840	Brandt 1837 p. 171;
			G. A. Brown's Journal.

Appendix 5 *Bibliography of Useful Works on Particular Merchant Banks*

Balfour, Williamson
Wallis Hunt, *Heirs of Great Adventure: the History of Balfour, Williamson & Co. Ltd.* (1951)

Barings
R. Hidy, *The House of Baring in American Trade and Financial ... 1763–1861* (Harvard, Mass., 1949).

Barnato Bros
H. Raymond, *B. I. Barnato: a Memoir* (1897).

Blount (Edward), **Laing** (Samuel) and the Railway Financiers
S. J. Reid (ed.), *Memoirs of Sir Edward Blount* (1902)
Dictionary of National Biography XXII Samuel Laing, Supp., Albert Grant.
D. A. Adler, *British Investment in American Railways 1834–1898* (Charlottesville, Va, 1970), ch. VII

Blyth, Greene and **Jourdain**
Augustus Muir, *Blyth, Greene, Joudain & Co. Ltd. 1810–1910* (1961).

Brandts
C. Amburger, *William Brandt and the Story of his Enterprises (typescript trans. from German, n.d.)*

Brown, Shipley & Co.
A. Ellis, *Heir of Adventure* (1960)
E. J. Perkins, *Financing Anglo-American Trade: the House of Brown 1800–1880* (Harvard, Mass., 1975).
J. C. Brown, *A Hundred Years of Merchant Banking* (New York, 1909).

Cassel
K. Grunwald, 'Windsor-Cassel – the last Court Jew', *Leo Baeck Institute Yearbook*, XIV (1969).
    C. Adler, *Jacob H. Schiff: his Life and Letters* (New York, 1928).

Cox & Co.
J. R. Winton, *Lloyds Bank 1918–1969* (1982), ch. 6.

Dreyfus
Dan Morgan, *Merchants of Grain* (1979).

Finlays
[C. Brogan], *James Finlay & Co. 1750–1950* (Glasgow, 1951).

R. Fleming & Co.
J. C. Gilbert, *A History of Investment Trust in Dundee 1873–1938* (1939).

Helbert Wagg
L. E. Jones, *Georgian Afternoon (1958)*.
W. L. Fraser, *All to the Good* (1963).

Kleinworts: 'Statistics Book' 1891–1923, Kleinwort Benson Ltd, Newbury Office Records Department.

Schröders: Miscellaneous historical records of J. H. Schröder Wagg Ltd, London. No data are available for any year before 1896.

Hambros: Guildhall Lib. Hambros MSS 19,034, 'Synopsis of Journals' 1867–1916.

Rothschilds: extracted from RAL ledgers VI/10/0–113.

Gibbs: Guildhall Lib. Gibbs MSS 11,064 'Balance Books' 1882–1925.

Brandts: London School of Economics Library, Brandts' ledgers (unlisted).

Notes:

Columns 1–7: any missing figures have been interpolated: the trend is shown in square brackets. The first six figures in the Schröder column have been extrapolated from the trend of subsequent data.

Column 8: lists the totals of the seven previous columns.

Column 9: has been calculated from the base of 1913 acceptances = £140m. (see Chapter 7). All other figures are a varying proportion of this figure determined by the totals in column 8, that is data in column 8 are multiplied by 3.07.

Appendix 4 *Acceptances of some leading London Accepting Houses 1890–1914 (£m.)*

	Barings (1)	Kleinworts (2)	Schröders (3)	Hambros (4)	Rothschilds (5)	Gibbs (6)	Brandts (7)	Totals (8)	calculated total acceptances (9)
1890	c.15.00	4.89	[3.5]	1.77	1.39	2.44	0.69	29.68	91
1891	3.46	4.85	[3.8]	0.86	2.12	0.72	0.54	16.35	50
1892	3.25	5.51	[4.0]	0.84	3.44	0.88	0.70	18.62	57
1893	3.04	5.57	[4.2]	0.61	2.79	0.39	0.59	17.19	53
1894	3.62	5.32	[4.5]	0.86	3.87	0.23	0.72	19.12	59
1895	4.91	6.56	[4.7]	0.93	3.93	0.72	0.84	22.59	69
1896	4.52	6.55	5.09	1.96	2.15	0.47	0.81	21.55	66
1897	4.68	6.61	4.74	1.20	1.56	0.47	0.67	19.93	61
1898	3.56	7.79	5.77	1.72	1.53	0.61	0.79	21.77	67
1899	3.90	7.75	5.65	1.94	1.44	0.62	[0.9]	22.20	68
1900	4.32	8.15	6.05	1.94	1.47	0.56	[1.1]	23.59	72
1901	4.49	8.91	6.12	2.00	1.94	0.62	1.18	25.26	78
1902	4.71	9.50	6.05	1.74	1.39	0.65	1.13	25.17	77
1903	3.83	8.55	6.72	1.72	1.17	0.93	[1.2]	24.12	74
1904	6.20	11.11	6.84	1.83	2.14	0.93	[1.4]	30.45	93
1905	7.42	11.69	8.78	2.23	2.66	0.89	1.53	35.20	108
1906	7.38	11.87	10.28	2.15	3.10	0.93	2.53	38.24	117
1907	5.39	12.12	11.74	2.60	5.02	1.03	2.34	40.24	124
1908	6.94	10.83	9.33	2.79	5.11	0.99	2.15	38.14	117
1909	7.77	10.76	10.18	2.41	2.44	1.16	2.34	37.06	114
1910	7.50	10.72	10.63	2.79	7.08	0.87	2.76	42.35	130
1911	6.05	13.44	11.29	3.40	2.18	0.89	3.64	40.89	126
1912	6.58	13.36	11.95	3.45	3.49	1.38	3.19	43.40	133
1913	6.64	14.21	11.66	4.57	3.19	2.04	3.33	45.64	140
1914	3.72	8.54	5.82	1.34	1.31	1.17	0.72	22.62	69

Sources:
Barings: T. Skinner, *The London Banks* (annual directory) 1892–1914.

Gibbs

J. A. Gibbs, *The History of Antony and Dorothea Gibbs* (1922)

W. Maude, *Antony Gibbs & Sons Ltd.* (1958)

Glyns

R. Fulford, *Glyns 1753-1953* (1953).

B. W. Currie, *Recollections, Letters and Journals 1827-96.* (1901).

Hambros

B. Bramsen and K. Wain, *The Hambros 1779-1979* (1979).

Hirsch

K. Grunwald, *Turkenhirsch: a Study of Baron Maurice de Hirsch, Entrepreneur and Philanthropist* (Jerusalem, 1966).

Huths

A. J. Murray, *Home from the Hill: a Biography of Frederick Huth, 'Napoleon of the City'* (1970).

S. Japhet

S. Japhet, *Recollection from my Business Life* (1931).

L. Dennett, *The Charterhouse Group, 1925-1979* (1979).

Knoop

G. von Schulze-Gaevernitz, *Volkswirtschaftliche Studien aus Russland* (Leipzig, 1899), pp. 91-106.

Kleinwort, Benson

S. D. Chapman and S. J. Diaper, *Kleinwort Benson in the History of Merchant Banking* (forthcoming, Oxford, 1984).

Knowles & Foster

(Anon.), *The History of Knowles & Foster 1828-1948* (1948).

Morgans

L. Corry, *House of Morgan* (1930).

A. Sinclair, *Corsair* (1981).

M. Hidy, *George Peabody, Merchant and Financier 1829-54* (New York, 1978).

Morton, Rose & Co.

D. Greenberg, *Financiers and Railroads 1869-1889: a study of Morton, Bliss & Co.* (Newark, Del. 1981).

R. McElroy, *Levi Parsons Morton: Banker, Diplomat and Statesman* (New York, 1930).

Ogilvy, Gillanders & Co.

J. S. Gladstone, *History of Gillanders, Arbuthnot & Co. and Ogilvy, Gillanders & Co.* (1910).

Rathbones

S. Marriner, *Rathbones of Liverpool 1845-73* (Liverpool, 1961).

William Rathbone VI, *A Sketch of Family History during Four Generations* (Liverpool, 1894).

Ricardo

P. Sraffa and M. H. Dobb, *Ricardo's Works,* X (1955), pt II, ch. 2.

Rothschilds

B. Gille, *Histoire de la maison Rothschild* (Geneva), 1965, 1967).

J. Bouvier, *Les Rothschild* (Paris, 1967).

Count E. C. Corti, *The Rise of the House of Rothschild* (1928) *The Rule of the House of Rothschild* (1928).

M. Samuel & Co.

F. C. Gerretson, *History of the Royal Dutch* (1953-7), II, 145-6.

Sassoons

C. Roth, *The Sassoon Dynasty* (1941).

Seligmans

Linton Wells, *The House of Seligman* (typescript, 3 vols, 1931) New York Historical Society Library.

R. L. Muir and C. J. White, *Over the Long Term . . . the Story of J. J. W. Seligman & Co. 1864-1964* (New York, 1964).

S. Birmingham, *Our Crowd: the Great Jewish Families of New York* (New York, 1977).

Wallace Bros

A. C. Pointon, *Wallace Bros.* (Oxford, 1974).

Werner, Beit & Co.

A. P. Cartwright, *The Corner House* (Cape Town, 1965).

R. V. Kubicek, *Economic Imperialism in Theory and Practice: the Case of South African Gold Mining Finance 1886-1914* (Durham, NC, 1979).

Index of people and places

Belgium 24, 30, 46, 87, 90

Belmont, August (& Co.) 19, 21, 22, 35, 37, 42, 49, 52, 67, 74, 84, 91, 92, 93, 96, 101, 157

Benecke, Souchay & Co. 139, 151

Benedicks, Herr 115, 116, 117

Bengal Railway 160

Benson, Robert (I) 129

Benson, Robert (II) 129

Benson, Robert (III) 129, 139

Benson, R. H. 153

Benson, Robert & Sons 44, 66, 96, 97, 101, 129, 133, 153,

Bentley, Thomas 5

Berlin 4, 8, 18, 37, 45, 47, 50, 61, 66, 83, 84, 123, 158, 168

Berliner Handelsgesellschaft 156

Berkfeld, Wm. & Co. 145, 146

Berne 4

Bethmann 18, 70, 84

Bettiah Raj 144

Biddle, Nicholas 66, 163

Bingham, Senator 26, 30, 36

Birmingham 13, 14, 41, 110

Bischoffsheim 133

Bischoffsheim & de Hirsch 95

Bischoffsheim & Goldschmidt 45, 47, 54, 60, 67, 95, 96, 134

Bismark, Otto von 52

Black Sea 60

Blackburn 91

Bleichroder, Gerson von 24, 37, 66, 160

Bliss, George 52, 53, 96

Blount, Edward 90, 134, 152

Blydenstein, B. W. & Co. 59, 120, 155

Blyth, Greene, Jourdain & Co. Ltd. 59, 114, 151, 162

Blyth, James 114, 162

Bodenkreditanstalt 160

Bolivia 130

Bombay 114, 120, 123, 131, 133, 140, 141, 143, 145, 146

Bombay Burma Trading Co. 143

Bonn, Max (& Co.) 61, 179

Borneo Co. 144

Boston (U.S.A.) 26, 27, 39, 41, 153

Boulton, Matthew 5

Boulton & Watt 6

Bourne, Sylvanus & Co. 6

Boustead, Anderson & Co. 153

Boustead Bros. 153

Boustead, Edward & Co. 153

Bouvier, Jean 174

Boyd, Benfield & Co. 4

Bradford 45, 115, 116, 117, 123, 136, 179

Bradford Banking Co. 117, 118

Brand, Hon. R. H. (Lord Brand) 65, 154

Brandenburg 2

Brandt, Arthur H. (& Co.) 55

Brandt, Augustus 61

Brandt, E. H. (& Co.) 11, 144

Brandt, William, Sons & Co. 44. 55, 60, 61, 62, 67, 105, 107, 108, 121, 122, 135, 144, 146, 151, 171

Brassey, Thomas 90

Brazil 60, 76, 86, 119

Bremen 2, 123, 124, 145

Bristol 10

British & Chinese Corporation 142, 174

British Thomson Houston Co. 99

British Westinghouse Co. 99

Brown, Alexander 42

Brown, (Sir) Alexander Hargreaves 154

Brown Bros. (U.S.A.) 153, 154, 157

Brown, Janson & Co. 119

Brown, Shipley & Co. 11, 22, 31, 35, 37, 39-45, 55, 60, 63, 66, 67, 72, 74-77, 87, 95, 97, 105, 121, 122, 126, 139, 152-5, 152-5, 157, 162, 177, 178

Brown, Waldron Post 154

Brown, (Sir) William 41, 63, 72

Brown, W. & J. & Co. 14

Brussels 45, 67, 95

Bryce, J. A. 63

Budapest Kreditbank 160

Buddicom 90

Buenos Aires 10, 78, 87, 122

Buist, M. G. 66

Bunge & Co. 172

Burgess, Henry 66

Burnham 43

Butterworth, Brooks & Co. 119

Calcutta 26, 27, 67, 111, 112, 113, 122, 123, 142, 143, 152

California 22

Canada 30, 87, 94, 95

Canton 27, 119, 131

Cape Colony 87, 147

Cassel, (Sir) Ernest 23, 37, 54, 67, 89, 95, 161, 168, 171, 178, 179

Cassis, Dr. Y. 171, 173

Catrine 140

Cazenove (& Ackroyds) 61, 159, 180

Cecco, Marcello de 173

Ceylon 153

Chaplin, Milne & Co. 135, 155, 176

Chaplin, Milne, Grenfell & Co. Ltd. 80

Index of Subjects